T5-BYX-276

DATE DUE

Maria Irene Fornes

Maria Irene Fornes is the most influential female American dramatist of the twentieth century. That is the argument of this important new study, the first to assess Fornes's complete body of work.

Scott T. Cummings considers comic sketches, opera libretti and unpublished pieces, as well as her best-known plays, in order to trace the evolution of her dramaturgy from the whimsical Off-Off Broadway plays of the 1960s to the sober, meditative work of the 1990s. The book also reflects on her practice as an inspirational teacher of playwriting and the primary director of her own plays.

Drawing on the latest scholarship and his own personal research and interviews with Fornes over two decades, Cummings examines Fornes's unique significance and outlines strategies for understanding her fragmentary, enigmatic, highly demanding theater.

Scott T. Cummings is Chair of the Theatre Department of Boston College, where he directs plays and teaches courses in playwriting and dramatic literature. He is the author of *Remaking American Theater: Charles Mee, Anne Bogart and the SITI Company*, as well as numerous performance reviews, journal articles, and essays on contemporary American theater and drama.

ROUTLEDGE MODERN AND CONTEMPORARY DRAMATISTS

Series editor: Maggie B. Gale and Mary Luckhurst

Routledge Modern and Contemporary Dramatists is a new series of innovative and exciting critical introductions to the work of internationally pioneering playwrights. The series includes recent *and* well-established playwrights and offers primary materials on contemporary dramatists who are under-represented in secondary criticism. Each volume provides detailed cultural, historical and political material, examines selected plays in production, and theorises the playwright's artistic agenda and working methods, as well as their contribution to the development of playwriting and theatre.

Volumes currently available in the series are:

J. B. Priestley *by Maggie B. Gale*

Federico Garcia Lorca *by Maria M. Delgado*

Susan Gaspell and Sophie Treadwell *by Jerry Dickey and Barbara Oziebo*

August Strindberg *by Eszter Szalczer*

Anton Chekhov *by Rose Whyman*

Jean Genet *by David Bradby and Clare Finburgh*

Future volumes will include:

Mark Ravenhill *by John F. Deeney*

Caryl Churchill *by Mary Luckhurst*

Brian Friel *by Anna McMullan*

Sarah Kane *by Chris Megson*

Maria Irene Fornes

Routledge Modern and Contemporary Dramatists

Scott T. Cummings

Routledge
Taylor & Francis Group

LONDON AND NEW YORK

First published 2013
by Routledge
2 Park Square, Milton Park, Abingdon, Oxon OX14 4RN

Simultaneously published in the USA and Canada
by Routledge
711 Third Avenue, New York, NY 10017

*Routledge is an imprint of the Taylor & Francis Group, an informa
business*

British Library Cataloguing in Publication Data
A catalogue record for this book is available from the British Library

Library of Congress Cataloging in Publication Data
Cummings, Scott T., 1953-
   Maria Irene Fornes / by Scott T. Cummings.
      p. cm. – (Routledge modern and contemporary dramatists)
   Includes bibliographical references and index.
   1. Fornes, Maria Irene – Criticism and interpretation.
   2. Theater – Production and direction – New York (State) –
   New York – History – 20th century. I. Title.
   PS3556.O7344Z68 2012
   812'.54 – dc23
   2012002519

ISBN: 978-0-415-45434-6 (hbk)
ISBN: 978-0-415-45435-3 (pbk)
ISBN: 978-0-203-81621-9 (ebk)

Typeset in Sabon
by Taylor & Francis Books

for Peter Ferran
(he knows why)

Contents

x   *Contents*

List of illustrations

While every effort has been made to trace and acknowledge ownership
of copyright material used in this volume, the Publishers will be
glad to make suitable arrangements with any copyright holders
whom it has not been possible to contact.

Acknowledgements

The research odyssey that has resulted in this book began at the Cornelia Street Cafe on May 23, 1985 when Edit Villareal and I interviewed Irene Fornes for an issue of *Theater* magazine. This first encounter catalyzed my decision to write my doctoral dissertation on Fornes at the Yale School of Drama, a project which benefitted from the wisdom and guidance of my advisor, Richard Gilman. At Yale, Stanley Kauffmann, Joel Schechter, Gitta Honegger, and especially Leon Katz sharpened my critical thinking and writing skills. Thanks is also due to Lynne Cummings for being there at the beginning.

In my work on Fornes over the years, a number of her colleagues and associates have done me the courtesy of sharing their experiences through formal interviews, casual conversations, and telephone and email communications. At one time or another, this has included Gwendolyn Alker, Devon Allen, George Bartenieff, Herbert Blau, Anne Bogart, Stephen Bottoms, Susan Letzler Cole, Migdalia Cruz, Sheila Dabney, Donald Eastman, June Ekman, Crystal Field, Susan Gregg, Rebecca High, Morgan Jenness, Larry Kornfeld, Janet Leuchter, Peter Littlefield, Bonnie Marranca, Marc Masterson, Patricia Mattick, Kelly Maurer, Michelle Memran, Anne Millitello, Aileen Passloff, Marc Robinson, Phyllis Jane Rose, Ed Setrakian, Alisa Solomon, and Caridad Svich. I thank all of them – and others who I must be overlooking – for their generosity and insight. In addition, I owe thanks to the many press representatives, publicity and marketing staffers at numerous theaters, and photographers who helped me gain access to production photographs and other Fornes materials.

A 2006–7 Research Incentive Grant from the Office of Sponsored Programs at Boston College made it possible for me to resume

Fornes research for the purpose of writing this book. I am deeply grateful to the George A. and Eliza Gardner Howard Foundation for a 2008–9 fellowship that supported a leave of absence from teaching at a crucial stage of the writing process. Over the years, a series of undergraduate research fellows at Boston College – Jenn Wade, Claire Darby, Dan Brunet, Marin Kirby, Megan Rulison, Sarah Lunnie, Dave Bruin, Sarah Lang, Han Cho, Evan Cole, Cam Cronin, and Cara Harrington – provided valuable nuts-and-bolts assistance. I was aided by my students in a different way when I directed *Abingdon Square* at Boston College in 2004, and I thank the talented student cast – Mairin Lee, Chris Tocco, Dan O'Brien, Emma Stanton, Marianne Frapwell, Jonathan Popp, Patricia Noonan, Lee Trew, and cellist Adrian Curtin – for their curiosity and dedication. I also want to acknowledge the support and encouragement of Morgan Jenness, Michelle Memran, and Gwendolyn Alker, whose commitment to preserving the Fornes legacy has been essential.

Patricia Noonan, Cam Cronin, Erica Stevens Abbitt, and Amanda Fazzone read all or part of the manuscript and made helpful suggestions and corrections. I am grateful for their time and attention to detail. As series editors, Maggie Gale and Mary Luckhurst have exhibited an astonishing patience with me over the years, as has Ben Piggott at Routledge all through production.

Janet, I love you and thank you for everything.

Most of all, I thank Irene. When she first agreed to cooperate with my research, I am sure she had no idea how many times I would turn up to request another interview, seek permission again to sit in on rehearsals, listen to her speak on a panel, see one of her plays, ask for a copy of a manuscript or doublecheck some information. Her willingness to share with me the intricacies and the intimacies of her creative process is a gift that cannot be measured. I am forever grateful. When I finished writing this book, I went to visit Irene in the adult care home where she lives in upstate New York. At that point, her dementia made conversation impossible, but when I asked her if she knew any good songs, her face brightened and she burst into singing "Guantanamera." I joined in on the chorus, as she sang verse after verse after verse. She loves to sing. She has joy in her heart and the song of life on the tip of her tongue. I am grateful for that, too.

Figure 1 Maria Irene Fornes in her Sheridan Square apartment with her
mother Carmen (1990).

Overview

Maria Irene Fornes pioneered a new American playwriting. Between 1960 and 2000, she created more than fifty works for the stage, including comic sketches, one-act plays, full-length dramas, musical plays, site-specific pieces, devised works, libretti for opera, and adaptations of modernist classics. This volume is the first book to examine the full range of Fornes's work, including unpublished plays and later works that have received little critical attention. Breadth of discussion has taken precedence over a narrow-but-deep focus on the best-known plays, a decision that stems from the conviction that Fornes is best understood in the context of her complete oeuvre. One of the hallmarks of her playwriting is her perpetual experimentation with different tones, styles, and subjects. The focus of most scholarship on a few major plays – *Fefu and Her Friends*, *Mud*, *The Conduct of Life*, *The Danube* – has inadvertently narrowed the perception of her work. A mild corrective is offered here.

This study takes a developmental approach in two different senses. First, it traces the trajectory of Fornes's career and the evolution of her techniques and themes over the last four decades of the twentieth century. Each decade commands one of the book's four parts. Her 1960s plays are rooted in the explosion of Off-Off Broadway theater that took place in and around Greenwich Village at that time. They are playfully absurdist, full of logic and language games, whimsical ironies, zany transformations, and fanciful incongruities. Her 1970s plays suggest a discomfiting period of growth and a search for a more personal voice, one which was signaled by her pivotal, groundbreaking *Fefu and Her Friends* (1977).

This is the decade in which she honed her skills as a director, in part by creating devised pieces from documentary sources. The plays of the 1980s, the period of her most enduring work, achieve a crystalline balance of lyricism, emotionalism, and formalism that reflected "an increasingly expressive relation to dread, to grief and to passion" (Sontag 1986: 9). This is also when she emerged as an influential teacher of playwriting, celebrated for her innovative exercises designed to release a writer's creative spirit. Her 1990s plays focus more explicitly on themes of survival and friendship, even as they revive a metatheatrical self-consciousness evident in the early work. These plays are ruminative, more personal, questioning, and sometimes tentative. They yearn for better days even as they manifest Fornes's resilient love and respect for life itself.

The approach here is also developmental in its attention to the origins of specific Fornes plays and to her creative process in general. Her playwriting cannot be understood independent of two collateral practices that also defined her career: teaching and directing. Early on, Fornes learned that she could not tolerate somebody other than her directing the first production of her plays. Over time, she developed a directing style that was praised for its compositional rigor and choreographic precision. Even when critics were befuddled or alienated by her latest play, they often commented on the sure-handedness of her staging. Fornes also began teaching early in her career; her eventual affiliation with INTAR in New York and the Padua Hills Playwrights Festival outside of Los Angeles led her to refine a pedagogy of playwriting – what she called "the anatomy of inspiration" – that had widespread influence. She developed a popular series of exercises designed to help a novice playwright gain access to the imagination, and in teaching those exercises, she wrote along with her students, generating raw material that often provided the seeds for a new play. As an extension of her creative process, teaching and directing enabled Fornes to construct her own idiosyncratic system for taking a play from initial conception to opening night.

In this she benefitted from sustained relationships with a number of theater artists and producing organizations: Al Carmines, Lawrence Kornfeld, and the Judson Poets' Theater; Max Ferra and INTAR; Crystal Field and Theater for the New City; Murray Mednick and Padua Hills Playwrights Festival; Julia Miles and the Women's

Project; the designers Donald Eastman, Anne Millitello, and Gabriel Berry; and a parade of actors over the years that included Florence Tarlow, Crystal Field, Aileen Passloff, Margaret Harrington, Sheila Dabney, and Patricia Mattick, among many others. This community assured that Fornes always had sympathetic collaborators and a supportive place to work, and she went on to receive numerous prizes, awards, and fellowships, most famously a total of nine Obie awards (for achievement in Off and Off-Off Broadway theater), more than anybody other than Sam Shepard.

The Fornes canon is bookended by two projects – *La viuda* (1961) and *Letters from Cuba* (2000) – based on letters written in Spanish by members of her family in Cuba. This coincidence draws attention not only to her Latina background but also to the importance in her plays of the reciprocal acts of writing and reading – "steps towards personhood" (Sofer 2006: 441) – and the operation of language in general. She came to New York City from Havana at age 15; when she took up writing fifteen years later, she wrote in English rather than her native Spanish. "My writing," she later remarked, "has an off-center quality that is not exactly deliberate, but that I have not tried to change because I know its origin lies in the temperament and language of my birth" (Delgado and Svich 1999: 268). Fornes's painstaking syntax, as well as her use of rhythm and repetition and a limited vocabulary, produces a dramatic idiom that is lyrical and deceptively simple. Her characters recognize that language has the power to transform. The erudite Dr. Kheal observes, "Words change the nature of things. A thing not named and the same thing named are two different things" (Fornes 1971: 68). In *Lust* (1989), the neurasthenic Helena dislikes a play she saw because of "the words the author used ... Words that are not real words. Like 'likewise.' False words that have nothing behind them ... No thinking goes into words like that ... People feel good using them, but they feel a little cheated later, debilitated. If you speak without meaning, you feel debilitated" (Fornes 2008: 137).

Fornes's characters speak with meaning, knowing that to name something is to change it, but the process is delicate and often difficult. Fornes described it metaphorically:

It is as if the words are dampness in a porous substance – a dampness which becomes liquid and condenses. As if there is a condensation that is really the forming of words. I want to catch the process of the forming of thought into words.

(Cummings 1985: 55)

This "struggle to translate thought into language, writing into speech, speech into action, action into coherent being" (Sofer 2006: 441) shapes the action of many plays. "Character is revealed through catechism" (Sontag 1986: 8), and tropes of literacy, language, and learning abound as part of the effort to capture the process of coming to thought. For her characters, this is tantamount to bringing self into being, which for some means vanquishing an existential vagueness. In that effort they demonstrate a rare combination of fragility and resilience, determination and helplessness, dignity and shame. They aspire to a purity that approaches the divine, yet they are subject to carnal impulses and adverse social conditions that seem to doom them to failure or at least to a profound frustration. If her characters suffer, they also benefit from Fornes's signature compassion for them.

For Fornes, life itself is so precious that her theater, in effect, wants to prolong life by slowing down time and zeroing in on stillness. Her plays are not concerned with the forward thrust of a narrative action or the strategic rush of a character towards some prized goal. Leading Fornes critic Bonnie Marranca (1984: 30) was among the first to credit her with lifting "the burden of psychology, declamation, morality, and sentimentality from the concept of character," freeing her figures from definition by intention or motivation and instead depicting them in "scenes that create a single emotive moment, as precise in what it does not articulate as in what does get said." These isolated moments of being – what this study will call "emotigraphs" – are the building blocks of Fornes's unique dramaturgy, juxtaposed one to the next without transition in a manner that asks the spectator to "bridge the gap" or "connect the dots" in order to complete the theatrical picture.

Fornes's depiction of isolated moments when the sensuous and the spiritual collide is informed by the social and demographic profile of her characters. They are defined as much by gender, ethnicity, class, and sexuality as they are by inner struggle. The personal and the political are radically intertwined, but at a moment when multiculturalism and identity politics came to play an increasing role in critical discourse, Fornes herself was wary about being categorized strictly as a woman or a Latina or a lesbian playwright. She neither proclaimed nor denied these identities. Despite her advocacy for Hispanic playwrights, her connection to feminist dramaturgy, her use of Catholic imagery and themes, her focus on the lumpenproletariat, and the sustained critique of heteronormative relationships in her plays, Fornes resisted classification by orthodoxy. Ethnography, queer theory, feminism, Marxist criticism, and other modes of analysis have much to reveal about her drama, but in the moment of performance Fornes sought a more visceral than ideological connection to events onstage.

To this day, Fornes's plays continue to be widely produced around the United States by small professional theaters, fringe companies, and university groups. Her work has always been revered by a coterie of in-the-know theater artists, critics, scholars, and students. But after a fleeting moment on Broadway in 1966 and the successful Off Broadway run of *Promenade* in 1969, she had no commercial productions and only a smattering of appearances at the growing network of not-for-profit resident regional theaters around the United States. Over the decades, she became more and more conspicuous as an outsider artist, a holdover from the 1960s whose work was ignored by the mainstream theater establishment. The average theatergoer has never heard of her. In a 1992 *Village Voice* essay titled "The Aging Playwright and the American Theater," Bonnie Marranca (1992a: 94) expressed outrage that "at the age of 62, after three decades of a richly committed life in the theater, Maria Irene Fornes is still working on the margins."

There is no simple explanation for this neglect. American philistinism is certainly a part of it. Marranca blamed the preoccupation with "new" playwrights and the failure of mainstream institutions to integrate proven experimentalists. The symbiosis between her playwriting and directing makes the merits of the texts themselves less apparent to directors and producers "shopping around" for an interesting play. There is also an economy of scale at work: most Fornes plays are shorter than a conventional full-length play and better suited to smaller studio theaters than large mainstage houses. This poses programming challenges for producers who need to round out a full evening's entertainment or fill more than a hundred seats a night. Still, the single biggest reason for Fornes's marginal status is the seemingly esoteric nature of the work itself:

> If Fornes remains on the periphery of the mainstream, it is because large, popular audiences come to the theater to have their most cherished beliefs reinforced, not challenged. They do not want to examine the implications of gender hierarchy or the dynamics of patriarchy too closely. Fornes's refusal to compromise, her refusal to write to please men, her rejection of romantic sentimentality ensures that she will remain on the fringe.
>
> (Schuler 1990: 227)

> The diversity of Fornes's plays, which makes them almost impossible to collectively "brand" by theme or milieu, is perhaps one reason why her work – though certainly fit to stand alongside that of Albee, Shepard, and others – has often been overlooked or underappreciated by critics. Another is simply the continuing, prejudicial tendency to assume that Fornes's own, multiply-othered status as a woman, a lesbian, and a Latina must somehow render her a playwright with "minority" appeal.
>
> (Bottoms 2004b: 22)

> Could it be that Fornes is underproduced (for a writer of her stature) precisely because her characters rebel with willful opacity against American theatrical notions about the clarity of intention?
>
> (Ruhl 2001: 194)

In short, a Fornes play insists on being taken on its own terms.

The main objective of this study is to make clear what those terms are by chronicling the transformation of her Off-Off Broadway ethic beyond its early communal preoccupations into a highly personal artistic vision. In performance, a Fornes play makes specific demands on a spectator, which include:

> a particular attentiveness or receptivity, a readiness to engage with the performance in ways which cannot be understood as

narrative or hermeneutic. It is an aesthetic which involves a concept of spectatorship as intimacy (intimate contact with the object of attention) depending on separateness, but not on the spectatorial distance of a masterful abstraction. For the spectator, what is on offer is a simple, direct, and moving pleasure; what is required, it seems, is a meditation of the same naivety and truthfulness as that in which the plays were written.

(Koppen 1997: 804)

Intimacy, pleasure, truthfulness, and an innocence willing to be taken by surprise – these are all crucial attributes of Fornes's theater.

Part I

The 1960s

"Let me be wrong. But also not know it."

1   Getting started

For Fornes, the 1960s was a period of discovery, one in which she began playwriting almost by accident and then never stopped. She had no aspiration to become a playwright, but from early on she had creative inclinations that first sought expression as a painter and a textile designer. At some point early in the 1960s – it is difficult to pinpoint exactly when – she found herself possessed by "this obsessive idea, as if you have a nightmare and for a while you can't shake it" (Cummings 1985: 51), and for three weeks, she wrote around the clock, calling in sick to work and stopping only to step out for groceries. The idea took shape as a one-act play. "Writing it was the most incredible experience," she later said. "A door was opened which was a door to paradise" (Savran 1988: 55). Later, when a friend of a friend told her about a theater on the West Coast that was looking for new plays, she sent the play off on a lark. It was selected for production, paired with another one-act, and presented in the theater's second space. On November 29, 1963, at age 33, with no formal theater training or practical experience, Fornes made her professional playwriting debut.

At that time, Fornes had been living for years in Greenwich Village, the neighborhood around New York's Washington Square long famous as an urban bohemia and center of artistic innovation. Following World War II, the avant-garde in contemporary art shifted from Europe to the USA, leading to radical developments in all of the arts in the 1950s: abstract expressionism and action painting, the Black Mountain poets, the New York School and the Beats, the experiments of composer John Cage and choreographer Merce Cunningham, bebop bending into modern jazz, the Living

Theatre, Happenings, and so on. These new forms, characterized by spontaneity, a restless, sometimes frenetic energy, and a rejection of traditional conventions, opened up realms of possibility for a new wave of artists who would define the 1960s: Warhol and other Pop Art pioneers, underground filmmakers, Fluxus, the Judson dancers, and the Off-Off Broadway theater movement. In a utopian pursuit of absolute freedom and close-knit community, these 1960s artists combined elements of elite and popular art in order to create what Sally Banes describes in *Greenwich Village 1963* as a kind of avant-garde, urban, folk art:

> For one thing, often the style of the works – low-budget, deliberately crude, home-made, nonrealistic, small scale, often humorous or playful, improvisatory, and personal in presentation – invited comparison with the rough-hewn vitality of naive painting, home movies, small-town civic pageantry, and festival occasions. For another, the content of these avant-garde works often recalled that of folk art – life's daily activities and objects, no matter how seemingly humdrum; the body in all its simultaneous grace and grotesqueness; the social life of the community. Finally, even the means of production and the functions of the avant-garde films, artworks, and performances of all kinds seemed folklike: the participants were family and friends; the materials were usually whatever was at hand; often the venues were not official stages or museums, but churches, clubs, lofts, storefronts, even homes; the audiences were local, sometimes learning about the performances through word of mouth; the times were often after-hours; the scale was intimate; and the unpolished amateur-style itself invited potential participation by anyone in the community.
>
> (Banes 1993: 93)

This is the context out of which Fornes's theater emerged, and her work cannot be fully understood without some sense of it. Her professional debut came in San Francisco, but she was a creature of New York, Greenwich Village, and the Off-Off Broadway theater community. Off-Off Broadway shaped Fornes and she, in turn, shaped it. Long after the movement had faded, she continued to make theater by much the same means.

Bohemian roots: growing up in Havana

Fornes came of age in New York City, but she was born and raised in Havana, Cuba, and her humble and eccentric family life there prepared her well for life as an artist. Born on May 14, 1930, she was the daughter of Carlos Luis and Carmen Hismenia (Collado) Fornes. Her father lived in Florida until age 7, when his family returned to Havana and his mother opened what became a successful school. Carlos himself received little formal education. He was a wanderer at heart, spending time with family friends in the USA and traveling through California as a hobo. At age 17, he met and fell in love with Carmen, a teacher at his mother's school, and two years later, after a tour of duty in the US Army, they were married. Like her husband, Carmen was a free spirit. Both of her parents had died before she was ten; her older brothers placed her and a sister in a convent school where she lived until she was 19. Carlos and Carmen had six children, three boys and three girls, Maria Irene being the youngest. The family was poor and moved often. In the early years of the Depression, they lived on an uncle's orange farm and later in the unused servant's quarters of an aunt's house in Havana. Fornes's father worked off and on as a low-level bureaucrat in Cuba's burgeoning civil service. Her mother stopped teaching to run the household and raise the children, occasionally taking in piecework sewing beach bags.[1]

Like anyone from a family of limited means, Fornes grew up learning how to make do with whatever was at hand. In *Letters from Cuba*, the boy Enrique reads from a letter that describes receiving canned food from a relative in the United States – "We liked food in cans. It had an American taste. A little taste of tin." – and then saving the empty cans for future use:

> It was good because we could use the cans as glasses to drink water, or pots to heat water for coffee or containers to put food in and save it in the refrigerator. We could make holes in the bottom and turn them into pots for plants ... We kept one (without the holes) to put on the roof to collect water when it rains. Mother likes to wash her hair with rainwater. I kept another in my room to hit with a spoon as a cowbell to use when I play music with my group. We also keep a candle in the

sardine can. When the lights go out, Mama lights the candle. We thank you for the light.

(Fornes 2007: 31)

This type of homespun inventiveness became a hallmark of Fornes's theatermaking. It made her a natural for the scavenger aesthetic of Off-Off Broadway, celebrated for being resource poor but rich in imagination. It made her a frequenter of second-hand stores, flea markets, garage sales, antique barns, and junk shops, where she would find costumes, props, and inspiration for plays she was working on. Fornes's fondness for found objects became a decisive element in her playmaking.

As Fornes and her siblings grew up, they knew that their family was somehow different, but they did not know how, as she explained it, "until the film *You Can't Take It With You* came to Havana. When we saw that we could finally identify ourselves" (Harrington 1966: 33).

Both my parents had Bohemian inclinations – at a time when there was no such thing as Bohemian life in Havana. Neither my father nor my mother thought that they were living in any special style, but they were. They were never concerned about ordinary, everyday, normal things. My father was a bureaucrat, but he had no education. My mother had a degree in teaching. It wasn't that there was a special emphasis on the arts, not that at all. But the difference with my parents – in my parents, in my parents! – was their thinking, the way they thought about life.

(Kelly 1990a: A8)

Her mother took the children to the local Catholic church more for social and cultural reasons than out of religious devotion. Her father kept a notebook filled with philosophical maxims and other musings about life. He organized family poetry readings and drawing contests. "He read all the time, and my mother read all the time. And they would talk books, books, books, ideas, ideas, ideas" (Kelly 1990a: A9). Fornes inherited their love of language and verbal expression, but she never became much of a reader herself, in part because she was dyslexic. Like her father, she had little formal education and tremendous intellectual curiosity. She attended

Escuela Publican No. 12 in Havana for three-and-a-half years; after that, she was an autodidact for life, gaining knowledge through experience, observation, travel, conversation, and going to museums and the movies. She learned, in effect, by osmosis.

Fornes grew up in Depression-era Cuba during the early years of the Batista regime, a time when Cubans moved to and from the United States more easily than under Castro. For years, her mother dreamed of moving to the USA with her family. Eventually, her father assented, promising to follow after in a year if she liked it there. Carmen was still in the process of obtaining a visa when Carlos died of a heart attack at age 53. Not long after, in October 1945, she and her two younger daughters, Margarita and Maria Irene, age 15, emigrated to New York, arriving from Miami on a train called the Silver Meteor. After living for a time in a basement room in the South Bronx, they settled on the West Side of Manhattan, living in an apartment on Columbus Avenue and 62nd Street which was later razed to make way for the construction of Lincoln Center. Fornes spoke little English when she arrived in the USA. With the help of Cuban nuns in New York, she was admitted to St. Joseph's Academy, a Catholic school in Washington Square; after six weeks she dropped out. In 1947, she took a folk dancing class at the New School for Social Research and found a new community in the post-war counter-culture of Greenwich Village. It became her home for most of her adult life. Initially, she lived in an apartment on 16th Street. Eventually, she took an apartment at One Sheridan Square in the heart of the West Village where she lived for the next forty years.

Bohemian roots: settling in Greenwich Village

Early on in her New York life, Fornes worked in a factory that made service medals and ribbons for the military, the first in a series of routine jobs that supported her while she pursued personal and artistic interests, including painting. She studied with celebrated teacher and pioneer abstract expressionist Hans Hofmann (1880–1966) at his studio on 8th Street and for one summer at his school in Provincetown on Cape Cod. From 1954 to 1957, Fornes lived and traveled in Europe. Her initial destination was a tiny fishing village on the Mediterranean coast of Spain, where she planned to paint the locals – "I thought I was Gauguin. The people of the village thought I was crazy." (Harrington 1966: 33) – but she soon relocated to Paris, where she lived la vie bohème for several years. She continued to paint but without conviction. Painting, she later said, "never really reached a personal depth for me. I always had to force myself to work. I never found that place where you're touching on something vital to your own survival, to your own life" (Cummings 1985: 52). Nevertheless, Hofmann's tutelage introduced Fornes to aesthetic principles that eventually influenced her approach to theater. As a teacher, he was famous for his "push-pull" theory, which

> stipulates that space in an abstract painting is created by juxtaposing forms and their surrounds in such a way that their color and placement cause them to appear to advance and recede in varying degrees ... The effect is a lively activation of space, imparting to the painting a sense of energy and vitality.
>
> (Colpitt 2002: 103)

Hofmann focused on how the two-dimensional form of painting could achieve a sense of depth without resort to perspective. Though Fornes gave up painting before she was 30, Hofmann's push-pull principle had a lasting, subliminal effect on her. In 1990, she said:

> I realized only recently that that had had a very strong impact on my playwriting, because I compose my plays guided not by story line but more by energies that take place within each scene, and also the energies that take place between one scene and the scene that follows. It's like Hofmann's push-and-pull in that the narrative doesn't control how the play proceeds, but the development of the energies within the play.
>
> (May and Lesniak 1990: 178)

Hofmann's theory also informed her composition of theatrical space as a director, particularly in the way that stillness in her stage pictures gained dynamism (the push-pull of advancing and receding) from her precise juxtaposition of figure (actor) and ground (scenery).

Figure 2 Maria Irene Fornes and Susan Sontag (*c.* 1960).

Another formative influence was the original Roger Blin production of Samuel Beckett's *Waiting for Godot* (1953), which Fornes saw in Paris. Even though she did not speak French, the play had a powerful impact:

> Imagine a writer whose theatricality is so amazing and so important that you could see a play of his, not understand one word, and be shook up. When I left that theater I felt that my life had changed, that I was seeing everything with a different clarity.
>
> (Cummings 1985: 52)

This oft-repeated anecdote has led some critics to exaggerate the immediacy of Beckett's effect on Fornes, who did not write her first play for another six years. By that time, she had also seen the 1958 production of *Ulysses in Nighttown* starring Zero Mostel and was impressed by his bravura performance, Joyce's muscular language, the play's non-linear structure, and the fact that it took place in an unconventional theater space.[2] "Still I didn't think I wanted to write a play," Fornes later claimed, "I just thought, 'How wonderful, what an incredible thing'" (Savran 1988: 55).

By her own account, Fornes took up writing on a whim. In a 1986 *Village Voice* profile, Ross Wetzsteon recounts how on a Saturday night in the spring of 1961, Fornes and the writer Susan Sontag were hanging out in Greenwich Village looking for a party. When Sontag voiced frustration about a novel she wanted to write, Fornes insisted that they give up their evening plans, go back to the apartment they shared, sit down at the kitchen table, and just set to work. When they got home, as if to prove how simple it was, Fornes sat down to write as well. With no experience and no idea how to start, she opened up a cookbook at random and started a short story using the first word of each sentence on the page. "I might never have even thought of writing if I hadn't pretended I was going to show Susan how easy it was" (Wetzsteon 1986: 42).[3]

By that time, Fornes had already taken a tentative step towards playwriting when she translated letters she brought with her from Cuba that were written to her great-grandfather from a cousin in Spain. "At first I was just translating them for myself, not for anyone else to read" (Betsko and Koenig 1987: 155), but in response to a playwriting contest announced by new Cuban President Fidel Castro, she decided to turn the original letters in Spanish into a script called *La viuda* (*The Widow*) (Winks 1986: 28). The correspondence takes place between 1899 and 1902, just after the Spanish-American War led to Cuban independence. It centers on a woman in her seventies named Angela, who dictates a series of letters in which she asserts from afar her legal rights as the widow of a husband from whom she was estranged for decades. The play was presented in Spanish in New York, broadcast as a radio play by the University of Mexico, and published in 1961 in Havana in an anthology of contemporary Cuban plays. Fornes never staged the play herself or translated it into English. In her career, it stands more as a precursor than a first play.

That distinction belongs to the first play she wrote in English, the one she dashed off in a nineteen-day flurry as a kind of exorcism and titled *There! You Died!* When she heard that the San Francisco

Actors Workshop was looking for new plays, she sent the play off with no expectation and was delighted that it was selected for production with James Schevill's *The Master* on a bill of one-acts, both directed by Herbert Blau, the theater's producing director.[4]

Tango Palace (1963)

Tango Palace – as Fornes later renamed the play – is a wild, claustrophobic, two-character drama that uses forms of social hierarchy (master/slave, warden/inmate, teacher/student, parent/child, even matador/bull) to explore the bounds and bonds of an ambiguously intimate relationship. Isidore is "an androgynous clown" described by one reviewer as "a wild, flamboyant horror, a bewigged, lipsticked half-man half-woman who prances and flutters in a lewd, hilarious travesty of womanliness" (MacKenzie 1963: D27). Leopold is "an earnest youth" dressed in a business suit and sporting a tattoo on his chest that reads "This is man. Heaven or bust." The play takes place in Isidore's lair, an ornately furnished room padlocked shut from the inside. In the beginning, Leopold emerges like a newborn from a large canvas sack and finds himself a prisoner subject to Isidore's fierce tutelage. Over the course of three scenes, these two eccentrics go from seeming strangers to partners so agonizingly enmeshed that one of them must die. Leopold's first lesson comes when Isidore grabs a whip that hangs on the wall and lashes Leopold, saying, "This is my whip. And that is pain." This sets the tone for a series of mind games, object lessons, and tender encounters that erupt into outbursts of escalating violence.

The first scene ends with a familiar practical joke when Leopold persuades Isidore to close his eyes and imagine something and then Leopold empties a pitcher of water over his head. The second scene ends with a more serious betrayal of trust when Isidore entices Leopold to "be a good bull and charge" at him and then thrusts a banderilla in his back. In the third and final scene, Leopold resolves once and for all to kill his mentor, but he cannot summon the will to do so – until Isidore provokes him into a duel and then allows Leopold to stab him in the heart. This is the lesson in pain that sets Leopold free. The stage darkens and the padlocked door magically opens. Isidore, instantly resurrected and dressed as an angel, appears against a clouded blue sky, beckoning Leopold to follow. Leopold walks through the door with cautious determination, headed for "Heaven or bust" (as his tattoo says) and "ready for the next stage of their battle" (Fornes 1971: 162).

Leopold starts off playing the waggish schoolboy to Isidore's flamboyantly strict schoolmaster, but ultimately, *Tango Palace* needs to be seen as a love story. In the second scene, Isidore tells Leopold to stop looking at him "like a lover. Transfigured by the presence of the beloved. Looking as though you want to breathe the minute bubbles of air imprisoned in each of my pores" (Fornes 1971: 146). Leopold is desperate to find a way to escape what he calls "this cave," but in the meantime, he yearns for tender mercies from Isidore and laments receiving only "nastiness ... and meanness and abuse" in return. In performance, Isidore's cruelty is leavened by what he calls "my unconventional pageantry" – a tango lesson in the first scene, a mock bullfight in the second, and a ritualistic dance with beetle masks in the third – but these are only momentary diversions. *Tango Palace*'s manic rhythm of trust and betrayal and forgiveness is the kind that often characterizes tempestuous love relationships. Isidore and Leopold are not explicit lovers, but they suffer each other the way lovers do. They seem to be at one only when they are at war or at play. Their emotional tango is the dance of power and passion between two people whose mutual bond is unbearable yet unbreakable.

A metatheatrical conceit

In addition to dances, games, and role-playing, *Tango Palace* includes a device that suggests an early self-consciousness about writing for the stage and, at the same time, forecasts a metatheatrical vein that runs through Fornes's subsequent work. In the text, Fornes stipulates that the stage direction "*(Card)*" indicates that "each time Isidore feels he has said something important he takes a card from his pocket or from a drawer and flips it across the room in any direction" (Fornes 1971: 129). These cards contain Isidore's wisdom, his pithy observations and witty watchwords for right living. When Leopold picks one up, reads it aloud, and finds a line of dialogue that was just spoken, Isidore explains:

Figure 3 Tango Palace at Theatre Genesis in New York (1973), directed by Fornes and Michael Smith. Bill Moor as Isidore (in white tunic with banderillas) and Ben Masters as Leopold. Fornes made the set out of bubble wrap she found on the street.

These are not my cards. They are yours. It's you who need learning, not me. I've learned already. *(Card)* I know all my cards by heart. *(Card)* I can recite them in chronological order and I don't leave one word out. *(Card)* What's more I never say a thing which is not an exact quotation from one of my cards. *(Card)* That's why I never hesitate.

(Fornes 1971: 134)

Isidore's cards recall the educational flashcards once used to teach arithmetic, foreign language vocabulary, and other rote subjects. When Leopold argues that he does not want to learn this way, Isidore insists that there is no other way to learn, lending a mischievous sense of predestination to the play, suggesting that *all* that takes place has already been determined, scripted, recorded for future playback. A letter from Fornes to Blau suggested a connection to the stiff paper punchcards used to program computers at the time of the first production. In her "original conception of the play, Isidore was not a man, but an IBM machine who communicated with Leopold by means of printed cards, lights, and sounds. The IBM machine was, to put it in very simple terms, the master mind of society" (Blau 1999: 79). This Orwellian notion gave way to an intense passion between teacher and student, with the cards functioning as the chief instrument of Isidore's pedagogical tyranny. But on a metatheatrical level, as the play progresses and cards litter the stage, the chaotic flurry suggests that the written text has the capacity to deconstruct or unwrite or reprogram itself. The order of speech seems as random as that of shuffled playing cards, implying a dada version of the play in which the lines are delivered in whatever order they come off the top of the deck.

Tango Palace introduces a number of motifs that came to characterize Fornes's work, including the dialectic of pleasure and pain, the related themes of love and violence, props that take on an iconic significance, brief outbursts of theatrical performance, and a puckish sense of irony. Two elements, one scenic and one concerning characters, prove to be especially important. The sets for Fornes plays often include a small, confined space within an already confined domestic interior. This enclosed area, which might be an alcove, a closet or vestibule, even a tiny room, is framed off by the surrounding area in a way that often makes it feel like an inner sanctum or cell, isolated, private, and potent. In *Tango Palace*, the space-within-the-space is Isidore's "shrine," an upstage recess decorated by flower-shaped light bulbs where Isidore sits Buddha-like at the start surrounded by an odd assortment of objects, including a guitar, a whip, a toy parrot that talks, a Persian helmet from the ancient battle at Salamis, two beetle masks, and a compass that points in the direction of joy. This cell, if not always called for in the script, appears in many productions Fornes directed. It becomes a scenic emblem of psychic interiority, a deeper inside or soul space, and it is often associated with a recurring archetypal character in Fornes's drama.

Leopold is the first instance of what I will call the Innocent. Unknowing, he is born out of his womb-like sack into Isidore's den, a prisoner of the world who hears a voice in his head that he cannot quite make out. He knows "there is a way out because there have been moments when I have been away from here ... I mean there are moments when I've felt this is not all there is" (Fornes 1971: 143). This intimation of realms of thought and experience not yet in reach will define many other Fornes characters, not all of them young and most of them, after Leopold, female. After the tyrannical Isidore and the bombastic Dr. Kheal, characters explicitly identified as teachers drop out of Fornes's plays, just as she herself dropped out of formal schooling at a relatively young age. But the presence of the Innocent and the corresponding focus on learning, gaining literacy, and the relation of cognition to imagination, emotion, sensation, and the conduct of life becomes a predominant feature. Fornes's theater is both an epistemology and an ontology.

Notes

1 Biographical information about Fornes comes from numerous sources: interviews, feature stories in newspapers, reference works. Two profiles in the *Village Voice* – Harrington (1966) and Wetzsteon (1986) – are among the most cited. The most thorough biography appears in Kent (1996), which includes information about the Cuban political and cultural context of Fornes's youth.

2 The play, which Fornes said "had this great impact on me" (Cummings 1985: 52), was performed at the Rooftop Theatre on the sixth floor of a former burlesque house at 111 East Houston Street. Conceived and directed by Burgess Meredith, the piece was adapted by Marjorie Barkentin

and Padraic Colum mainly from the Nighttown section of James Joyce's *Ulysses*. Zero Mostel received an Obie Award for his portrayal of Leopold Bloom.

3 A different version of this story can be found in Delgado and Svich (1999: 255). Though it was not widely known until the *New York Times* published excerpts from Sontag's diaries in 2006, she and Fornes were lovers who lived together in Sontag's apartment on West End Avenue in New York from 1959 to 1963, a formative time in their respective careers. Sontag was soon to launch her career as a celebrated author, cultural critic, and public intellectual; Fornes was about to discover theater as an outlet for her creativity. For more on Fornes and Sontag, see Rollyson and Paddock (2000) and Sontag (2008).

4 When Blau wrote to Fornes in the early 1960s to ask permission to do her play, "the letter came back, return to sender. By an amazing coincidence, Blau happened to pick up a novel which was dedicated to Ms. Fornes, tracked down the novelist and finally Ms. Fornes. It was like fate" (Winks 1986: 28). The novel in question is Sontag's *The Benefactor* (1963), which, in fact, is dedicated to Fornes.

2 Off-Off Broadway: the good scene

By the time of Fornes's San Francisco debut in 1963, a theatrical development of major importance was well under way in Greenwich Village. More and more small, independent, loosely organized theater groups with very little money began producing plays in unconventional venues such as churches, coffeehouses, storefronts, galleries, and bars. The work was boisterous and willfully amateur in spirit, presented with little regard (if not outright disdain) for Broadway and the growing number of professional Off Broadway theaters. It was, in the best sense, a community theater, presented by and for a generation of bohemians who gravitated to Greenwich Village without, for the most part, professional training or ambition. This theater – first dubbed "Off-Off Broadway" on November 24, 1960 by the *Village Voice* theater listings – was the collective effort of a burgeoning counter-culture reacting on one hand to the main-stream, white-bread conformism of the Eisenhower years and to the radical innovations of the 1950s artistic avant-garde on the other. It sought a theatrical language that combined European aesthetics with American restlessness, that harnessed the anti-logic of the so-called "Theatre of the Absurd" to a parody of popular culture, and that expressed the inchoate values of a new generation.

Of the many early influences on Off-Off Broadway, none was more important than the Living Theatre. Through the 1950s, Julian Beck and Judith Malina worked with painters, poets, actors, and musicians in an effort to forge a new American lyric drama, one that focused more on language, sound, and image than on personal psychology and family relationships. In the 1960s, this led to "experiments with putting actuality on stage which led eventually to eliminating the separation between art and life, between dramatic action and social action, between living and acting, between spectator and performer, and between revolution and theatre" (Shank 1982: 9). Beck and Malina's effort to create a more visceral, more confrontational experience was signaled by their seminal 1959 production of Jack Gelber's *The Connection*. The play, which presents a group of junkies waiting for a fix, used the torpor of heroin addiction as a metaphor for a more pervasive, existential entropy.[1] In its radical form and taboo subject, *The Connection* affirmed a range of possibilities that Off-Off Broadway theaters would explore for the next decade.

Cino, Judson, La MaMa, and others

Off-Off Broadway was not a movement so much as "a loose constellation of enterprises, whose aesthetic concerns often seemed wildly divergent: there was never a single leader or a manifesto for this movement, or even a coherent set of objectives. There was, however, a clear sense of shared community, and a shared resistance to the economic imperatives of mainstream American culture" (Bottoms 2004a: 3). Starting around 1960, vest-pocket theaters began to spring up in makeshift locations around Washington Square and the Lower East Side. Many were short-lived, but four emerged as the leading Off-Off playhouses. Each was founded and led by a charismatic impresario with an interest in new plays and a commitment to artistic freedom. Joe Cino opened a coffee house at 31 Cornelia Street in December 1958; occasional poetry readings led to play readings, and by 1960, Caffe Cino was mounting fully staged productions on a tiny platform (eight feet by eight feet) set up on wooden milk crates. Reverend Al Carmines joined the Judson Memorial Church in 1961 as assistant minister and head of its arts program with a mandate to expand the church's performance activities; on November 18, 1961, the Judson Poets' Theater debuted with a pair of one-acts performed in the church's choir loft. On the model of the Caffe Cino, Ellen Stewart, a fashion designer from Chicago with Louisiana roots, opened Café La MaMa in a basement on East Ninth Street in 1962. Harassed by municipal authorities over zoning restrictions and code violations, the theater moved several times before settling in a former meatpacking plant at

Figure 4 Fornes at the Caffe Cino with (from left to right) composer Al Carmines, fellow Off-Off playwright Harry Koutoukas, and director Lawrence Kornfeld (*c.* 1965).

74 East Fourth Street; in the process, the name was changed to La MaMa ETC (for "Experimental Theatre Club"). Ralph Cook converted a second-floor meeting room in the parish hall of St. Mark's Church in the Bowery into a black box theater and opened it as Theatre Genesis in July 1964. That October, he presented *Cowboys* and *The Rock Garden*, a pair of one-act plays by a 20-year-old waiter at the Village Gate named Sam Shepard.[2]

Each of these theaters, like its founder, had its own unique personality, but they were united in their mission to promote a downtown theater that would give aspiring actors, directors, and especially playwrights a platform to express themselves. Before each performance at La MaMa, Ellen Stewart greeted spectators by ringing a bell and saying in her mellow, Cajun-inflected voice, "Good evening, ladies and gentlemen. Welcome to La MaMa, dedicated to the playwright and all aspects of the theatre." In addition to Caffe Cino, Judson, La MaMa, and Theatre Genesis,

American Place Theatre, New Dramatists (a playwrights organ-
ization founded in 1949), the Playwrights Unit (funded with
profits from the Broadway run of Edward Albee's *Who's Afraid
of Virginia Woolf?*), and other operations concentrated on
readings, workshops, and low-budget productions of new plays.[3]
Off-Off Broadway nurtured a generation of playwrights, including
H.M. Koutoukas, Sam Shepard, Megan Terry, Jean Claude van
Itallie, David Starkweather, Tom Eyen, Soren Agenoux, Ruth
Krauss, Lanford Wilson, Leonard Melfi, Doric Wilson, Paul Foster,
Robert Heide, Rosalyn Drexler, Rochelle Owens, Ronald Tavel,
Murray Mednick, Robert Patrick, Maria Irene Fornes, and many
others. Most faded into obscurity, moved on to other pursuits, or
continued to work on the margins, but Sam Shepard, Lanford
Wilson, and Fornes went on to become major American playwrights
with sustained careers.

The hallmark of Off-Off Broadway was an unfettered spirit that
reveled in the freedom to explore, to experiment, to say or do anything and to fail, with impunity. Most plays ran less than an hour
in performance, and pairing two or more one-acts as an evening's
offering was common practice. The general lack of funding eliminated
commercial pressure and promoted creative ingenuity. Plays were
produced on shoestring budgets, often with materials that were
picked up off the street or borrowed from friends. Admission was
minimal, if not free. Actors worked for no money or a share of
donations collected at the door. The venues were small, accom-
modating audiences of less than one hundred; the close proximity of
actor to actor, and actor to spectator, fostered a performance
dynamic that was intimate one moment and confrontational the
next. Talented professionals worked side by side with rank ama-
teurs, and an inchoate Off-Off acting style developed that favored
sheer energy and theatrical flair over genuine technique. Over the
course of the 1960s, a number of successful productions, such as
Fornes's *Promenade*, Megan Terry's *Viet Rock*, and Jean Claude
van Itallie's *America Hurrah*, attracted commercial producers and
were remounted in Off Broadway houses. But the phenomenon was
sustained more by a perpetual sense of possibility than a consistent
record of artistic achievement. In commemorating the thirtieth
anniversary of the Obies, Richard Gilman listed some of Off-Off
Broadway's less appealing traits:

There was widespread lack of skill, sometimes compensated for by ardor and ideality but more often not. And also: self indulgence; juvenile acting-out; theory run amok; false gurus; fake avant-gardism; dreary imitations of Beckett, Ionesco, Pinter; a dispiriting hunt for modern "myths"; an equally dispiriting idea that you could devise "rituals" as though they were party games; an obnoxious belief that if you shouted "Love!" and "Freedom!" loudly enough you would bring them about; and other instances of nonsense, witlessness, and dreck.

(Gilman 1985)

Nevertheless, Off-Off Broadway had a spirit, energy, and infectious idealism that compensated for its shortcomings. Just often enough, these raw ingredients would combine with enough talent and imagination to create a genuine theatrical sensation. A reporter for the *New York Times Magazine* captured the zeitgeist when she wrote:

The last Off Off Broadway show I saw, an actress in a negligee accidentally tripped into my lap during the performance. The time before that, I got into an all-night bull session with the playwright after the show. The plays? Man, they're alive. Even when they stink, they're alive! And you get it all for a buck. Can you beat that anywhere?

(Lester 1965)

Michael Smith (1966), who chronicled Off-Off Broadway as the theater critic for the *Village Voice*, simply called it "the good scene."

The Open Theatre connection

Fornes was a theatrical neophyte when she wrote *Tango Palace*, but she soon made a concerted effort to develop herself as a playwright. She began to apply for and receive grants and awards, starting with fellowships from the John Hay Whitney Foundation in 1961 and the Centro Mexicano de Escritores in 1962. She joined the Playwrights Unit of the famous Actors Studio, where she was able to get feedback from Lee Strasberg and others in response to workshop presentations of her writing. She took a Method acting course at the Gene Frankel studio. The Actors Studio sponsored a one-night "special performance" of *Tango Palace* (still titled *There! You Died!*) on April 6, 1964, which then traveled to the Spoleto Festival in Italy. She submitted her second play, *The Successful Life of 3*, to Arthur Ballet's Office of Advanced Drama Research at the University of Minnesota, which underwrote the play's premiere (on a double bill with *Tango Palace*) at the Firehouse Theatre in Minneapolis in January 1965. That winter in New York, she participated in a series of workshops with the Open Theatre, a group with which she would have a loose affiliation for the rest of the decade.

Started in 1963 as an ongoing workshop, the Open Theatre became the most important ensemble theater company in New York City. In the beginning, members met once or twice a week to conduct physical, vocal, and improvisational exercises (many invented on the spot) that would take them beyond their Method training and help them to create a performance vocabulary better suited to the non-naturalistic dramaturgy of Brecht on the one hand and Beckett, Genet, and Ionesco on the other. Early on, the Open Theatre included playwrights Megan Terry, Jean Claude van Itallie, and Michael Smith, critics Richard Gilman and Gordon Rogoff, and more than a dozen actors, including most notably Joseph Chaikin, who emerged as the charismatic, if reluctant, leader and artistic director of the group. Chaikin had been a member of the Living Theatre since 1959, but when the Living left for Europe in 1964, he chose to stay behind in order to pursue a new way of acting that was more physical than psychological, more expressive than behavioral, and more abstract than referential.[4]

The Open Theatre was always animated by a creative tension between being a laboratory conducting open-ended experiments and a company creating original work intended for an audience. That process-versus-product dynamic led to limited, public showings of the group's work in progress. In the winter and spring of 1965, on alternate Monday nights, the Open Theatre performed a series of eight different programs at the Sheridan Square Playhouse, marking "the climax of the Open Theatre's work in the bright-spirited, pyrotechnical vein," a period marked by a pop sensibility and an inclination towards social satire (Pasolli 1970: 69). Fornes's *The Successful Life of 3* was performed as part of these showcases, directed initially by Chaikin and then restaged by Gilman. Over the next few years, Fornes maintained an affiliation with the group. In

1966–67, she was one of three writers who participated in a workshop led by director Jacques Levy that sought to devise a play on the theme of assassination. The piece was to be modeled after Peter Brook's phantasmagoric *US*, but difficulties in collaboration contributed to the project's breakdown before coming to fruition. In the politically charged summer of 1968, wanting an anti-war piece for their tour of Europe, the Open Theatre performed Fornes's satirical *The Red Burning Light*, which was revived a year later for a run at La MaMa on a bill with her *A Vietnamese Wedding*.

While Fornes was not an official member of the Open Theatre, her Off-Off Broadway plays share an affinity with the group's aesthetic and with two fundamental Open Theatre techniques in particular: transformation and role-playing. For the Open Theatre, a transformation was an abrupt and radical shift in the circumstances governing an improvisation. Without warning or transition, even in mid-sentence, an actor changes when or where a scene is taking place or the theatrical style of the improvisation or even the identity or nature of his character. Other actors are expected to make their own immediate adjustments in order to keep the transformed situation alive and moving forward. Initially, this exercise was used to develop an actor's focus and spontaneity, but the practice lent itself to scripted "transformation plays," such as Megan Terry's *Calm Down Mother* and *Keep Tightly Closed in a Cool Dry Place*. Fornes's *The Successful Life of 3* is a transformation play. And the principle behind transformation – a radical discontinuity of time, place, and situation – became a general trait of Fornes's plays, which often take the form of a series of short, discontinuous scenes that shift abruptly and without clear narrative logic. Emphasis is on an ever-changing here-and-now.

The Open Theatre also did an exercise called "Perfect People," which was rooted in the contemporary understanding of social behavior as a kind of mask concealing and protecting personal identity.

> Perfect people are the sanitized, regularized, and glamorized types which the image-makers have us all secretly believing we ought to be – those clean-cut men and virginal women who live a kind of half-life with double intensity in the magazine advertisements and television commercials.
>
> (Pasolli 1970: 37)

The Open Theatre developed a series of exercises that placed these stereotypes of perfection in less than perfect situations, testing their ability to maintain their composure in the face of, say, a social taboo or a natural disaster. For example, in an exercise called "The Odets Kitchen," a tranquil family scene would suddenly be turned inside out. In the middle of dinner, parent and child or husband and wife would break out and express their hidden fears, secret fantasies, or unspoken feelings in a manner that was physically, vocally, and emotionally extreme, before resuming an outward calm that was then seen as a façade or role holding back an inner anguished truth.

Fornes did not write plays based on this exercise per se, but she did create characters based on this model. After *Tango Palace*, her 1960s plays are populated by two-dimensional characters known only by pronoun (He, She), number (3, 103, 105), letter (I, O, U, R, S, T), or occupation (Servant, Mother, Mayor, Soldier). The cardboard aristocrats of *Promenade* suggest a version of Perfect People as they maintain a blithe indifference and unruffled demeanor in the face of poverty and war. *Molly's Dream* is populated by idealized stereotypes drawn straight out of popular culture. *The Successful Life of 3* presents a triangle of generic figures so dispassionate in their pursuits that they make a mockery of emotion. The absence of true feeling here is so conspicuous that it seems to imply a paradoxical, comic pathos. When feeling is expressed, it becomes a performative gesture, just another part of the show and nothing that would crack the veneer of insistent nonchalance. Fornes accentuates this histrionism by borrowing theatrical or paratheatrical structures to organize the action. *The Successful Life of 3* is subtitled "a skit for vaudeville." *Dr. Kheal* takes the form of a mock lecture, *The Red Burning Light* a variety show, *Molly's Dream* a Hollywood western. *A Vietnamese Wedding*, altogether different in tone, enacts a ceremony. In one way or another, these first plays all emphasize role-playing, showmanship, striking a pose. They seem superficial, yet they suggest there is something heartfelt going on beneath the surface. Therein lies their peculiar charm.

The Successful Life of 3 (1965)

The Successful Life of 3 presents a trio of generic characters – He, a handsome young man; She, a sexy young lady; and a third character named 3, a plump middle-aged man – caught up in a plot that has the sweeping arc of a Hollywood romance played on fast forward. It presents a "life" of sex, love, marriage, money, career, and adventure so dispassionately pursued and easily achieved as to undermine their value and render the very idea of "success" meaningless. The play has ten scenes, making it Fornes's first experiment in writing a play in a series of brief, episodic, often inconclusive scenes. The result is a dizzying, deadpan comedy that exemplifies Fornes's delightful, often mischievous sense of humor.

In scene one, He and 3 both meet She in a doctor's office. In scene two, all three go on a date. By the third scene, He and She have married, and all three characters have lived together for ten years and had more children than they can count. Soon, She abandons the two men and 3 decides to go into business selling nylon rope to fishermen and becomes an instant tycoon. The play continues at the same whirlwind pace. Characters come and go at random. 3 begins a life of crime, goes to prison, escapes, becomes a mob gangster and then adopts a Zorro costume in order to steal from the rich and give to the poor. In the play's final moments, a policeman enters to arrest 3, and 3 shoots him dead, which leads into a finale called "Song of Ignorance" sung by all three characters with a chorus that repeats:

> Let me be wrong
> But also not know it.
> Be wrong,
> Be wrong,
> And, oh, not to know it.
> Oh! Let me be wrong.

(Fornes 1971: 199)

In a manner typical of Off-Off Broadway plays of the 1960s, *The Successful Life of 3* rejects dramatic logic regarding the relationship between cause and effect. Events of great magnitude are compressed into units of theatrical time so exaggeratedly brief as to make them trivial – to great comic effect. 3 goes off to start his business and returns seconds later in top hat and furs, a millionaire. Critic Richard Gilman, who staged the 1965 Open Theatre production of the play, described the revolving-door rhythm of the play:

In the scene in the doctor's office at the beginning of the play, one of the men is ushered into an inner room; we assume he is seeing the doctor but learn, when he comes back, that he has "banged" the nurse who led him in. The script merely indicated that they return, but our actors came back instantly, which suggested that the act had been consummated with blinding, unheard-of speed. It struck us all as wonderfully funny and, more than that, as being exactly true to the way Irene Fornés organizes her stage time and, by extension, her stage space. Things happen outside chronologies and beyond known boundaries; the center of the action is sometimes in language, sometimes in gesture or sheer mise-en-scène, but always in a dimension unlocatable by any of our ordinary means of determining the whereabouts of what we consider truths.

(Gilman 1971: 1)

The entire play is, in effect, a series of these transformational "quickies." Success, be it criminal, coital, or capitalist, becomes as easy as walking on and off the stage. But the pattern of instant gratification, funny as it is, also has a discomfiting effect, reducing great ambition and passionate desire to hollow impulse. Robert Pasolli described it this way:

They meet all the random events of their lives with the same low intensity of feeling, that of matter-of-fact acceptance. They are vaudeville characters (the play is subtitled a "skit for vaudeville") and live a routine of double takes, punchlines, non-sequiturs, freezes, incongruities, and blackouts. Vaudeville is their life-style, not merely their style of self-presentation; it is a matter of essence rather than one of illustration. They are cardboard funnymen, brightly entertaining, quirkily energetic and ingratiating. But the play's silliness has an edge to it, for the cumulative foolery is a deadened routine. These people are mechanisms engaged in a kind of verbal slapstick, indifferent to one another, giving and taking at whim, valuing no one thing above anything else. They are not people as we like to think of people; they are people as we are made to see them from Maria Irene Fornes's peculiar angle of vision. Their charm and appeal make us accept them, but what we've got then isn't very pretty.

(Pasolli 1967)

The Office (1966)

The most unusual chapter in Fornes's early career came in 1966 when she became the first Off-Off Broadway playwright on Broadway. While Fornes was a member of the Playwrights Unit of the Actors Studio, portions of a comedy she was writing called *The Office* were workshopped there. The Establishment Theatre Company, led by movie mogul Joseph E. Levine, the anti-establishment British comedian Peter Cook, and the Off Broadway producer Ivor David Balding, acquired the rights to the unfinished play and hired director/choreographer Jerome Robbins, fresh off the success of his *Fiddler on the Roof*, to stage the play on Broadway. Robbins, most renowned for his ballet and Broadway musical work, had also directed Arthur Kopit's black comedy *Oh, Dad, Poor Dad, Mama's Hung You in the Closet and I'm Feelin' So Sad* for the Phoenix Theatre in 1962 and Brecht's *Mother Courage and Her Children*, starring Anne Bancroft, on Broadway in 1963. For Fornes, it was an early, sudden, and short-lived leap into the commercial mainstream.

The Office takes place around Christmas-time in the offices of Hinch, Inc., a shipping company in sharp decline since the recent death of its founder. The action centers on the bumbling, neurotic office manager Albert Pfancoo, who hopes to lead the business back to prosperity. He is beleaguered by three comic female figures: Princess, Hinch's plump, sensuous widow; Miss Punk, a strait-laced spinster secretary who refuses to be fired; and Shirley Bisbee, the misfit girl-Friday he wants to hire in her stead. The comedy takes a strange, magical turn when it turns out that a Portrait of the late, lamented George Hinch can talk and soon confesses love for Shirley. The play ends with Shirley alone and uncertain whether to go or stay. "I just don't belong. I've never belonged anywhere," she laments, and then, as the lights fade, she and the Portrait dance about the stage together, singing a love song with the refrain:

For 'tis love, and love alone,
The world is seeking:

And 'tis love, and love alone,
That can repay!

The Office was scheduled to open at Henry Miller's Theatre on
May 12, 1966 with a noteworthy cast that included Elaine May
(Shirley), Jack Weston (Pfancoo), Ruth White (Princess), and Doris
Roberts (Miss Punk). But after ten preview performances, the producers closed the show, anticipating negative reviews. The play had
the same zest and whimsy as Fornes's other 1960s plays, but the
effort to channel it into a conventional situation comedy was
unsuccessful. Eight years later, critic Clive Barnes recalled *The
Office* as "a New York evening that never officially opened, but is
still well-spoken of by a loyal preview public" (1974: 53). Fornes
never returned to the play or to the commercial arena of Broadway.
Not altogether by choice, she became an outsider playwright,
working on the theatrical margins where resources and recognition
were limited but artistic freedom was assured.

Dr. Kheal (1968)

Dr. Kheal, the only one-character play Fornes ever wrote, takes the
form of a half-hour mock lecture given by a learned professor.
Dr. Kheal holds forth on a variety of subjects, asking rhetorical
questions for which he always has ready answers, illustrating his
ideas with charts, figures, and equations, abusing his imaginary
students for their stupidity, and concluding with a little song about
a spider. Each time Dr. Kheal takes up a new subject, he writes its
name on the blackboard. On Poetry. On Balance. On Ambition. On
Energy. On Speech. On Truth. On Beauty and Love. On Hope. On
Cooking. Coming early in Fornes's career, this list can be seen as a
cheeky prolegomenon to the body of work to come, an outline of
themes and principles that will surface in her plays again and again.
There is the persistent aesthetic concern with harmony, balance,
lyricism, and beauty, and there is the dual preoccupation with
language and with love, two metaphysical webs in which her
characters are often caught.

Dr. Kheal – whose name elides the words "kill" and "heal" – is
Fornes's contribution to theater's long tradition of bombastic wise
men, a lineage that stretches back to commedia dell'arte's Il

Dottore. These Learned Doctors assume a posture of intellectual superiority that eventually gives way to an amusing pedantic lunacy. Kheal's fiery temper, flamboyant egomania, and tyrannical insistence on his superior knowledge recall Isidore in *Tango Palace*, as much demagogue as pedagogue. "Wrong, wrong, wrong, wrong, wrong, wrong, wrong. Damn it! You're wrong," he harangues his students, echoing in a way the "Song to Ignorance" at the end of *The Successful Life of 3*. Richard Gilman (1971: 3) calls *Dr. Kheal* "an exercise in plausibility, a seeming parody of pedagogy but in fact a brilliant investigation of the myths of knowledge." While on the surface it derides the didacticism of institutionalized learning, its undercurrent celebrates the power and practice of thought and the pursuit of metaphysical truths. However absurd or silly Dr. Kheal's individual insights may be, the idea of having ideas gains legitimacy and appeal, leading to his final triumphant declaration: "There! That is what it is all about. Man is the rational animal."

The mock-lecture format allows Fornes to present intellectual ideas in an openly discursive manner. In the process, in addition to cataloguing Fornes's abiding themes, Dr. Kheal articulates two key principles of her dramaturgy.

> Don't you know that you can take a yes and a no and push them together, squeeze them together, compress them so they are one? That in fact that is what reality is? Opposites, contradictions compressed so that you don't know where one stops and the other begins?
>
> (Fornes 1971: 72)

Like the push-pull of Hans Hofmann, the compression of yes-and-no lends dynamism to Fornes's theater. This strategy of juxtaposition or conflation is contrasted moments later by a strategy of containment and indirection, one that reflects Dr. Kheal's (and Fornes's) ambivalence about language. "Truth," he says, "you name it and it vanishes." And then he stands like a bullfighter (again, similar to Isidore) and makes three quick passes with an imaginary sword. "There is truth. Three quick passes. Name it here, here, and here. Surround it, and you'll have it. Never touch it. It will vanish. That is truth ... elusive" (Fornes 1971: 69). At its best, Fornes's theater operates much the same way, using yes-no contradictions, witty

songs, charming characters, and short, inconclusive scenes to surround a slippery truth on three sides, capturing it for a fleeting
moment before allowing it to vanish into thin air.

A Vietnamese Wedding (1967)

This indirect approach can be seen at work in *A Vietnamese Wed-
ding*, a piece that Fornes created in 1967 for Angry Arts Week, a
New York City festival of protest against American involvement in
Vietnam. The text begins with a disclaimer:

> *A Vietnamese Wedding* is not a play ... The four people con-
> ducting the piece are hosts to the members of the audience who
> will enact the wedding, and their behavior should be casual,
> gracious, and unobtrusive.
>
> (Fornes 1971: 8)

What follows is a scenario for a theater event that uses four
facilitators and ten audience members to act out a Vietnamese
wedding ceremony. When first presented on February 4, 1967 at
Washington Square Methodist Church, the facilitators were Fornes
and three other regulars from the Judson Poets' Theater: Remy
Charlip, Aileen Passloff, and Florence Tarlow. In lieu of character
names, their names appear in the published text.

For the re-enactment, members of the audience volunteered or
were drafted to play the bride and groom and members of their
families. They were escorted to designated seats onstage and out-
fitted with sashes around their waists and garlands on their heads.
Florence described some of the customs surrounding the arranging
of a traditional match, including a visit to an astrologer to see if the
match is favored by the stars. The astrological signs of the volunteer
bride and groom were checked on a chart and the match was
declared desirable. Aileen described the families' ritual exchange of
betel nuts and areca leaves – symbols of conjugal love and goodwill – as a custom rooted in an ancient, tragic tale of two devoted
brothers who both fell in love with the same beautiful woman. The
formal wedding ceremony began with Vietnamese music and a
procession through the theater and back to the stage. Candles were
lit. Gifts of jewelry and money were given to the bride. Reading

from index cards, the father of the groom made a solemn request for the bride's hand for his son and the father of the bride offered his agreement. A message to the genie of marriage, the Rose Silk Thread God, was written on a red sheet of paper which the groom signed and then burned for good luck. With that, the couple was, in the fiction of the piece, officially married. Music played, whistles blew, and the four hosts led the wedding party and the audience through the theater and out into the street.

A Vietnamese Wedding is political theater at its most sublime. In 1967, with the war in Vietnam still escalating and the nightly news focusing mainly on American casualties, the piece made a profound anti-war statement. Military propaganda promotes a war effort by demonizing the enemy. The Fornes re-enactment did the opposite by emphasizing shared values and common practices. Once the volunteer participants and their sympathetic audience committed to the fiction of the wedding, the political argument became incontrovertible. In the emotional calculus of the event, what might otherwise be dismissed as a false syllogism – something like "I believe in marriage/the Vietnamese believe in marriage/therefore, I believe in the Vietnamese" – became a compassionate recognition of the humanity of Americans and Vietnamese alike. The ingenuity of the piece was the utter absence of the war itself, which is never mentioned, thus instigating a gap between the performance and the political-historical context framing the performance. With their knowledge of current events, the audience, so to speak, "supplied" the missing term of the war just as, in a different way, it supplied the "actors" that make the enactment happen.

A Vietnamese Wedding is as profoundly occasional as anything that Fornes ever created. While its immediacy passed with the Vietnam Era, Fornes continued to use the Kheal-like technique of surrounding a missing term and an unnamed truth on three sides. The oppression of women, the threat of nuclear destruction, political tyranny in Latin America, the AIDS epidemic, and institutionalized poverty are all political issues whose presence at the heart of a Fornes play is more implied than explicitly invoked and commented upon. This method can be traced back to aspects of Symbolist dramaturgy, as seen in a play such as Maeterlinck's tension-filled one-act *The Intruder* (1890). In that play, a worried family sits up late at night in virtual darkness awaiting the death of the ailing

mother in the next room. As they experience a series of phenomen-
ological cues – the wind in the trees, the squawk of startled swans,
a noise on the stair – the spectral approach of the figure of Death
itself is made palpable without ever being identified or represented
as such. As Dr. Kheal says, "Surround it, and you'll have it. Never
touch it. It will vanish." Pinter's comedies of menace pursue a
similar strategy, as does Beckett, famously, in *Waiting for Godot*,
which invites audience speculation about the title character by
refusing to say who or what he is. The Judges in *Fefu and Her
Friends* and the unexplained but worsening catastrophe in *The
Danube* are two prime examples of Fornes's use of this symbolist
technique. The action onstage focuses on the characters, their
domestic situations and personal, often passionate relationships,
even as it is circumscribed and pressured by an implicit (that is,
withheld in crucial ways) social or political condition. The true
event of the play happens in the space in between.

The Red Burning Light Or: Mission XQ3 (1968)

If A *Vietnamese Wedding* is sublime, Fornes's other anti-war play is
ridiculous, intentionally so. *The Red Burning Light Or: Mission
XQ3* excoriates American imperialism and what in the 1960s was
known as "the military-industrial complex" by presenting it in the
form of a traveling burlesque revue that one character calls "our demo-
cratic caravan of love." Drums roll, cymbals crash, and a buffoonish
General Kikkeelost, more master of ceremonies than military com-
mander, introduces his invading army as "the show ... that
leveled ... the world!" The cast marches out and performs a
patriotic opening number, during which a sexy young lady in khaki
panties, Private Lily, keeps saluting in a way that pops her shirt
open, exposing her breasts. "Oops, me little titty's showing," she
squeals. The General warns her to keep it clean, but by the end of
the opening number, the entire cast is displaying all manner of crude
and lewd behavior, bumping and grinding, burping and farting,
scratching their asses and picking their noses. This sets the stage and
the tone for a series of slapstick bits, running gags, clownish sex
acts, and upbeat musical routines, all in the service of the omnivorous
American war machine and its mission to spread "enlightenment,
truth, peace, and, in one word, our message, around the world."

The Red Burning Light is typical of agit-prop plays of the period: overtly theatrical in style, satirical in tone, unsubtle in political analysis. It was first performed by the Open Theatre on their 1968 European tour, directed by Fredric de Boer, choreographed by James Barbosa, with Open Theatre regulars such as Ron Faber, Ralph Lee, and Paul Zimet in the cast. It shares an affinity with the Open Theatre's *Viet Rock* (1966), although its cartoon violence, anarchic spirit, willful bad taste, and grotesque humor are more akin to Alfred Jarry's infamous *Ubu Roi* (1896). In April 1969, Fornes and Remy Charlip joined de Boer and Barbosa in restaging *The Red Burning Light* at La MaMa on a bill with *A Vietnamese Wedding*. The stark contrast of the two pieces must have highlighted the weaknesses of the former. In coupling runaway libido with reckless US militarism and presenting both ironically as music hall entertainment, Fornes aimed for a dark political comedy and, even for her most sympathetic critics, missed the mark. "Fornes's characteristic light touch is not well suited to protest themes and bitterly mocking satire," wrote Bonnie Marranca (Marranca and Dasgupta 1981: 60). "In her only out-and-out failure," echoed Ross Wetzsteon (1986: 45), "the disparity between the buffoonery of the characters and the destructive consequence of their behavior was too great to be bridged by even the most charming obliviousness." In 1987, when Marranca and PAJ Publications re-issued the original 1971 Winter House anthology of Fornes plays, *The Red Burning Light* was omitted.

Notes

1 Audiences were stunned by the play's meandering and fragmentary plotlessness, characters shooting up onstage, the jazz improvisations at each performance, and a framing device involving a film crew that treated the performers as actual drug addicts being recorded for a documentary film. Following their production of *The Brig* in 1963, the Living Theatre left the USA for political exile abroad and a long history of organizational struggles and changes. Julian Beck died in 1985 – Fornes's *The Conduct of Life* is dedicated to him – but as recently as April 2011, Judith Malina (aged 84) participated in the Third New York City Anarchist Art Festival at the Living Theatre.

2 For book-length studies of Off-Off Broadway, see Bottoms (2004a) and Crespy (2003). For more of a "you-are-there" perspective, read the

theater pages of the *Village Voice* from the time, especially the writings of Michael Smith.

3 For a thorough and trenchant overview of new play development in New York circa 1968, see Pasolli (1968).

4 For a full discussion of Joseph Chaikin and the Open Theatre, see Pasolli (1970) and Blumenthal (1984).

3 Key play: *Promenade* (the apotheosis of Judson)

Fornes's work in the 1960s was animated by a sense of free play that sometimes can be traced back to a play's conception. "Most of my plays start with a kind of fantasy game, just to see what happens," she said (Fornes 1977: 30). On one occasion, this effort "to take her own subconscious 'by surprise'" (Bottoms 2004a: 139) led her to create two stacks of cards, one with a different setting on each card and one with different character types. She randomly picked a card from each pile and found herself writing a scene for "Aristocrats" set in "Jail." The play that developed out of this exercise was *Promenade*, which she submitted to the Judson Poets' Theater in 1964, after seeing Rosalyn Drexler's *Home Movies* there.

Promenade debuted in April 1965, and for the next few years, she was as close to a house playwright as the Judson had. In May 1967, *The Successful Life of 3* was produced there as part of the Judson Arts and Happenings Carnival, and a month later, this production was coupled on a bill with *Celebrations*, a two-part exercise in Mariolatry. For *Celebrations*, Fornes staged *The Annunciation* in the church's garden. A variety piece about the archangel Gabriel's visit to the Virgin, it featured a patchwork of popular songs and religious texts that included Tim Hardin's "If I Were a Carpenter" and Rilke's *The Life of Mary*. A year later, in August 1968, *Dr. Kheal* ran for a series of Judson performances with David Tice in the title role. And in June 1969, a revised, full-length version of the Judson *Promenade* opened for a successful commercial run uptown. During this period, Fornes also designed and made costumes for a number of Judson productions. While Fornes's work was presented at many Off-Off Broadway venues in the 1960s, it was the Judson Memorial Church, just a few blocks from her Sheridan Square apartment, that provided her true artistic home.

The Judson Poets' Theater

Located on Washington Square in the heart of Greenwich Village, the Judson Memorial Church has been a community-oriented institution since its opening in 1892. In the 1950s, its activities turned more and more towards the arts. In 1956, head minister Howard Moody instituted the Judson Gallery, which displayed the early works of Claes Oldenburg, Tom Wesselman, Jim Dine, and others. In 1958, Allan Kaprow created the first Happening in New York City at the Judson Gallery. Al Carmines, then a student at Union Theological Seminary, was in the audience. Three years later, Moody invited Reverend Carmines to begin a theater program as assistant minister and head of Judson's arts program. With the help of Bob Nichols, a landscape architect, playwright, and member of the congregation, Carmines launched the Judson Poets' Theater in the fall of 1961 with a double-bill of Apollinaire's proto-surrealist play *The Breasts of Tiresias* and Joel Oppenheimer's mock-western *The Great American Desert*.

A year later, Carmines offered the church's basement gymnasium to a group of young choreographers who had studied with Robert Dunn, Merce Cunningham, and Ann Halprin. This loose-knit collective, which came to be known as the Judson Dance Theatre, included Yvonne Rainer, Steve Paxton, Lucinda Childs, Trisha Brown, David Gordon, Deborah Hay, and others. On July 16, 1962, they presented "A Concert of Dance," the first in a series of sixteen historic concerts over the course of the next two years that would set the course for postmodern dance.[1] The presence of a dance company, a theater, and an art gallery under one roof made Judson a low-budget, community-based, experimental performing arts center where painters, poets, dancers, musicians, and actors crossed paths on a regular basis, leading to numerous collaborations across disciplines and both practical and theoretical examinations of what makes dance dance, what makes theater theater, and so on. This open dialogue between art forms and the blurring of the boundaries between them became an essential part of the 1960s avant-garde centered in Greenwich Village.

The Judson Poets' Theater soon became distinct among Off-Off Broadway theaters. Every other month, a double-bill of original one-act plays was presented for four consecutive weekends in the church's choir loft. In the early years, each production had a budget of $37.50. Admission was free and donations were accepted at the door. Carmines chose the plays along with the directors, one of whom, Lawrence Kornfeld, became a co-artistic director. In the first five years alone, they produced fifty-nine plays by forty-three authors in twenty-nine different programs (Confessore 1968: 27). Kornfeld, as director, and Carmines, as composer, were responsible for many of Judson's noteworthy productions. They came to define the theater's aesthetic, which from production to production mixed camp sensibility, abstract movement, social commentary, zany and grotesque humor, bright melodies, grinning irony, pop culture symbols, surrealistic flights of fancy, open sexuality, and, above all else, an unapologetic joy in life. The plays did not promote church orthodoxy, but for Carmines and the Judson leadership, art and performance were an extension of ministry, so it was natural that an ecumenical and somewhat programmatic celebration of life became a Judson hallmark. Two key traits of the Judson Poets' Theater – a free and experimental approach to performance events and a madcap often ironic delight – became important aspects of Fornes's work in her first decade as a playwright. Nowhere is that affinity more apparent than in *Promenade*, her most Judsonesque play.

Promenade as a one-act with "a lot of music" in 1965

Promenade is the type of play that challenges the synoptic powers of critics. Jerry Tallmer (1965) likened the original 1965 production to "a Jeanette MacDonald movie co-scripted by Bertolt Brecht and Jean Genet, directed by Groucho Marx." Robert Massa (1983: C8) described a revival eighteen years later as "a mixture of *Candide* and Samuel Beckett viewed through Lewis Carroll's looking glass." With its extensive musical score and large cast, *Promenade* worked baroque variations on the themes and techniques of Fornes's other early plays, adding enough social commentary to border on satire.

The action begins in the prison cell of two inmates known only by their numbers, 105 and 106. As they dig a tunnel to escape, they sing a song that announces them as Fornes Innocents:

Unacquainted with evil we are.
This shelter protects us from wrong.
To discover the appearance of sin
We must go where the dog takes a leak.

(Schroeder 1968: 6)

With that, like Alice down the rabbit hole, 105 and 106 disappear into their tunnel and enter into a world of comic adventure that takes the form of a series of object lessons. They surface first at a banquet attended by a half-dozen high-society types who sing a song in praise of unrequited love. None of them notices when 105 and 106, joined by a housemaid referred to as Servant, fill sacks with their wallets, purses, jewelry, silverware, candlesticks, and other loot. In subsequent scenes, 105, 106, and Servant turn up in a park, a city street, and another private party, thumbing their noses again and again at the rich and powerful. At one point, 105 announces that he has "just discovered what life is all about" and sings an exuberant lyric that has often been cited as quintessential Fornes:

To walk down the street
With a mean look in my face,
A cigarette in my right hand
A toothpick in the left.
To alternate between the cigarette
And the toothpick
Ah! That's life.
Yes, I've learned from life.
Every day I've learned some more.
Every blow has been of use.
Every joy has been a lesson.
What surprises me
Is that life
Has not learned from me.

(Schroeder 1968: 18)

In the end, the play comes full circle and they return to jail, where they are tucked in by their Mother, who sings them to sleep with an ironic song about the many poor people in the world. "Did you find evil?" she asks, and when they say no, she tells them not to worry: "You'll find it some other time." With willful naïveté, the prisoners conclude "All is well in the city." And the play is over.

Similar to He and She and 3, the characters of *Promenade* all display a defiant nonchalance and happy-go-lucky attitude that draws attention to what it would ignore: all is not well in the city. But 105 and 106 just don't see that or they pretend not to. They seem oblivious, just as the wealthy socialites are so preoccupied with their hedonistic pursuits that they are oblivious to 105 and 106. The characters in *The Successful Life of 3* sing their "Song to Ignorance" with the telling refrain, "Let me be wrong/But also not know it." Here it is as if 105 and 106 are singing, "Let me know wrong/But also not see it." Like Leopold coming out of his sack in *Tango Palace*, the child-like prisoners are born out of their Edenic prison cell as innocents, "unacquainted with evil," lacking knowledge or experience of the world. In their adventures, they learn that the luxuries of the leisured class have an anesthetic effect. They bring a loss of feeling. Through word games, food games, and sex games, genuine sensation is reduced to conspicuous consumption. No wonder then that in the end 105 and 106 choose to return to the cloister of their jail cell and whatever state of innocence it might confer, like the lunatics who return to the asylum after finding the free world to be the true madhouse.

When first performed as a one-act by Judson Poets' Theater in 1965, the play was titled *The Promenade* and presented on a bill with *Devices* by Kenneth H. Brown. Lawrence Kornfeld directed both plays, and Al Carmines composed one of his most celebrated scores. The production was a cult hit with the Off-Off Broadway coterie, bringing Fornes her first Obie.[2] Michael Smith (1965) captured the paradoxical spirit of the piece in his *Village Voice* review:

> The dominant emotion is romantic melancholia but the tone is vapid frivolity, and the delicate tension this creates gives the event its distinction. Only occasionally do we come upon the bitter rejection implied by cynicism; more often we confront ironic acceptance.

The show attracted the attention of producers Edgar Lansbury and Joseph Beruh, who optioned the play for a commercial Off

Broadway production which eventually opened in an expanded version on June 4, 1969 at the brand new Promenade Theatre, named after the Fornes play as its inaugural production, at Broadway and 76th Street.[3]

Promenade as a full-length musical in 1969

The full-length version of *Promenade* became an instant hit. Broadway designers Rouben Ter-Arutunian, Willa Kim, and Jules Fisher were teamed with the original downtown trio of Fornes, Carmines, and Kornfeld and a new fifteen-member cast (except for the returning Florence Tarlow as Miss Cake, who was a sensation in the original). This unusual and happy confluence of Broadway professionalism and Off-Off Broadway ebullience helped the show to run for 259 performances, far and away the longest run of any single Fornes production. Critics quibbled or carped about the book being thin or cryptic or nonsensical but forgave its perceived flaws in the face of Fornes's free-spirited lyrics, Carmines's imaginative score, and musical talent that was hailed by many as second to none at the time.

For many, the evening belonged to Carmines, whose score now featured thirty-three songs that flowed from one to the next more like an operetta than a standard book musical of the time. Reviewers applauded the eclecticism of Carmines's music, which drew on a wide range of popular sources: polkas and czardas, Jacques Brel and Kurt Weill, cabaret and honky-tonk, Sigmund Romberg and W.C. Handy, torch songs and show tunes, Blitzstein and Bernstein, ragtime and gospel. Some found the music derivative, but Marilyn Stasio (1969) hailed Carmines as "a genius at assimilating every musical style from grand opera to gut blues and transforming them into an ecstatically slap-happy style that is clearly his own." She described the show as "structured on a mood, a kind of manic exuberance so exultantly good-natured that it would take a rigid soul indeed to resist it." Walter Kerr (1969: 10) characterized it as "the best of both worlds – up-to-date sassy and remember-when fond."

The mainstream reviews suggest that the uptown *Promenade* captured the play's peculiar downtown charm. But for the *Village Voice*'s Michael Smith, the critical conscience of Off-Off Broadway, the show had sold its soul to the devil of commercialism:

In its new version, in sum, there is virtually no life to the show, no heart, no warmth beneath the shiny surface. The irony has gone flat, like leftover champagne. I wonder why they killed it. For money, I guess.

(Smith 1969)

Smith's judgment draws attention to the cultural divide separating Off-Off Broadway from Broadway in the 1960s and how quickly the spirit and innovation of one was appropriated and commodified by the other.[4]

Broadway of course took whatever it considered usable in Off-Off Broadway, especially the nudity, the scatological language and the naive vitality. But since it did so without understanding the impulse behind elements which were rooted in a broader philosophy it did little more than consumerise those elements – proof, if such were needed, that Off-Off Broadway experimentation was not a question of testing new forms but seeking a redefinition of the purpose and possibilities of theatre. That process of redefinition brought an energy to the American theater it had formerly lacked. Seeking no validation beyond the immediate authenticity of the moment, the magic of the performance, it remains in some final sense immune to critical attack. Its naiveties were its strengths as well as its weaknesses.

(Bigsby 1985: 73)

The revision of *Promenade* for its move uptown was mainly a matter of sprucing it up and padding it out to make a full evening for a paying audience. Songs were added and shifted, scenes lengthened, gags cut, character names altered, and dialogue re-assigned.[5] A 1995 interview with Lawrence Kornfeld lends some credence to Smith's assessment that something was lost in the revised and expanded *Promenade*. "At Judson it was a play with a lot of music. When it went uptown it became a musical," Kornfeld (1995: 25) said. "The production uptown was fascinating, accessible, wonderful. But the one at Judson had a scale to it ... [it] was smaller, more beautiful." This change stemmed in part from different scenic designs. At Judson, Malcolm Spooner created a series of cartoon-like hand-painted backdrops set up to be turned like pages of a book each time 105 and 106 surfaced in a new location. "I wanted the feeling of *Promenade* to be that people are in one place, and the world keeps changing around them," Kornfeld explained. Rouben Ter-Arutunian's 1969 unit set featured a sparkling maze of suspended bicycle wheels, brightly lit by Jules Fisher.

> When we went uptown, it became in a sense more abstract, more decorative ... and therefore Irene's book was more hidden, although it was very strong, it was very much there, it became covered. The production at Judson, the book was much stronger, not because it was changed, but because it was just more apparent.
>
> (Kornfeld 1995: 26)

The uptown production reflected the rapidly changing, post-1968 political climate in the USA and the rising opposition to the Vietnam War. In 1969, the second act began with an entirely new scene set on a battlefield where two heavily bandaged soldiers talk about how they were hoodwinked into joining the army. Then, 105 and 106 are hurled onto the stage wounded and bandaged, and as bombs explode, Misses I, O, U and Misters R, S, T stroll through as if at a garden party, oblivious to the war all around them, pausing long enough to dance around the wounded soldiers using their head bandages as Maypole ribbons while they sing "Spring is here." The addition of this sardonic anti-war scene helped to make *Promenade* what Clive Barnes (1969) called "a protest musical for people too sophisticated to protest." The social commentary about class differences and the callousness of the rich toward the poor was made more pointed and overt throughout. Sounding a theme that would echo through Fornes's subsequent work, a new song gave the piece an explicit message:

> I know what madness is.
> It's not-knowing how another man feels.
> A madman has never been
> In another man's shoes.
> Madness is lack of compassion,
> And there's little compassion
> In the world.
>
> (Fornes 1971: 254)

The other significant revision in the 1969 *Promenade* amounted to expanding the role of Servant, played by Broadway newcomer Madeline Kahn, who possessed what Kornfeld called "one of the great coloratura voices in America when she was young" (Kornfeld 1995: 25). Carmines composed new songs specifically for Kahn, and lines were added in almost every scene that made the Servant less moll and more partner-in-crime with 105 and 106. In the 1965 script, the Servant fades into the background in the later scenes, whereas in 1969, her exit from the play took the form of a three-minute torch song called "Listen, I Feel," which included the lyric:

> Listen ... I feel ...
> I'll tell you in a moment ... what I feel.
> I have a thought somewhere in my head.
> It's a fine thought. I'm sure it is.
> It feels like a fine thought. Like a fine day.
> And I know just what makes it fine.
> Listen I feel, and I know just what I feel.
> Listen, listen I feel. Listen I feel. Listen I feel.
>
> (Fornes 1971: 271)

In revisions to the text after the 1969 production, Fornes cut this song. Nevertheless, it voices what will become a defining trait of many Fornes characters: the feeling of having "a thought some-where in my head," a nascent thought rising towards articulation from just below the threshold of consciousness. The theme was introduced in *Tango Palace* by Leopold, who sensed there was a way out of Isidore's lair without knowing what it was. In the 1969 version of *Promenade*, the assignment of this trait to the Servant signals a gender shift and foreshadows the female heroes of such subsequent plays as *Fefu and Her Friends*, *Evelyn Brown (A Diary)*, *A Visit*, *Mud*, *The Conduct of Life*, *Sarita*, *The Trial of Joan of Arc in a Matter of Faith*, and *Abingdon Square*, all of whom have moments where they, like the Servant, are left alone to listen to the thoughts in their heads. The first instance of this shift is *Molly's Dream*, Fornes's first play – discounting the precursor *La viuda* – to center on a female protagonist. Molly's preconscious thought takes the form of an extended dream that constitutes the action of the entire play.

Molly's Dream (1973)

Though not fully produced until 1973, *Molly's Dream* belongs with Fornes's 1960s Off-Off Broadway plays. It features cartoonish characters who display an insistent nonchalance that masks an odd depth of feeling; complex ironies that combine whimsy and world-weariness; a mischievous sense of humor that signals an underlying joy in life; songs, dances, and other performance bits that give the play an overt vaudevillian theatricality; and Fornes's favorite theme: frustrated love. Written in two scenes separated by a musical interlude, the play looks at the yearning for perfect romance in a manner that is part lampoon and part lament.

Set in an old-fashioned saloon, the action centers on a waitress named Molly, who starts off alone onstage, drinking a cup of coffee, smoking a cigarette, and reading a romantic story in a pulp magazine. A Young Man appears, and they exchange meaningful glances. He turns and walks away. She puts her head down on the table and drifts quickly off to sleep, and the rest of the play is Molly's dream. It begins with the entrance of Jim, as handsome as a fairy-tale prince and played by the same actor as the Young Man; he is trailed by five fawning females known as the Hanging Women, jilted lovers who cling to him like ivy. Soon, Molly is hanging around his neck as well, offering her love. When he rejects her, she transforms into a version of Marlene Dietrich in *Blue Angel*, complete with German accent, top hat, and sultry demeanor. After a musical interlude in which Jim asks again and again, "Am I the wrongdoer or the wronged?", the action grows even more surreal. Alberta, a 27-year-old incarnation of child star Shirley Temple, enters and tap-dances about. She rejects Jim's advances in favor of the cowboy John, who wears "holsters with guns from his ankles to his armpits." In his pursuit of Alberta, he transforms first into Dracula and then into Superman. They sing songs of love to each other, kiss, and exit the stage in a wedding procession, trailed by the Hanging Women. Alone again, Molly and Jim speak of what might have been and he leaves. She puts her head down and sleeps again. The Young Man from the beginning of the play enters again, orders a drink, watches Molly sleeping, picks up his bags and leaves. Only then does she awaken from her dream. She stares at his empty seat as a blue spotlight narrows around her and fades out. The man of her dreams turns out to be just that.

Molly's Dream was first seen in 1968 in two different workshop productions sponsored by writers groups, the Boston University Writers Conference and New Dramatists. Neither was reviewed, but Off-Off Broadway playwright Robert Patrick later remembered the New Dramatists showcase, directed by Fornes with music by Cosmos Savage, as "the single most perfect and memorable and dazzling production of any play I've ever seen anywhere in the world" (Bottoms 2004a: 353). Five years later, in June 1973, Fornes and Savage teamed up on the world premiere, presented as part of the New York Theatre Strategy Festival at the Manhattan Theatre Club. The *Village Voice* described it as "a chilling, trance-like comedy" and "succinct and aloofly devilish, a kind of bitch cunning stained with human concerns informs the work" (Sainer 1973). After that, the play received little attention beyond college campuses until 2003, when it was mounted by both Boston Theatre Works and the reputable SoHo Rep in New York. *The New York Times* dismissed the play as "a relic, a curiosity in the career of an accomplished playwright" (Weber 2003), and the *Voice* called it "a little gem" and "a revealing critique – and celebration – of hetero romance" (Solomon 2003).

An early Fornes scholar put a feminist spin on the play's action when she wrote that Molly's dream reflects her "psychic journey from sexual attraction, through heartbreak and feigned indifference, to acknowledgement and restraint of this particular desire since its satisfaction would cost her autonomy and individuality" (Kent 1996: 111). In this view, Molly's failure to wake up is an act of sub-conscious will that has liberated her (at least for the moment) from the heteronormative pressures so deeply ingrained in the icono-graphy of popular culture that they penetrate our dreams. Perhaps so, but an anecdote from Fornes suggests otherwise:

> I remember having what became almost an argument with a friend who is very political. It was about my play *Molly's Dream.* She said it was romantic and meant it as a criticism and I said, "Yes, isn't it?" and meant it as a high compliment. I remember we were in a bar, we were drinking beer, and I said, "Have you ever been with a person when just being with them

makes you see everything in a different light. A glass of beer has an amber, a yellow that you've never seen before and it seems to shine in a manner that is" – and she said, "Yes!" and I said, "That is romantic! That is romance!" and she said, "Well, in that case ... " I said, "It *is* more beautiful. It isn't that you want it to be more beautiful or that you are lying to yourself. It *is*. Your senses are sharpened ... When the glass of beer looks like the most beautiful amber, there's no deception, because it *is* actually. Everything is beautiful."

(Cummings 1985: 55)

Here Fornes declares herself not only an unapologetic romantic but also an untutored phenomenologist. For Fornes characters, perception is shaped by emotion. When Servant in *Promenade* sings "Listen I feel," she conflates outward sensation and inward feeling. In *Molly's Dream*, Alberta sings a song about the five senses, which includes the lyric, "Love, love, love. Love, love, love, love./You have brought me to my senses/You have made sense of me" (Fornes 1971: 199). Throughout Fornes's work, love, in one form or another, activates and sharpens the senses of her characters, and those senses in turn change what is True and Real and Beautiful for that character. It is a matter of transformation, not appearance or illusion or self-deception.

Notes

1　For the history and significance of Judson Dance Theatre and postmodern dance, see the writings of Sally Banes, among others.

2　Obie, short for Off Broadway, is the nickname – in the manner of Oscar or Tony – for a series of awards first presented in 1955 by the *Village Voice* to celebrate achievement in Off Broadway theater and extended to include Off-Off Broadway in 1964. There are no fixed Obie award categories; they change from year to year based on the work the judges want to recognize. Fornes's first Obie was for "Distinguished Plays" for both *Promenade* and *The Successful Life of 3*. The Obie Committee that year was Richard Gilman, Gordon Rogoff, and Michael Smith.

3　The Promenade, the only Off Broadway theater *on* Broadway, went on to become the home for dozens of productions, including the five-year run of *Godspell*, David Rabe's *Hurlyburly*, Edward Albee's *Three Tall Women*, and Sam Shepard's *A Lie of the Mind*. In 2006, it was shut down and converted into a Sephora cosmetics store.

4 The most conspicuous signal of this trend was *Hair: The American Tribal Love-Rock Musical*, which inaugurated Joseph Papp's Public Theatre on Lafayette Street in October 1967. Six months later, reworked by director Tom O'Horgan, *Hair* moved to Broadway and ran for 1750 performances. Gerome Ragni, an Off-Off actor who wrote the book and lyrics with his friend James Rado, dropped out of the 1967 Judson production of *The Successful Life of 3* in order to concentrate on *Hair*.

5 The 1965 one-act version of *Promenade* is published in Alson and also in Schroeder. The 1969 full-length version can be found in the 1971 Winter House anthology of Fornes plays, in Richards's *Great Rock Musicals*, and on an original cast recording issued by RCA Victor. By the time of that recording, Madeline Kahn had left the show and the role of the Servant is sung by Sandra Schaeffer.

Part II

The 1970s

"If we're showing what life is, can be, we must do theatre."

4 Finding a way

For Fornes, the 1970s was a period of transition, one in which her playwriting took a back seat to work as a director and a producer. The Off Broadway run of *Promenade* had given Fornes her first and only true commercial hit. *Newsweek*'s Jack Kroll (1969) called it "the apotheosis of Judson," and in a way, it was the apotheosis of Off-Off Broadway as well, which was becoming more and more institutionalized as a breeding ground for professional careers and commercial projects.[1] By 1970, innovation in downtown theater was associated more with directors: director-driven ensembles such as Joe Chaikin's Open Theatre and Richard Schechner's Performance Group; early experiments by visionary directors such as Richard Foreman and Robert Wilson; and influential European directors such as Jerzy Grotowski, Peter Brook, and Andrei Serban. The playwright was no longer in the spotlight.

Fornes adjusted to this changing climate in two ways: she co-founded a playwrights theater called New York Theatre Strategy and she began to direct her own plays. The goal was to maximize artistic control in the creation of her work. In this regard, she benefitted from lasting relationships that she forged in the 1970s with four producing groups: INTAR, Padua Hills Playwrights Festival, American Place Theatre and its offshoot Women's Project and Productions, and Theater for the New City. Collectively, for the rest of her career, these organizations provided her with an artistic home where she could develop her plays with total freedom. From the mid-1970s on, with few exceptions, each new Fornes play received its initial workshop or world premiere at one of these theaters. They made it possible for her to carry forward the ethos and working methods she came to know Off-Off Broadway, something she herself did for other playwrights with New York Theatre Strategy.

New York Theatre Strategy

The New York Theatre Strategy (NYTS) grew out of the Women's Theatre Council, a short-lived group organized in 1972 by six female playwrights – Julie Bovasso, Rosalyn Drexler, Fornes, Adrienne Kennedy, Rochelle Owens, and Megan Terry – to promote plays by women, mainly their own. Within a year, the group re-organized, changed its name, and broadened its membership to include a number of their male Off-Off cohorts. Fornes described the climate that led to the group's formation:

> When theatres started getting funding and when Off Off Broadway became a transition to doing plays in the commercial theatre, there were a great number of new Off Off Broadway theatres started. And then they started saying, "Well, submit a play. If you want to do a play, submit a play. We will read the play." And that was really what happened. I thought that I would never submit a play to this person, who would be somebody I felt had no great sense of what theatre was, no great intelligence, no great knowledge, no great taste – nothing. And that person was saying to me, "I am going to read your play and I am going to decide whether I want to put it on or not." Now, that person was not investing a large amount of capital to put it on, that person was not paying me anything to put it on, that person was not paying the actors anything to put it on. All that person had was a space and a very small budget to pay for a little ad and flyers and five hundred dollars for a set. And for that, that person was the person choosing and deciding – and I was horrified. I thought I would never accept that kind of situation. It was then that I and some other writers started the New York Theatre Strategy.
>
> (La Tempa 1983: 46)

Run as a cooperative, NYTS served as an umbrella organization and production company committed to the idea that "writers should be able to choose the context and collaborators for any given project, rather than having to make do with the circumstances and personnel offered by existing venues" (Bottoms 2004a: 352). In the spring of 1973, Manhattan Theatre Club helped to launch NYTS by hosting a five-week festival of twenty short plays. Over the next five years, NYTS presented twenty more productions in various performance spaces around lower Manhattan. Fornes emerged as the prime mover in the organization, serving variously as co-founder, office manager, fundraiser, production coordinator, costumer, publicist, bookkeeper, and president, duties that brought her own playwriting to a virtual halt.[2]

While New York Theatre Strategy employed directors sympathetic to new plays, such as Larry Kornfeld and John Vacarro, playwrights were given the opportunity to stage their own work. This policy stemmed in part from Fornes's first experiences of seeing her plays staged by others. In the early 1960s, as a member of the Playwrights Unit of the Actors Studio, her work was presented in a director's workshop.

> The actress was standing and she said a few lines, looked around, and then she walked and stood behind a chair. And I said, "That is wonderful! That is wonderful!" and I stood up and walked around the way she had gone and I said, "but instead of stopping here, you can continue on ... " Everybody was looking at me and I thought, "I must be doing something wrong." But I couldn't figure out what it was. Then the director came to me very politely and he said, "Please, Irene, any kind of comment that you want to make I am happy to hear. You make a note of it and then, after rehearsal, we go and have a cup of coffee and talk about it." This seemed to me like the most absurd thing in the world.
>
> (Cummings 1985: 52)

Fornes soon discovered that a playwright in the rehearsal room was expected, in effect, not to speak until spoken to. She was told that because playwrights did not understand the actor's process they should channel their comments through the director.

This protocol made no sense to Fornes. When *Molly's Dream* was selected as part of a playwrights workshop in western

Massachusetts in the summer of 1968, she asked Bobby Lewis, director of the program and esteemed veteran of the Group Theatre and the Actors Studio, if she could direct her own play. The answer was no, and when the chosen director took a much different approach than what she imagined, she resolved to exert herself. When New Dramatists hosted another workshop of *Molly's Dream* later that year, she insisted on directing it. And when New York Theater Strategy produced the play in 1973, she directed it again. From then on, she directed the initial workshops and productions of each new play. For the rest of her career, she was her own director.

As a result, playwriting and directing became such radically integrated processes for Fornes that she regularly began rehearsals for a new play without a complete script in hand. Staging a play became an extension of the writing process. She also began to experiment with staging the words of others, interviewing performers about personal experiences and then drawing on verbatim transcripts to fashion a script that was then further developed in rehearsal. In 1972, she worked with four actors from Cincinnati Playhouse-in-the-Park and artistic director Word Baker on a piece called *Baboon!* that was based on the actors' dreams. In 1975, at INTAR in New York, she worked with an ensemble of eight Hispanic American actors on *Cap-a-Pie*, a series of scenes, songs, and monologues that examined their bi-cultural identities. These forays into what is now called devised theater eventually led Fornes to create productions based on found texts and historical documents. While these projects proved to be ephemeral compared to Fornes's better-known, published plays, they underscore the extent to which the traditional practice of writing a play and handing it over to a director was unnatural and unacceptable to her. As she gained experience in working with actors and designers, she became a hybrid writer-director – a playmaker – who added a vital dimension to her texts through her distinctive mise en scène. A full understanding of her plays requires consideration of her initial staging of them.

Aurora (1974)

In its five-year existence, New York Theatre Strategy produced three Fornes plays: *Molly's Dream* in 1973 (see Chapter 3), *Aurora* in 1974, and *Fefu and Her Friends* in 1977 (see Chapter 5). *Aurora* was dismissed by reviewers and never published or produced again, but it merits brief attention as a transitional play which demonstrates that Fornes's unique blend of whimsy, slapstick, melancholy, and camp do not always harmonize. It takes place in the fairy-tale duchy of Gyurko, a vaguely Central European realm imbued with Pre-Raphaelite romanticism. Over the course of six scenes, each of which includes one or two songs, the action presents the exploits of William, an adventurous young swain who sets out for a place "where I can learn what is possible and what is impossible for me ... where every moment is unfamiliar and I can test myself as a man."[3] William is accompanied by a sidekick named Bill, who represents his spirit. In the second scene, they arrive at the castle of Desno, Duke of Gyurko, where a series of social indiscretions leads to a duel at dawn between William and Desno. A wizard-like priest named Galindo tries to stop the fight, and in the fracas William deals the duke a mortal blow. The remaining scenes present the romantic pursuits of the courtiers around Desno and the palace intrigue surrounding his prolonged dying, which erupts in a final orgy of murder and death that seems like a parody of Jacobean revenge tragedy.

The crux of the action reveals William as an early variation on the Fornes Innocent. Bill announces that he is leaving William to become Desno's spirit instead. Bill stands over the sleeping William and says, "You are now unconscious of my act and yet your eyes will open to a knowledge you didn't have when you last closed them." Bill sinks magically into Desno's bed, and with his disappearance, William loses innocence, protection, and companionship and gains responsibility, his own reason, and consciousness of "the knowledge that nature puts into a man." Or he would if the resuscitated Desno, now speaking with Bill's voice, did not murder William on the spot. More often than not in Fornes, the metaphorical birth of coming into being coincides with some form of death. The play ends with a Russian Angel stepping forward to sing an ironic song that summons all the dead to their feet for the long journey to heaven as if it were a bus tour of Mexico:

> Put your money in a safe place.
> And count every penny you spend.
> Drink bottled water at first.

Faucet water might be bad for your tummy.
Eat plain things till you get used to the diet.
Wine is good but it might taste bitter at first.
You can talk your own language at first.
But try soon to learn the native tongue.
They'll think you're rude if you don't.
What's that expression on your faces?
Smile, they'll treat you nice up there.
Arise, arise, we're going on a journey.
Aurora, aurora.
The sun is rising it is dawn.

Aurora baffled its critics. Michael Feingold called it

> a series of disconcertments of ideas. Just as you expect it to be
> about something (like identity and the maturation process), it
> turns a meaning-corner, usually to great comic effect, and pre-
> tends to be about something else for a while, till it sees the
> hated pigeonholes moving in to categorize it again, and scuttles
> off in a new direction.
>
> (Feingold 1974: 76)

This refusal to mean something led others to dismiss the play as
"pretentious nonsense" (Barnes 1974: 53) or "a silly intellectual
exercise" (Sears 1974) or "too obtuse to put its message across
clearly" (Marranca and Dasgupta 1981: 60). In hindsight, Fornes
herself questioned the play: "I think in *Aurora* I tried to repeat
Promenade. It wasn't conscious. And *Molly's Dream*, too, in a way.
Those plays were more charming than substantial. They had less
muscle" (Savran 1988: 66).

INTAR and the Hispanic Playwrights-in-Residence Laboratory

For nearly twenty-five years, Fornes played a vital role in the cultural organization known as INTAR (International Arts Relations),
which was started in 1966 as a kind of Latin American Off-Off
Broadway theater. Seven young Cubans and Puerto Ricans banded
together to rent a loft on Sixth Avenue and 21st Street where they

presented plays in Spanish under the name Association de Arte Latinoamericano (ADAL). In 1971, they changed the name to INTAR, organized as a not-for-profit group, and moved to a disused tenement on 53rd Street west of Tenth Avenue provided by the City of New York. Early seasons focused on Spanish-language productions of significant plays by modern Europeans (Garcia Lorca, Ionesco, Durrenmatt) and Latin Americans (Egon Wolff, Alfredo Dias Gomez, Ariano Suassuna). In 1977, INTAR became the Hispanic theater in residence on Theatre Row, an urban renewal project on West 42nd Street that replaced peep shows and massage parlors with a block of small- and mid-sized theaters. Under the guidance of artistic director Max Ferra, one of the founders, programming expanded and emphasis shifted to creating new plays that reflected the experience of Hispanic Americans and to performing them in English for the widest possible audience. The addition of an art gallery, touring exhibitions, a children's theater, community and school projects, a developmental theater program which included commissions, residencies, readings, and services to Hispanic actors made INTAR the leading Hispanic arts center in New York.[4]

Fornes's long and fruitful association with INTAR began in 1975 when she created *Cap-a-Pie*, her first play on Hispanic themes since her fledgling *La viuda*. In 1977, she wrote and directed *Lolita in the Garden*, a children's play that toured the city, and in 1979, she wrote and directed *Eyes on the Harem*, a play about the Ottoman Empire. In the early 1980s, she translated and adapted Garcia Lorca's *Blood Wedding* and Calderón's *Life Is a Dream* for presentation at INTAR. *Sarita* (1984) and *Lovers and Keepers* (1986) received their world premieres at INTAR, as did *Terra Incognita* (1997), commissioned by INTAR's Hispanic American Music Theatre Laboratory. All of these plays had direct connections to INTAR's mission of developing new plays by Latin American playwrights and examining Hispanic American cultural heritage. This mission also led to Fornes's most important contribution to INTAR. In 1981, aided by a Ford Foundation grant, INTAR launched the Hispanic Playwrights-in-Residence Laboratory (HPRL or the Lab), with Fornes as its director and teacher. Each year for the next decade, Fornes selected a small group of budding Latino/a playwrights to study with her off and on for a year in a series of writing workshops. Many of them – including Eduardo Machado,

Ana Maria Simo, Milcha Sanchez-Scott, Migdalia Cruz, Cherrie Moraga, Lisa Loomer, Josefina López, Edit Villareal, Octavio Solis, Caridad Svich, and Nilo Cruz – went on to become "a virtual 'Who's Who' of Latina and Latino playwrights," prompting eventual recognition of Fornes as the inspiration and "Godmother" of a generation of new voices in the American theater (Huerta 2000: 61).

Cap-a-Pie (1975)

When it opened in May 1975, *Cap-a-Pie* was the first original theater piece produced at INTAR. Fornes began by gathering an ensemble of eight Hispanic actors – Ivan Acosta, Jose Rafael Arango, Vicenta Aviles, Doris Castellanos, Vira Colorado, Iris Diaz, Ruben Rebasa, and Johnny Robles – some with little acting experience. Several were born and raised in the USA, but most came from Puerto Rico, Cuba, Mexico, Colombia, or the Dominican Republic. Fornes conducted a workshop with this group that generated memories, fantasies, confessions, and anecdotes about their bi-cultural identities. She shaped this raw material into monologues, brief scenes, and tableaux, and added a handful of musical numbers for which she wrote the lyrics and José Raul Bernardo composed the music. Fornes staged the material as a series of vignettes on a small platform stage with a simple cloud-filled backdrop, using a handful of props, a set of Christmas tree lights, and a chair for each performer.[5]

Cap-a-Pie – the title means "from head to toe" – was simple, personal, and honest, more psychohistory than ethnography. There were no characters, plot, or setting. The performers simply played themselves, recounting personal experiences directly to the audience in a casual manner that enhanced the immediacy of the event and even allowed for on-the-spot variations or embellishments from one performance to the next. The piece avoided mention of historical events or familiar place names in favor of evocative memories of childhood. Johnny recalled his days as a kid bottling, labeling, and selling bleach water in the projects. Vicenta remembered waking up early one morning when she was three just in time to glimpse the wings of an angel as it flew out the window after her mother gave birth at home. Jose Rafael recreated the construction of a nativity scene that each Christmas season took over a room in his mother's house. Ivan summoned up the many smells on the sugar plantation in Cuba where his uncle worked: the orange blossoms, the soil "when it's damp y el olor del estierol que olía bién," the manure of cows who eat fresh grass instead of hay, and the café con leche made with warm milk straight from the cow.

The play began, significantly, in Spanish. Ruben sat in a chair and spoke:

> Yo, cuando estoy en un lugar bello, es una cosa que me satis-face el espiritu. I can be in a place, just sitting. In a park. And I feel content and satisfied. Y me puedo estar hora que no tengo sentido del tiempo ni nada. I have been in the Cloisters and I have spent a whole Sunday sitting in the garden. Nada más que sentado. Just looking. Así, mirando.[6]

This opening speech, with its Fornesian sentiment of serene contentment, established the piece's practice of shifting between languages, an unusual convention in 1975. Some sections were entirely in English, others entirely in Spanish, but more often than not, the speaker switched back and forth from sentence to sentence or phrase to phrase, sometimes providing an immediate translation and at other moments simply continuing a train of thought back and forth in Spanish and English, like a linguistic swinging door. The bilingual idiom – what some would call Spanglish – came to represent the rich bicultural heritage shared by the cast, even as a well-tuned ear could detect accents that pointed to their different countries of origin.

This undercurrent of celebrating difference-in-sameness surfaced in the first-act finale titled "Divino Manjar/Sublime Supper." The performers arranged their chairs in a semicircle and one by one, almost as if ordering in a restaurant, they named their favorite native dishes, occasionally explaining to the audience and each other what a food is or how it is best prepared.

> VICENTA: Tostones, and yellow rice with black beans, and pernil asado.
>
> DORIS: Lechón asado, but with mojo. Avocado salad. Plátanos maduros, and green too.
>
> IRIS: Carne asado. Tostones y yuca.

JOHNNY: Harina de maíz with beans. And boiled viandas con
ensalada de bacalao.

As it moved from main courses and side dishes to salads and des-
serts, the imaginary feast grew into a virtual cornucopia, until it
was capped off when Johnny blurted out in English, "And apple
pie." The company turned to him in mock disapproval of this
stereotypical all-American food, and he replied, half-apologetically,
"I like apple pie" (19). When the ensemble sang a final chorus
reciting many of the foods already mentioned, Johnny topped off
the list by saying, "Y apple pie." The short, seemingly negligible
shift from "*And* apple pie" to "*Y* apple pie" is precisely the gap of
alienation that *Cap-a-Pie* sought to bridge. In its gentle, playful look
at cultural identity, it captured both the pure joy of memory and the
melancholy of nostalgia.

Cap-a-Pie was, in effect, another Fornes vaudeville, an occasional
piece devised by the ensemble and shaped by the director as a kind
of Hispanic revue. Still, it anticipated changes that would characterize Fornes's playwriting in the years to come, as Fornes herself
was the first to recognize: "I think *Fefu* comes straight from *Cap-a-Pie*
because that play was based on the personal experiences and dreams
and thoughts of the cast. Dealing so intimately with the realistic
material left me with a desire to continue working in that manner"
(Marranca 1978: 111). Fornes's approach to character began to
change. She came to focus on a character's subjective experience in
an unabashed, almost confessional manner. Whimsy, irony, and an
outward nonchalance became less insistent, and a tenderness
entered the writing that made the plays more intimate and lyrical.
Eventually, the plays zeroed in on individual female protagonists,
but two plays from the late-1970s – *Fefu and Her Friends* and *Eyes
on the Harem* – extended *Cap-a-Pie*'s focus on a group protagonist
defined by gender and ethnicity.

Eyes on the Harem (1979)

Eyes on the Harem is Fornes's first play on an explicitly historical
subject: the 600-year history of the Ottoman Empire. The play
begins on April 27, 1909, the day on which Abdul Hamid II, the last
of the Ottoman emperors, was deposed. "In my veins is the blood

of all the sultans," he says and then names all 28 of them. This introduced a mordant series of sketches, songs, monologues, and tableaux that catalogued, often in grisly detail, the Turkish sultanate's legacy of cruelty and violence, especially but not exclusively towards women. Fornes drew raw material – some of it used verbatim – from Mary Mills Patrick's autobiographical *Under Five Sultans* (1929); N.M. Penzer's history of the Grand Seraglio, *The Harem* (1965); and Noel Barber's comprehensive account, *The Sultans* (1973). But her treatment was governed by the same puckish irony found in *Aurora* and many of her 1960s plays. A belly dancer did a tap dance. A lecture on Turkish syntax devolved into gibberish. A group of fawning courtiers, each in a fez, watched as their monarch writhed in what seemed like religious ecstasy, only to have it revealed that he was squatting over a chamber pot relieving himself. In a bizarre parody of a fashion show, runway models struck alluring poses that were rendered clownish by the layers of traditional garments that encumbered them.

Not all of the segments verged on satire or slapstick. The salat, the ritual prayer recited five times a day by Muslims, was performed. Passages from the sources on Ottoman history and culture were read, including a graphic description of the castration procedures that created eunuchs. In this way, *Eyes on the Harem* shifted mood and tone from one scene to the next in Fornes's familiar vaudevillian manner, careening from grotesque to whimsy to chilling horror, generating a "juxtaposition of improbabilities ... a series of images and moments thrown against each other for whatever resonances they can create" (Syna 1979). In a manner that was by turns heavy-handed and light-hearted, the piece conjured the Orientalist myth of the seraglio as the exotic realm of male desire and then undercut it with a chronicle of savage violence or barbaric cruelty leavened by laughter. As one critic noted,

> This tone is very difficult to maintain. When Fornes is at her sharpest the mockery tellingly skewers romantic myth in the timeless, universal way she intends. In some less well-honed segments, one has the uncomfortable feeling that the contemporary, American audience is amused from a sense of cultural superiority.
>
> (Jenner 1979: 9)

Reviewers of the 1979 INTAR production agreed that the most affecting sequence in *Eyes on the Harem* was a scene in which three veiled harem women fantasized together about a future in which they would be free to eat in public, go without a veil, even go out with a man. Their conversation broke off several times for them to sing the bouncy chorus from the song "Meet Me in St. Louis," which includes the line "We will dance the hoochee koochee" (American slang for a belly dance). With each rendition of the song, their singing grew slower and more melancholy. "It is a hallucinatory moment; an extraordinary progression from comedy to seriousness, an audacious and successful theatrical rendering of a complex vision of feminine history" (Eder 1979: C17). If not as sublime as this, the rest of *Eyes on the Harem* displayed the same audacity – flirting with the politically incorrect, making humor of atrocity, rendering suffering beautiful – in order to expose a culture of misogyny, oppression, and violence against women. "The evening is fascinating," wrote Michael Feingold in the *Village Voice*, "because of the lurid extremes of the subject matter and Fornes's hypnotic, visually brilliant direction" (1979: 104), for which she received her third Obie.

Notes

1 For example, within a year of closing *Promenade*, its producers discovered a quirky, upbeat, college musical at La MaMa and fashioned it into *Godspell*, which ran Off Broadway for five years before moving to Broadway and beyond.

2 Fornes's roll-up-your-sleeves approach is evident in an anecdote told by Peter Littlefield, a stage manager and general assistant at New York Theatre Strategy. When Rochelle Owens's *He Wants Shih!* was about to open in a rundown theater on Second Avenue, a serious leak over the stage was discovered; Fornes masterminded the effort to jerry-rig an overhead catch basin out of a large plastic sheet, a wooden frame, and a hose to siphon water off into a garbage can. "She had a preference for home-made solutions, and she seemed to operate in a realm of timelessness," recalled Peter Littlefield (Delgado and Svich 1999: 187).

3 Quotations come from a photocopy of the typewritten manuscript provided to this author by Fornes.

4 For more on the rise of Hispanic theater and drama in the USA in the 1970s and 1980s, see Huerta (2000), Pottlitzer (1988), Ramirez (2000), and Lopez (2006).

5 Coincidentally, the initial run of *Cap-a-Pie* overlapped with the premiere of another, more famous play based on the lives and experiences of

the performers: *A Chorus Line*. A year and half after the first *Cap-a-Pie* production, it was remounted under the title *Cap-a-Pie II*. Five of the original cast members (Aviles, Castellanos, Colorado, Diaz, and Robles) were joined by three newcomers (Manuel Martinez, Ilka Tania Payan, and Victor Romero).

6 Quotations come from a photocopy of the typewritten manuscript provided to this author by Fornes.

5 Key play: *Fefu and Her Friends* (turning over the stone)

"My husband married me to have a constant reminder of how loathsome women are." This is the provocative first line of *Fefu and Her Friends*, a play about eight women who gather in the spring of 1935 to plan, prepare, and rehearse for a fundraising event. The play opened on May 5, 1977 at a little-known venue on the Lower East Side, and within six months, it won an Obie (Fornes's second) and was remounted at the American Place Theatre. The play circulated more and more widely, thanks in part to its publication in an early issue of *Performing Arts Journal*. Within two years, Fornes also directed the play at the Padua Hills Festival, the Pasadena Community Arts Center, and the University of Wisconsin-Parkside. Professional productions soon followed in San Francisco and Seattle. The play offered what one scholar called "a progress report" (Kent 1996: 144) on the continuing struggle for equal rights and "women's liberation." Over time, it became recognized as "a foundational text in feminist theatre" (Farfan 1997: 450) and one of the most important American plays in the last quarter of the twentieth century.

Fefu and Her Friends signaled a more explicit focus in Fornes's writing on female characters seeking to break free of dependent or oppressive relations with male characters, a shift that lasted for more than a decade and led to Fornes's categorization as a "woman playwright" and a feminist. Her plays were produced by women's theater collectives, discussed in studies of the rising tide of female playwrights, and published in anthologies of plays by women. Fornes herself participated in international women playwrights conferences in Buffalo in 1988 and Toronto in 1991, but she was wary about being pigeon-holed strictly as a feminist in the heightened political sense of the day. Some activist feminists took issue with some of her playwriting choices, challenging the portrayal of characters (Fefu, Julia, and the others, Mae, Sarita, Leticia and Nena) as victims and calling for more aggressive (and successful) resistance to patriarchy as part of the dramatic action.[1] But Fornes resisted the notion that her characters should be role models or mouthpieces:

> I am a feminist in that I am very concerned and I suffer when women are treated in a discriminatory manner and when I am treated in a discriminatory manner because I am a woman. But I never thought I should not do certain work because I'm a woman nor did I think I should do certain work because I'm a woman.
>
> (Cummings 1985: 55)

She set *Fefu and Her Friends* in 1935 partly to avoid direct participation in ongoing political debates regarding women and feminism. "I prefer for the play to be more personal thoughts" (Fornes, Follies interview). The play, she said, "is not fighting anything, not negating anything" (Marranca 1978: 109) in explicit political terms. Still, the play's depiction of the women's psychic struggle to free themselves from oppression by men is palpable and powerful.

Fefu and Her Friends: the basic action

The surface action of *Fefu and Her Friends* is disarmingly simple. Written in three acts – Fornes calls them Parts – the play unfolds with a rhythm that is casual, playful, and Chekhovian, governed by the simple ebb and flow of a social gathering rather than by characters with competing aims caught up in a conflict. Part One takes place in the living room of the New England country home of Stephany Beckmann, affectionately known as Fefu. Christina and Cindy are the first to arrive, and Fefu shocks them when she picks up a shotgun, opens a French door, and shoots at her husband across the lawn outside. She explains that the gun is loaded with blanks and the shooting is part of an odd marital game they play. With that, Fefu goes off to repair a broken toilet. Over the remainder of Part One, the other women arrive in ones and twos: first

Julia, who is confined to a wheelchair, then Emma, Paula, and Sue, and finally, Cecilia. They make small talk until the whole group is there and ready for lunch.

Part Two takes place in four different rooms around Fefu's house and presents four intimate conversations in which the women talk about romance, love, and sex. Three of the scenes begin on a tranquil or whimsical note. On the lawn, Emma and Fefu fantasize about "a divine registry of sexual performance" which sends passionate, devoted lovers to heaven and "the duds" to hell. In the study, Cindy and Christina wonder what actually happens to the feet "when a person is swept off their feet" in love. In the kitchen, Paula calculates the duration of a love affair with mathematical precision. But each scene takes an ominous and disturbing turn before it ends. Paula has an awkward, painful reunion with her former lover, Cecilia. Cindy reveals a terrible dream in which she is harassed and molested by a series of male figures. Fefu confesses to being in spiritual anguish, a condition associated with a mangy stray cat that shits all over her kitchen floor. The fourth scene is the most foreboding: it shows Julia alone in bed in a dark room, caught up in a convulsive hallucination, twisting and turning as if being beaten under interrogation as she murmurs about "the judges."

In Part Three, as afternoon turns to evening, the action returns to the living room where the women conduct the meeting that has brought them together. They plan the agenda for what seems to be a fundraising event to support arts education. Fefu will introduce "the project" and talk about "the stifling conditions of primary school education." Paula will speak about "Art as a Tool for Learning." Sue, the treasurer, will explain the finances and ask for pledges. Emma will perform an interpretive reading, which she rehearses on the spot, with flamboyant gestures and expressive poses suggestive of Isadora Duncan or Mary Wigman. As they exchange ideas, they re-arrange the order of events until they reach consensus, and when the formal meeting winds down, they simply relax together, singing an old song, serving and sipping coffee, reminiscing about their school days together. At one point, several of the women get in a rambunctious water fight. All this while, little biographical information about these women is revealed, beyond that they are friends who share a common cause, the details of which remain sketchy.

This principle of narrative indeterminacy erupts into full-blown mystery when Julia arrives midway through the first act. She is wan, subject to petit mal seizures, and still paralyzed from the waist down more than a year after a bizarre hunting accident. A hunter in the woods took aim and fired a shot, killing a deer but also bringing Julia to the ground, bleeding from the head, semi-conscious, and muttering deliriously about persecution, torture, and keeping silent. In the bedroom scene in Part Two, Julia's raving suggests that at the time of the accident she was initially killed but then allowed by the "judges" to live, albeit weak and wheelchair-bound, as long as she abided by their "prayer." Julia says, "They say when I believe the prayer I will forget the judges. And when I forget the judges I will believe the prayer. They say both happen at once. And all women have done it. Why can't I?" (Fornes 1992: 35). In an ambiguous incident in Part Three, Fefu observes the disabled Julia walk into the living room and out again under her own power, raising questions about Julia's paralysis or Fefu's vulnerability to hallucinations like Julia's. Both women seem to be under attack by a pernicious, unrelenting, invisible enemy.

The mystery climaxes in the play's stunning final moments when Fefu confronts Julia, shaking her wheelchair violently and commanding her to "Fight with me!" again and again. When Christina walks in on their confrontation, Fefu asks for forgiveness, grabs the shotgun leaning against the wall, and heads outside. A moment later, a shot rings out. Julia grabs her head. Fefu enters and stands behind Julia, a dead rabbit in her hands. Julia's head falls back, bleeding. The other women enter and surround her in shock as the lights fade to black. This abrupt and violent ending triggers an immediate desire to know exactly what happened and what it means, but the play frustrates such an urge, ending on a note of profound ambiguity that leaves it open to a wide range of interpretation.[2]

Whatever this final sequence represents – Is Julia dead? Did Fefu kill her? Is Fefu acting of her own volition or is she now an agent of "the judges"? What does the rabbit symbolize? – the play examines the powerful potential of women recognizing each other as women, both as individuals with their own personal preoccupations and private struggles and as a community gathered together for a purpose. "Women are restless with each other," says Fefu, ever the

Figure 5 Fefu and Her Friends at American Place Theatre in New York (1978), directed by Fornes. Margaret Harrington as Julia and Rebecca Schull as Fefu.

provocateur: "They are like live wires ... they are always eager for men to arrive. When they do, they can put themselves at rest, tranquilized and in a mild stupor ... The danger is gone, but the price is the mind and the spirit" (Fornes 1992: 15). But no men arrive in the play – Fefu's husband Phillip, his brother, and a gardener remain offstage – and in their absence the restlessness of women manifests itself in a variety of ways, some playful and relaxed, some agitated and ill at ease, and some that suggest that "the mind and the spirit" of women carries with it the force of its own oppression or liberation.

Julia's debilitating medical condition develops as a complex and resonant metaphor for the ways in which women internalize the stifling forces of patriarchy and misogyny. The "prayer" which "the judges" force Julia to recite makes this plain:

> The human being is of the masculine gender. The human being is a boy as a child and grown up he is a man. Everything on earth is for the human being, which is man ... Woman is not a human being. She is: 1 – A mystery. 2 – Another species. 3 – As

yet undefined. 4 – Unpredictable; therefore wicked and gentle and evil and good which is evil.

(Fornes 1992: 35)

Onstage, in the fever pitch of Julia's delirium in the bedroom, this prayer may come out sounding like nonsense, the pitiable raving of an hysteric, but on the page it clearly implies that over the centuries women have been, in effect, brainwashed to view themselves as less than human and have served thereby as unwitting accomplices in their own domination by men. Conversely, in the larger context of the play, it also suggests that if Woman – as gender, as "another species" – is unpredictable, mysterious, and undefined at present, then the process of women defining themselves has the potential to be joyful, transformative, and explosive, in Fefu's words, "as if a god once said 'and if they shall recognize each other, the world will be blown apart'" (15).

Fefu and Her Friends: the experimental second act

Fefu and Her Friends had an unusually long gestation period. As early as 1964, Fornes wrote a scene based on an old Mexican joke about two men at a bullfight that evolved into the eventual first scene of the play. In 1972, a "new work" by Fornes titled *Fefu and Her Friends* was announced as part of the Women's Theatre Council's first season (Gussow 1972: 44). But progress on the play proceeded in fits and starts, slowed by her commitment to New York Theatre Strategy. Eventually, as a way of forcing the issue, Fornes withdrew from her administrative duties, set a performance date for the unfinished play, and began the search for a suitable place to present it.

> I saw this place, the Relativity Media Lab on lower Broadway, and looked at the main performing area and thought it wasn't right. But I liked the place and the general atmosphere very much. The people who owned the place took me to different parts of the loft and said, "This room could be used for a dressing room," and I thought this room is so nice it could be used for a room in Fefu's house. They took me to another room and said, "This you can use as a green room," and

> I thought this is nice, this could be a room in Fefu's house. They took me to the office where we were to discuss terms, dates, etc. I thought this could be a room in Fefu's house. Then right there I thought I would like to do the play using these different rooms ... I went home and continued writing the play with this new concept in mind.
>
> (Marranca 1978: 108)

This inspiration led to a radical experiment in dramatic form that became central to the experience of the play. Fornes wrote the four scenes of Part Two to be staged in four areas away from the main playing area, which represents Fefu's living room. At each performance, at the end of Part One, the audience is to be divided into four groups and guided in turn to the secondary spaces that represent the study, the kitchen, the lawn, and the bedroom before re-assembling for Part Three. As spectators move from room to room, they catch glimpses of other groups moving between scenes or hear snatches of dialogue from a scene already seen or yet to come. They become aware that all four scenes – both in the fiction of the drama and in the moment of performance – are taking place simultaneously and being repeated four times for four different sub-audiences. This requires precise timing: Fefu appears in three of the four scenes, leaving Emma on the lawn to go get some lemonade, poking her head in the study to see if Cindy and Christina want to play croquet, and then entering and exiting the kitchen after taking a pitcher from the fridge.

Unusual when the play premiered in 1977, this formal convention triggers self-consciousness about being an audience. "The very act of getting up and moving from room to room breaks the passivity of conventional realism and reminds the spectator of her or his presence at a constructed theatrical event" (Wolf 1992: 25). The kinesthetic and experiential aspects of Part Two – chance eye contact with other spectators, crowding in close around the actors in a tiny acting area, catching sight or crossing paths with other groups, gradual recognition that the four scenes are all taking place at the same time, and so on – spark a curiosity about the experience of others that constitutes a form of identification with them. "In each view of each scene of *Fefu* our position as audience members is re-accentuated and our relationship to the characters is re-mediated" (Keyssar 1991: 100). The intimacy of these four scenes, both in content and manner of presentation, heightens the sense of a shared experience marked by multiple, variable points of view on the same action.

> Through her reconfiguration of the actor/spectator relationship and her manipulation of aesthetic distance, Fornes fosters community by facilitating identification. At the same time, however, she insists on the need to recognize difference within community by representing multiple and simultaneous perspectives on – and/or versions of – the action in Part Two.
>
> (Farfan 1997: 449)

By the time the four sub-audiences re-assemble in the main playing area for Part Three, the individual spectator is conscious of being part of "a self-evidently theatricalized body, an 'audience,' a community sharing irreconcilable yet interdependent experiences" (Worthen 1989: 180). This recognition parallels the process that offers itself to women who are able to resist internalized self-loathing and misogyny while preserving the difference-within-sameness that is essential to their humanity. Part Three begins with Cecilia saying, "Well, we each have our own system of receiving information, placing it, responding to it," and she goes on to argue for the need to remain sensitive to difference while finding "a common denominator" in a community of others (43). The action of Part Three – the formal meeting followed by several forms of play (singing, making jokes, reminiscing about school days, and a water fight) – rehearses a genuine, if momentary, community of women, which is eventually disrupted (but not necessarily shattered) by the final confrontation of Fefu and Julia. The stunning final tableau "provides an ending that reinforces the ambivalent, unpredictable nature of empathy among female characters" (Lee 1996: 182). In its disarmingly simple focus on women being together as women, reinforced by the experimental second act, *Fefu and Her Friends* explores "the politics of consciousness" in a manner that is "deeply feminist in its perspective and guiding spirit" (Marranca and Dasgupta 1981: 61) without insisting on a specific feminist orthodoxy.

Fefu and Her Friends at At the Foot of the Mountain

When it opened in 1977 at an anonymous loft in the East Village, the play represented an early experiment in what eventually became known as "site-specific theater," an umbrella term for theatrical events conceived for and staged in natural environments or in architectural spaces originally built for non-theatrical purposes.[3] *Fefu and Her Friends* is not site-specific in the narrowest sense of the term – that is, it does not foreground a unique site as essential to the performance at hand – but Part Two's inspiration by the architecture of the Relativity Media Lab asks for a localized site-specific approach whenever the play is produced. This limits where the play can be done effectively. When Fornes remounted the original downtown production at American Place Theatre, she found suitable areas around the building to use for the kitchen, bedroom, and lawn, but the study scene had to be staged at one end of the living room. A comparison of two notable productions of *Fefu and Her Friends* helps to demonstrate its delicate and crucial relationship with the physical space where it is staged.[4]

In the summer of 1986, Fornes directed the play in Minneapolis with members of a feminist theater collective called At the Foot of the Mountain. Performances took place at the Mixed Blood Theater, an aging, former firehouse on an out-of-the-way street near the West Bank theater district. Everything about Fornes's staging served to connect the play to the building and the street and city beyond. The living-room set incorporated architectural features of the firehouse itself: doors leading to other rooms, a set of stairs, the windows in the old wooden garage doors, and so on. Pre-show music was piped out into the street as the audience arrived. A toy wagon full of vegetables outside the building's entrance turned up as a prop onstage later on. Fornes shifted the setting of two scenes in Part Two. The study scene took place in an old wooden rowboat set up on blocks in the driveway of the theater, with Cindy and Christina sitting at opposite ends reading and talking and the audience standing on either side. The lawn scene was staged amidst boulders and trees in a large vacant lot across the street, with Emma and Fefu picking vegetables in a garden rather than playing croquet. At the end of that scene, silhouetted against the Minneapolis skyline at twilight, Fefu walked away, crossed the street, and approached Cindy and Christina in the rowboat to ask if they would like some lemonade.

Just as the two exterior scenes expanded the playing area to include the city outside the theater and make characters visible at great distances, the two interior scenes contracted space and took audiences deeper inside the old firehouse to small, confined rooms on the second floor. To get to the "kitchen," spectators had to walk up onto the stage, cross the "living room," and go up the same actual stairs in the firehouse used by the characters in Parts One and Three. The "bedroom" was located in a small room down a narrow hallway that felt all the more claustrophobic by comparison to the wide-open feel of the outdoor scenes. In her characteristic fashion, Fornes directed the play in direct response to the physical site at hand, obscuring the boundary between stage set and theater architecture, between inside and outside, between dramatic event and daily life, creating a volatile liminal zone that at any moment was subject to the demands of either the theater or the street. The production instigated a spectatorial self-awareness that was immediate and thrilling and that strengthened a sense of intimacy and identity with the audience as a whole and with the cast of female characters.

Fefu and Her Friends at the Yale Repertory Theatre

In the winter of 1992, Lisa Peterson directed *Fefu and Her Friends* at the Yale Repertory Theatre in New Haven, Connecticut. This production also instigated a metatheatrical self-consciousness, but in a manner that undermined the dynamic of the play. Spectators entered the theater not through the main entrance but through the stage door, filing past a video monitor that allowed them to see themselves entering and past open dressing rooms that allowed them to see actors getting ready for the show. The staging of the four scenes of Part Two mediated between the audience and the actors in an explicit manner that drew attention to itself and away from the characters. The library scene was staged against the rear wall of the main auditorium, with Cindy and Christina positioned high overhead atop two library ladders and the audience standing thirty feet below, leaning back and craning their necks to look up at the scene. In the bedroom scene, Julia tossed and turned in a vertical bed set up on the apron of the main stage, with the audience looking on as if from above, either from onstage at the sides or the first rows of the house. For the kitchen scene, the audience was guided through a makeshift television studio, with a camera crew and a complete kitchen set, to a small viewing room where they watched the scene on monitors while the actors performed in the adjacent studio.

The Yale Rep production understood the play's emphasis on spectatorship and bearing witness, but the cleverness of its staging strategy backfired. So did the method for dividing the audience in four groups for Part Two. In Minneapolis, artistic director Phyllis Jane Rose made a simple, friendly announcement at the end of Part One and the audience went off in four different directions led by volunteer ushers. In New Haven, a recorded announcement told people to look for a colored dot on the cover of their playbills and then move to the corner of the auditorium where a Yale undergrad wearing a bright sweatshirt of the corresponding color was waiting to guide them to the four locations. The start of each Part Two scene was signaled by a series of recorded chimes, as was the stipulated moment to move to the next location. This "answering the bell" by actors and spectators had an undesirable Pavlovian effect that made the experience of the play more mechanical and consumerist, as if the audience were tourists at some arty theme park being led past a series of living dioramas. Rather than bringing the audience to an intimate identification with the characters and their fellow spectators, the Yale Rep production interposed itself between them, privatizing the experience of the play and blunting its emotional impact.

Part of this problem stems from the logistical challenge of staging *Fefu and Her Friends* in a theater much larger than the one for which it was written. The Yale Repertory Theatre seats 500; even half a house divided by four means groups of fifty or more people moving from scene to scene and standing around Julia in bed or Cindy and Christina in the library or Paula and Sue in the kitchen. The more compelling Minneapolis production had an audience of one hundred or less. This issue is not limited to *Fefu and Her Friends*. Most of Fornes's plays are written for intimate performance spaces similar to the ones where she cut her teeth Off-Off Broadway. The shift in style signaled by *Fefu and Her Friends* led to plays in the 1980s that resonate with silence and stillness; they do not readily scale up to the larger venues of resident regional theaters around the USA and elsewhere, making them less attractive to producers and artistic directors who have subscription seasons to program and lots of seats to sell. This predicament of scale is a matter of time as well as space. *Fefu and Her Friends* is a three-act play, but many other Fornes works run an hour or less in performance, prompting a need to pair them with other works to round out an evening, a practice that has its own marketing and production challenges.

Over the years, Fornes received numerous inquiries from theaters interested in *Fefu and Her Friends* but unable to accommodate the multiple locations called for by Part Two. When Muhlenberg College in Pennsylvania invited her to direct the play in 1996, she took the occasion to adapt the script for a single setting. Part One and Part Three remained the same, but the four scenes of Part Two were rewritten to take place in Fefu's living room as well. Fornes eliminated business that was specific to the kitchen or the lawn and wrote new dialogue for Part Two that would lead characters in and out of the living room as needed. The only significant addition came in the bedroom scene. Julia is resting on the living room sofa (instead of a bed) when she hallucinates her torture by "the judges;" at the height of her terror, Fefu walks in unnoticed, sees exactly what Julia is seeing, and recoils in fright, strengthening the sense that both Julia and Fefu are under attack in the play.[5] Even though the substance of the play remained the same, Fornes's decision to reconfigure the play for one setting is radical for those who regard the environmental second act as essential to the play's meaning and experience. It demonstrates a playwright's desire to have her work seen as widely as possible and Fornes's particular attitude towards her plays as never altogether finished.

Notes

1 For example, at a panel discussion following the performance of the Omaha Magic Theatre production of *Mud* at the 1986 Boston Women-in-Theatre Festival, several audience members objected to the play as

> an anti-feminist, negative portrayal of women. They found the ending especially disturbing: "Why did Mae have to die?" Fornes replied that she too would like to see women liberated, but to allow Mae to escape from her situation in any way other than death would not be true to the dramatic situation or to the relationships.
> (Curb 1986)

2 In a chapter entitled "Fefu and Her Critics," Kent (1996: 119–38) provides a thorough overview of the critical and scholarly responses to the play, concluding with a summary of "key issues for interpreters."

3 In the USA, site-specific theatre has its historical roots in experimental performance forms from the late-1950s to the early-1970s, such as the Happenings of Allen Kaprow, Robert Whitman, and others and the postmodern music and dance innovations of Meredith Monk and Trisha Brown. Off-Off Broadway's standard practice of turning churches, storefronts, and industrial spaces into performance venues – more a matter of expediency than innovation – also catalyzed the move towards site-specific theater. In recent years, the term has been displaced by a descriptive label originating in England – "immersive theater" – which suggests how the spectator is surrounded by the theatrical event and, in some cases, invited to participate in the action in some way.

4 The discussion here is based on this author's direct experience of the two productions in question.

5 Information about the single-set version comes mainly from a telephone interview on May 1, 2009 with Devon Allen, the Muhlenberg faculty member who played Fefu in the otherwise all-student production. "It was all very fluid," reported Allen, "with characters popping in and out, interrupting the scene for a moment. It didn't feel gerrymandered at all. It felt like that was the way she had written it." Despite Fornes's desire to prepare a version of the play that might be more widely produced, she never assembled the Muhlenberg revisions into a clean script. The single-set *Fefu and Her Friends* has not been published or performed again.

Part III

The 1980s

"I have to learn how to
lead my life."

6   Found

For Fornes, the 1980s was a period of fruition, one that secured her reputation as a major American playwright. While she approached each new play as an experiment, her body of work could now be seen to feature recurring elements: characters imbued with a pre-cognitive innocence and often caught up in a thwarted romance; a sequence of short, often fragmented scenes that present a dramatic landscape more than a plot; a deepening mystery that envelops the action with metaphorical import; a pared-down language that is lyrical in its simplicity and often opens up into song; the inclusion of found or borrowed textual material; and an ironic relationship between the characters' situation and the manner of its presentation. On balance, the plays of the 1980s took on a less whimsical tone, but in production they retained underlying traits of her earlier work: "first, a passionate clarity – a transparency in all dimensions – movement, color, text, even the lyrics for the many songs she writes; and second, a consistent and elegant charm that is not superficial and does not supersede the seriousness of purpose which animates Fornes's vision" (Falk 1980: 60).

The 1980s was also an astonishingly prolific decade for Fornes. Starting with *Eyes on the Harem* in 1979, she wrote and directed a new play at the rate of more than one a year for ten years. In that same period, she also directed productions of Calderón's *Life Is a Dream*, Ibsen's *Hedda Gabler*, Chekhov's *Uncle Vanya*, Virgilio Piñera's *Cold Air*, Ana Maria Simo's *Exile* and *Going to New England*, Leo Garcia's *Dogs*, and Cherrie Moraga's *Shadow of a Man*. And she taught playwriting on a more regular and sustained basis, in the summers at the Padua Hills Playwrights Workshop starting in 1978 and at her Hispanic Playwrights-in-Residence Laboratory at INTAR starting in 1981.

Fornes's collateral work as a teacher and a director facilitated her remarkable productivity as a playwright. In her classes, Fornes wrote along with her students, following the same writing prompts that she gave them in order to generate raw material for a new play. Each summer, the Padua Hills workshop gave her the opportunity to stage a preliminary version of a work-in-progress, which often led to further development in a production at Theater for the New City or INTAR. On these occasions, Fornes did not hesitate to start rehearsals without a finished script. Just as she used her own classes to start a new play, she used the rehearsal-and-production process – including the looming deadline of scheduled public performances – to finish it, sometimes making script changes during final rehearsals or the run of the show. Both teaching and directing allowed Fornes to extend the writing process into the more structured and social environments of the classroom and the rehearsal hall, providing a measure of external discipline and a hedge against the solitude of sitting alone at a desk writing. In this way, Fornes established her own unique personal system for taking a play from first impulse all the way to opening night and beyond. On a practical level, this system depended on her relationships with several producing organizations, particularly two with roots in 1960s Off-Off Broadway theater.

Theater for the New City

Theater for the New City (TNC) was formed in 1971 by Crystal Field, George Bartenieff, Lawrence Kornfeld, and Theo Barnes, veterans of the Judson Poets' Theater who wanted to carry the Off-Off mission forward into the 1970s.[1] The goal was to foster new plays, experimental theater, cross-disciplinary collaboration, and a community of artists in an atmosphere free of commercial pressures and constraints. TNC's first venues were in Greenwich Village on the Hudson River: first, in Westbeth, an artists' community in the abandoned Bell Laboratories building; and then in a former seaman's hotel on Jane Street. In 1977, the operation shifted to the East Village, first to a Ukrainian church and eventually settling into a former WPA building at 155 First Avenue. The performing arts complex that took shape there eventually came to include four theaters and an art gallery.

Under the artistic direction of Crystal Field for four decades, TNC remains an important cultural resource for the Lower East Side, known for its commitment to the surrounding multi-ethnic neighborhood, radical political theater, and nurturing theatrical innovation, new playwrights, and fledgling theater companies. TNC presents as many as forty productions a year, including the annual New York appearances of the Bread and Puppet Theater and the Thunderbird American Indian Dancers. Longstanding TNC traditions include an annual Halloween costume ball and an original street theater production that tours the five boroughs of New York City each summer.

Fornes directed six new plays at Theater for the New City between 1980 and 1986. Three of them – *Evelyn Brown (A Diary)* (1980), *A Visit* (1982), and *A Matter of Faith* (1986) – were one-off Fornes experiments in staging found texts; none was ever remounted or published. The other three – *The Danube* (1983), *Mud* (1983), and *The Conduct of Life* (1985) – are major Fornes plays that were published, along with *Sarita*, in a 1986 PAJ collection that made Fornes's plays available to a much wider audience.

Padua Hills

Padua Hills Playwrights Festival and Workshop was organized in 1978 by Murray Mednick as a workshop and summer retreat for playwrights. Mednick was a regular Theatre Genesis playwright who moved to California in 1974 and grew to miss the creative community he had known in Greenwich Village. He recruited fellow Theatre Genesis playwrights Sam Shepard and Walter Hadler, as well as Fornes, and in the summer of 1978 they led a four-week playwriting workshop on the grounds of a beautiful old estate surrounded by eucalyptus trees, olive groves, and the red clay foothills of the San Gabriel Mountains east of Los Angeles. A small theater on premises was unavailable for use, so when the time came to showcase work in progress, plays were performed elsewhere on the premises, mainly outdoors. "The participants were fascinated with the potentiality of the Padua Hills environment, and most of the plays directly evolved from the artistic and personal interaction between the playwrights and the environment" (Aaron 1979: 122). Thus began the Padua tradition of concluding the workshop with a festival of new plays by the workshop leaders performed outdoors at chosen sites around the grounds.[2]

With Murray Mednick as artistic director, Padua Hills convened every summer but two between 1978 and 1995, developing "a maverick reputation" for "spawning edgy work that features short, filmic scenes or poetically minimalist dialogue" (Breslauer 1994). It became a bastion of new play development for West Coast play-wrights, including John Steppling, John O'Keefe, Kelly Stuart, Susan Mosakowski, Marlane Meyer, Julie Hebert, and Jon Robin Baitz. Lack of administrative infrastructure led to financial instabil-ity and a peripatetic existence. In its fifteen seasons, Padua Hills had numerous homes and sponsors around Los Angeles, including University of La Verne, Pomona College, California Institute for the Arts, Chapman College, Cal State-Northridge, Woodbury University in Burbank, and finally the University of Southern California.[3] Wherever the workshop took place, apprentice and master play-wrights alike were encouraged to create plays for the architecture and landscape at hand.

Fornes embraced this practice whole-heartedly. For the first fes-tival, she staged a piece titled *In Service* in a long dining hall on the estate. The cast consisted of "six actors in white aprons and dressing gowns – a regimented, maniacally cheerful work force."

> The piece utilizes group incantation and non-matrixed actions to create a frightening collage of imposed work. The actors sweep, clean, polish, pray, and chant. The group is relieved when a disenchanted member reluctantly takes up her broom again. They next gather by the kitchen to order pie at a "res-taurant," echoing a real luncheon of the playwright and two actors earlier in the week. The actors then sit in a circle and take notes on how to make eggplant casserole, chanting, "My chest is as empty as the Bank of England is large."
>
> (Aaron 1979: 125)

In Service's depiction of work as a form of slavery was Fornes's direct response to a second-stage Los Angeles smog alert in effect at the time of the workshop. As she explained, "At first I thought the environment here was romantic. But then with the smog and heat, it becomes oppressive. And the piece changed as a result. I brought a piece as sort of a back-up but the place dictated something different" (Aaron 1979: 124).

At Padua in 1983, Fornes worked on *Mud*, which took its name from the red clay hill where she set up a stage for the play. A year later, she worked on *No Time*, an early version of *The Conduct of Life*, on the grounds of Cal Arts in Valencia. The play's subject is political and sexual violence in Latin America. Fornes situated much of the action on a terrace which looked out over a large, grassy field that stretched out to a two-lane road in the distance; at moments, she extended the play's setting to include the field and road below. Martin Epstein, one of Fornes's colleagues that summer, recalled one serendipitous moment:

> The final scene, played around sunset, had Nena (Sheila Dabney), running up the empty highway, right to left, while the death squad, driving slowly in a large car, bumped her to her knees several times before throwing her inside and driving off. It was a devastating ending, made more so for one particular performance when a local jogger in red shorts suddenly appeared and continued his slow inclining trot in the wake of the car. So the audience thought they were watching Irene's final providential touch. And who's to say they weren't.
>
> (Delgado and Svich 1999: 34)

Fornes played a crucial role in the history of Padua Hills, and it in turn served her well as an incubator for her work. The plays she started there were not conceived to be site-specific so much as they drew inspiration from the chosen site. Her lifelong penchant for making use of whatever materials were at hand – found spaces, found texts, found objects – became a cornerstone of her practice.

Fondness for the Found

In the late 1970s, Fornes and some friends were browsing around an antique shop in Massachusetts. One of them found an old hand-written diary from 1909 that originally belonged to a New England houseworker named Evelyn Brown, one of nine children in an

Anglo-Irish family that lived in the small town of Melvin Village, New Hampshire. The diary provided a matter-of-fact catalogue of Evelyn Brown's daily activities, starting with a mention of the weather and followed by a list of chores completed, visitors received, and news of anyone who had fallen ill or died. As Fornes said, "I was just looking at this diary the way you look at an old photograph. You could either read it and say, 'My God, what a boring manuscript,' or 'What a beautiful sense of rhythm about this life.' It took me" (Falk 1980: 57). The diary became the basis of *Evelyn Brown (A Diary)*.

A year or two later, Fornes chanced upon a stack of old 78 rpm records in a Greenwich Village thrift shop, and on a lark she bought one for a dollar. It contained a Hungarian language lesson that took the form of a series of simple dialogues, first in Hungarian and then repeated in English, built around commonplace situations like ordering at a restaurant or talking about the weather. "There was such tenderness in those little scenes," Fornes said, "that when Theater for the New City asked me to do an antinuclear piece, I thought of how sorrowful I felt for the bygone era of that record, and how sorrowful it would be to lose the simple pleasures of our own era" (Wetzsteon 1986: 43). These language records provided the inspiration for *The Danube*.

A similar incident occurred at Padua Hills in the summer of 1983.

> When I wrote the first scenes of *Mud* in a writing workshop I was doing at Theater for the New City, I didn't envision the characters in the country. In my mind they were in some European city. It was very general and vague. They were in some kind of basement, and they were very poor. When I arrived in California ready to start rehearsal all I had was that one scene. In fact, I was already a week late. They had already set up auditions for me. I thought, "I'll work on that scene because it wasn't even finished so I have a good scene for auditions and the actors think there is a play behind it." The next day some people were going to a flea market near where we were, and I went with them because I often need objects or furniture to get a hold on a play. I need the props. We were at a flea market and I was looking for my set. (Also, you know, we had to put on these plays for hardly any money at all so

when you find something cheap, then you write a play about that.) There were two little country chairs that were, for the two of them, only $5. They were very nice. They had been stripped down to the wood, and they were wonderful, and I said, "That's very good." Then we went a little further, and there were a hoe, and axe, and a pitchfork, also very cheap. The axe was $10. The hoe and pitchfork were 2 for $5. And I thought, "This is a sign. I think it's going to be a play in the country." Then I went a little further and there was the prettiest little ironing board for $3. Those things are antiques. You know, they cost $30, $50, $70 anywhere. So I said, "That's it, that's my play. Now I know where they live, they live in the country. The play takes place in their living room or wherever they have two chairs, and I know what he does, he works the land, and I know what she does, she irons." The reason why she's ironing all the time is because that ironing board was so pretty and so cheap.

(Frame 1984: 30)

These anecdotes illustrate the importance of found objects for Fornes. She always had a fondness for rummaging around flea markets, junk shops, antique barns, yard sales, Goodwill and Salvation Army stores, and all those places where people go in search of hidden treasures that others have discarded or sold off. For Fornes, these abandoned items represented both an object of delight and a way of life that was passing out of existence. As something already owned or already used, the found object has a secret history that gives it the authority of an artifact and the charm of an antique. When repurposed as a stage prop, it takes on a new usefulness and seems to exist in both the present and the past at the same time. "Each object (pitcher, bowl, chair, bucket, broom) has perfect grace and purity," wrote Erika Munk (1980) of the props in *Evelyn Brown (A Diary)*, "Vermeer stripped of color, the possessions of a dream-world New England grandmother."

A similar dynamic pertains to Fornes's use of found space and found texts. The original production of *Fefu and Her Friends* is Fornes's most celebrated use of found space. Padua Hills gave her the opportunity to experiment with site-specific theater. But even in conventional theaters, she staged her plays as if the theater at hand was a found space, holding off on scenic designs until she was familiar with the theater so she could look for ways to incorporate elements of the building itself into the play. For example, in 1993, Fornes directed the world premiere of *Enter the Night* at the New City Theatre in Seattle. The play takes place in a loft apartment, and the set designed by Donald Eastman included a large wooden staircase constructed to come up to the stage floor from the actual basement below. Characters entered by coming up these stairs, but before they came into view, they were often heard slamming a door below or shouting upstairs or tromping across the basement on their way in. This wedding of fictive setting and theatrical venue can be traced back to Off-Off Broadway's conversion of lofts, churches, coffeehouses, and social halls into makeshift theaters; at that same time, Happenings extended the place of performance into art galleries, storefronts, and outdoor locations. The practice brings to mind a passage about hermit crabs that the character of Mae in *Mud* reads aloud from her primer about marine life: "He is called a hermit because he lives in empty shells that once belonged to other animals" (Fornes 1986: 29). Throughout her career, Fornes staged plays in empty spaces that once belonged to other activities, theatrical shells that were already occupied or already used for other purposes.

Fornes also incorporated found or borrowed texts into her plays. Both her early work, *La viuda*, and her last play, *Letters from Cuba*, are based on letters by members of her family. The plays in between include many pieces of writing she did not write herself: excerpts from books, diary entries, popular songs, official documents, a few stanzas from Dante, newspaper clippings, even the list of backstage chores of the assistant stage manager for the Ridiculous Theatrical Company production of Everett Quinton's *Tale of Two Cities*. In *Fefu and Her Friends*, Emma recites a passage from Emma Sheridan Fry's "The Science of Educational Dramatics" and Shakespeare's Sonnet 14. In *Terra Incognita*, the character of Steve recites lengthy passages from *History of the Indies* by Bartolomé de las Casas, the Spanish cleric who recorded the early atrocities inflicted upon the aboriginal peoples of the Caribbean.

Fornes was far from the only American playwright at the end of the twentieth century to borrow the writing of others and work it into a play. Charles Mee, for example, gained notoriety for his practice of taking passages from a wide range of sources – internet posts, popular magazines, memoirs, interviews – and incorporating them verbatim into his plays as monologues or dialogue.[4] Mee's cut-and-paste technique blurs the boundary between what he wrote and what others wrote, whereas Fornes situates a found or borrowed text in a manner that sets it apart somehow, frames it as a quotation or a citation, and thereby confers upon it the authority of a document. In its new context, the passage retains not only its original form and content but also its status as already written. Like the found object or the found space, the found text invokes the time of its origin even as it asserts its new place in the present tense of the action. Fornes's use of the Found – the already owned object, the already occupied space, the already written text – recuperates the past without altogether assimilating it into the present. The tension that results lends a kind of truthfulness or ontological depth to her plays, as if the immediacy of the Now is fortified by the historicity of the Already.

Evelyn Brown (A Diary) (1980)

Nowhere did Fornes make greater use of a found text than in *Evelyn Brown (A Diary)*, which ran for five weeks at Theater for the New City in 1980 and was never seen again. It is not a play so much as a theater poem composed of choreographed movement, music, a little dance, and many verbatim recitations from the 1909 domestic's diary that Fornes found in a Massachusetts antique shop. The diary is stunning in the monotony of its unadorned, telegram-like prose.[5]

> January 16th Very cold. got breakfast washed dishes sweeping dusting washed three floors, made two kinds of cake, fried doughnuts, made beds, and did lots of little things. Mrs Gordon and Mr Porter went to Mr Frisbey's to day. Lizzie Lord called.

> Saturday February 27th. Warmer. Got up and got breakfast and washed the dishes, but had about all I could do to sit up. Trimmed the lamps, and washed the floors. after dinner Mr. Porter brought me and baggage down to Charlie's.

> Sunday 21st. March. Cool this morn, but fine this P.M. did up the work this morn Sed went up to Bertha this P.M. went down

to see Jennie Doe, sick with cold. Have been reading some and
wrote letters. Plumie Heath died today we hear.

The chronicle goes on like this day after day, unrelieved by humor,
gossip, emotion, personal confession, or self-reflection. In sentence
after sentence, the grammatical subject, the first-person pronoun
"I," is left out of the writing, and that sense of an absent "I" or
missing person was preserved in Fornes' presentation of Evelyn
Brown as a mysterious figure with no apparent personality or feelings. She was a woman defined instead by a seemingly endless series
of menial chores.

Fornes staged the piece in a plain, empty room of unfinished
knotty pine designed by Donald Eastman and described in the script
as "a wooden temple suggestive in its lack of décor of a puritan
place of worship. However, its shape is closer to the interior of a
mausoleum." The set featured a series of passageways and narrow
white doors that led to other passageways, suggesting a kind of
unending interiority. Fornes made the shrewd decision to cast two
actors – Margaret Harrington and Aileen Passloff – rather than one
as Evelyn Brown. Both women wore kerchiefs and plain homespun
work clothes, which Fornes herself dyed in spinach and onions to
get the color just right.[6] Differentiated in the script only as Evelyn
and Evelyn Brown, their relationship onstage was ambiguous, their
interaction minimal. "They are simply both there, not there together.
The feeling is of overwhelming solitude; the work implies children,
families, shopkeepers, a community, but extraordinary loneliness
triumphs" (Munk 1980).

After a brief prologue, the play began with Evelyn reciting diary
entries for the first week of the new year, pausing between each one
to crisscross the stage in a repetitive, diagonal pattern. A series of
routine activities followed. Evelyn and Evelyn Brown carried a table
onstage and proceeded to mix ingredients and knead dough
according to "Mrs. Hiram Hill's recipy for domestic bread." The
litany of diary entries resumed, punctuated more and more by signs
of fatigue, sighs at first and then an unnatural series of actions that
had both women leaning on and stretching across a long table in
postures of exhaustion. At another point, an American folk tune
was heard, and the two women danced a few polka steps, but
mechanically, without joy or spirit. "In and out, up and down the

Figure 6 Evelyn Brown (A Diary) at Theater for the New City (1980), directed by Fornes. Margaret Harrington (in plaid apron) and Aileen Passloff as two manifestations of the diarist and homemaker. Set design by Donald Eastman.

actresses move, like rats in a maze, the sterility of their surroundings accenting that of their chores" (Hill 1980). Eventually, live speech gave way to recordings of more entries, and then words stopped altogether as the piece concluded with a long non-verbal sequence in which Evelyn and Evelyn Brown carried six different tables onstage and proceeded to set each one with a ritual purposefulness that was as precise as it was opaque.

Evelyn Brown (A Diary) was a theatrical meditation on the poetics of housework, a testament to the tedium of domestic labor and the humanity of the women who perform it. "Although they seem trapped in a comforting but deadening cycle of repetitive 'women's work,' they transform this work into a holy rite, related to their senses of self" (O'Malley 1989: 103). Though only produced once, it confirms the importance of simple, everyday work – ironing a shirt, sweeping the floor, cleaning dry beans – in Fornes's theater. "Cleaning is a very beautiful activity," Fornes said. "Something is dirty and you clean it – it's like magic. But the beautiful which has to do with despair is slavery" (Falk 1980: 57). Fornes rendered the woman she found in the diary without judgment, but the austerity of the set, the precision and monotony of the routines enacted there, and the lack of feeling or self-awareness in the dull prose all combined to suggest a stifled spirit, a lonely woman lost in the mundanity of everyday life. "Not a breath of distaste or contempt is shown for this life; the sadness is hard to bear precisely because Evelyn Brown's dignity is upheld with a great tenderness ... a tenderness completely without sentimentality, without deception, and not for interpretation" (Munk 1980).

A Visit (1981)

A Visit is *Evelyn Brown (A Diary)* turned inside out. The situation is again domestic, but the monotony of work and a life without pleasure are replaced by a carnival of sexual delight and a spirit of pure, unrepentant play. Set in 1910, the play centers on another Fornes Innocent, a sweet young woman named Rachel who is about to matriculate at the University of Lansing. En route, she stops to visit the country home of the well-to-do Tyrrell family and finds herself the object of desire of virtually every member of the household, from the master to his wife to their bachelor son to the son's fiancée to the parlor maid who first opens the door to welcome her in. And she is more than willing to be initiated in the secrets of the flesh, pausing at one moment to exclaim, "Oh, I have never been so happy in my life as I have been this day."[7] As one reviewer observed, "this play is not a bawdy satire on Victorian values, although it is at times satirical. It is not slapstick comedy although it is at times comic. It is written as erotic poetry" (Mitchell 1982). Michael Feingold (1981) called it "a whole new genre – humane pornography."

The key to the play's erotic fun was a theatrical conceit: the characters all wore their libido on the outside, literally. Each male character had an erect white porcelain penis protruding from the fly of his pants. Each female had a pair of white ceramic breasts beneath her blouse, which were exposed at moments of sexual excitement. These private parts made public were clownish one moment and titillating the next. In the second scene, when the son, Michael, asks Rachel for a token of her love, she bares her breasts and he sucks on her ceramic nipple. "What does it taste like?" she asks, and he answers with a long list of sweet treats ranging from pear flambé to frozen velvet meringue, tasting her again and again until he brings her to climax with an exclamatory "Zabaglione!" Moments later, as she straddles Michael on the sofa and moves up and down on him, she muses out loud:

> Years afterwards, when I am a woman, the sunlight falling on the wall through the skylight over the staircase will bring back this moment to me, the moment when the world first began to open itself before me and puzzle me.

This schoolgirl romanticism, as self-conscious as the sexual behavior is uninhibited, stems from the play's sources, two Victorian novels written for young ladies in the flower of their youth, one in English by Rosa Mulholland and the other in Spanish by Emilia Pardo Bazan. Fornes borrowed paragraphs, characters, and situations from the novels and stitched them together with her own writing, a few original songs, and an array of sexually explicit behaviors. Grandpa masturbates while reciting Longfellow. Michael stares through a stereoscope at pornographic nudes. A swordfight between Rachel and Margery, Michael's jealous fiancée, turns seductive when Rachel exposes her breasts – "white as doves" – and a combative clinch between the two women melts into a passionate kiss. Mrs. Tyrrell, something of a sex scientist, watches insects copulating and takes notes on their positions for future reference. From start to finish, the characters cavort with neither the guilt nor the guile typical of bedroom farce. Still, the play was "faithful to the paradox of Victorian pornography: its genteel, keepsake quality that suggested not so much hypocrisy as a strange pathos of twisted idealism" (Kroll 1982).

The only production of *A Visit* opened at Theater for the New City in late December 1981 and ran three weeks into the new year. Critics were split along uptown/downtown lines. In the *New York Times*, Mel Gussow (1981: 86) dismissed the play as "a quaint, impossibly cute musical trifle" which "quickly succumbs to coyness and redundancy as the characters rendezvous in predictable sequence, producing a kind of domino effect." In the *Village Voice*, Michael Feingold (1981: 69) admitted that Fornes's "gnomic, playful approach gives the piece a scattershot quality" but credited it as "a pixilated entertainment which, as usual with Fornes, reveals enough new facets of her artistic persona to seem an almost total surprise." The particular surprise here was her unabashed embrace of pansexual promiscuity, an explicit attempt on Fornes's part to "reclaim [the Erotic] so that fun-loving people can enjoy it" (Barnes 1982). The sexually explicit behavior and ribald impulses of *A Visit* surface again and again in Fornes's plays, especially in *Oscar and Bertha* and in *Lust*, the third play of the *What of the Night?* cycle.

The Trial of Joan of Arc in a Matter of Faith (1986)

Fornes returned to the asceticism of *Evelyn Brown (A Diary)* when she staged *The Trial of Joan of Arc in a Matter of Faith*, a theatrical adaptation of transcripts from the trial of Joan of Arc in Rouen in 1431 on charges of heresy against the Roman Catholic Church. The historical Joan has been brought to the stage innumerable times, in plays by Shakespeare, Schiller, and Shaw, in Carl Dreyer's silent film, an oratorio by Arthur Honegger, and a modern dance by Martha Graham, to name only a few. Fornes's treatment is perhaps the most austere. She eschewed the battlefield pageantry of the Hundred Years War and Joan's sensational burning at the stake in order to concentrate on the inquisition conducted by Pierre Cauchon, Bishop of Beauvais. Even then, *The Trial of Joan of Arc in a Matter of Faith* is not so much a history play as what critic Gordon Rogoff called "the most solemnly aesthetic collection of images and rhythms I have seen in years" (1986).

The first and only production took place at Theater for the New City in March 1986.[8] Everything about Fornes's rendering served to abstract the play from its historical context in order to present a stark, intimate, direct confrontation between a young woman and her male interrogators. The set suggested a marbled grey cell, with a narrow passageway upstage leading out, a deep recessed window, a column, and a wide shelf that served as a bed. The lighting was precise, severe, and expressionistic, casting long shadows at moments or leaving characters in dim light at others. While there were dozens present at the actual trial – eminent theologians and clerics all sitting in judgment – Fornes reduced the cast to three: young Joan and two older unnamed clerics, one in black vestments, the other in red. In a series of sessions punctuated by blackouts, they questioned her about her claims to hear the voice of God, her visions of St. Margaret and St. Catherine, her practice of wearing men's clothes, and other subjects. Unlike the simple prose of Evelyn Brown's diary, the trial transcripts are linguistically elaborate and legally technical; Fornes's redaction worked to simplify sentence structure and reduce vocabulary as much as possible.[9]

Joan of Arc is an interesting variation on the Fornes Innocent. She was an uneducated peasant girl of thirteen when she first "heard a voice from God to help and guide me," a voice that was "seldom heard without a light."[10] She heard the voice while she slept and did not understand it; when awake, it gave her strength "to answer without fear." This voice from another realm recalls the voice heard by the adolescent Leopold in *Tango Palace* and the internal, semi-conscious promptings of other Fornes characters. "Because you are an unlettered and ignorant woman," says Joan's inquisitor, "we offer to provide you with wise and learned men who could duly instruct you." But the Fornes Innocent does not learn from a male authority, be it holy father or Isidore or Dr. Kheal. She listens to the voice within, however remote or mysterious. She attends to the faint light in the distance, like the starfish that Mae reads about in *Mud*. And in the case of Fornes's Joan, she is already in a state of

Figure 7 The profane and the sacred: *A Visit* (1981) and *The Trial of Joan of Arc in a Matter of Faith* (1986), both directed by Fornes at Theater for the New City in New York. Mary Beth Lerner as the innocent Rachel (left) and Penelope Bodry as her rival, then lover Margery. Costume design by Gabriel Berry. Sheila Dabney as Joan and Bennes Mardenn (seated) and George Bartenieff as her inquisitors. Set design by Donald Eastman.

grace, which lends her a strength of will and a capacity for suffering. Fornes is not interested in Joan of Arc as a French national hero or even as a religious martyr but as a paragon of devotion. Her trial in a matter of faith sheds light on the struggle of any Fornes character caught in the crucible of her own being.

Notes

1 Kornfeld and Barnes left the operation in short order; Bartenieff partnered with Field until he left in 1994 to pursue more of his own work. As TNC approached its fortieth anniversary, Field was still at the helm.

2 The most complete account of the Padua Hills Playwrights Workshop and Festival can be found in Onstad (2009: 115–51).

3 Padua Hills was closed in 1992 and 1993 and revived in 1994 and 1995, before shutting down altogether. In 2001, a version of Padua was revived as Padua Playwrights Productions, with Guy Zimmerman as artistic director and Murray Mednick as playwright-in-residence, workshop leader, and eminence grise.

4 For a detailed discussion of Mee's playwriting, see Cummings (2006).

5 All quotations from the play are from an unpublished, typewritten manuscript provided to this author by the playwright.

6 Personal interview with Aileen Passloff (February 15, 2009).

7 All quotations from the play are from an unpublished, typewritten manuscript provided to this author by the playwright.

8 Sheila Dabney played Joan, and the two inquisitors were Bennes Mardenn and George Bartenieff (who played 105 in the original 1965 production of *Promenade*). The designers were Donald Eastman (set), Anne Militello (lights), and Tavia Ito (costumes).

9 Fornes based her script on the 1932 translation of the original Latin and French documents by W.P. Barrett, available at http://www.maidofheaven. com/joanofarc_trial_barrett.asp (accessed June 2, 2009).

10 All quotes come from an early draft of the play provided to this author by Fornes at the time of the original production. Each page contains cross-outs and revisions penciled in. Anecdotal evidence suggests that Fornes continued her practice of changing a script right up until a play opened. Sheila Dabney, the actor playing Joan, describes Fornes coming to her in the dressing room shortly before the first performance with twenty pages of revisions, which led to a script-in-hand performance that night in which the actors tossed each new page up in the air as they finished it (Robinson 1999: 161).

7 The PAJ Plays

In the spring of 1982, Fornes received her fourth Obie, this time for "Sustained Achievement." In 1984, she was awarded her fifth and sixth Obies – one for writing and one for directing *The Danube*, *Mud*, and *Sarita*. A year later, *The Conduct of Life* won her a sixth Obie for Best New American Play. At that point, more than twenty years into her career, Fornes was still relatively unknown outside of New York's downtown theater community. But the critical attention attracted by these four plays – aided by their publication in 1986 by PAJ Publications – led to wider interest around the United States and abroad. Scholars began to write about her plays. University theater programs and Off-Off-type companies around the country began to produce them more often. By the end of the decade, she was widely regarded as a playwright of national importance.

The PAJ Plays, as these four might be called, demonstrated what Bonnie Marranca, her publisher and leading critic, called "a new language of dramatic realism."

> What Fornes, as writer and director of her work, has done is to strip away the self-conscious objectivity, narrative weight, and behaviorism of the genre to concentrate on the unique subjectivity of characters for whom talking is gestural, a way of being. There is no attempt to tell the story of a life, only to distill its essence.
>
> (Marranca 1984: 29)

As Marranca suggests, by this time in Fornes's career, playwriting and directing were virtually inseparable and equally precise in their composition. In a 1986 *Village Voice* profile, Ross Wetzsteon, another close follower, enumerated the key traits of Fornes's directing style:

> a gestural and intonational formality, an emphasis on decla-matory line-readings in particular, that rejects the cumulative effect of naturalistic detail in favor of the spontaneous impact of revelatory image, that rejects emoting, behavioral verisimilitude, and demonstration of meaning in favor of crystallization, painterly blocking, and layers of irony.
>
> (Wetzsteon 1986: 43)

In both the writing and staging, a principle of compression came to govern the work; as a result, Fornes's theater became more rigorous and more demanding, for actors and audiences alike. Though not without moments of humor, these plays present characters in the midst of an ordeal that is both physical and spiritual, one that often pivots on acts of reading, writing, or speaking that reveal language as the crux of a troubled subjectivity. The 1986 PAJ collection fea-tured a preface by Susan Sontag that celebrated "the steady ripening of this beautiful talent": "Fornes's work has always been intelligent, often funny, never vulgar or cynical; both delicate and visceral. Now it is something more" (Sontag 1986: 9).

The Danube (1983)

In 1938, in a cafe in Budapest, Hungary, a young American busi-nessman named Paul Green meets a customs house clerk named Mr. Sandor who introduces him to his daughter, Eve. The two young people fall in love and marry, but Eve and then Paul are stricken with a strange illness that eventually afflicts the entire city. Conditions worsen and tensions mount until Paul packs a suitcase to return to America with Eve, who bids a sad farewell to her father, her beloved Budapest, and the beautiful Danube River.

This is the plot, such as it is, of *The Danube*, the Fornes play inspired by an old Hungarian language record found in a Greenwich Village antique store. Each of the play's fifteen scenes is introduced as if it was a practice dialogue: a tape-recorded voice announces, for example, "Unit Ten. Basic sentences. Paul Green visits Mr. Sandor.

They discuss the weather." For some scenes, the first few lines of dialogue are also heard on tape, first in English, then in Hungarian, and then spoken by the character in the scene. On this model, the dialogue throughout maintains the stilted and rudimentary tone of a language lesson. The vocabulary is repetitive and mundane. The syntax is simple. The speech is so deliberate and unadorned as to make the characters appear naïve, almost brittle. They are capable of only the most superficial forms of expression, yet "as they find their existences growing more complex, their language devolves from a bridge connecting their lives to a wall separating them from each other" (Antholis 1985). The tension between their growing need to articulate their experience and their limited ability to do so comes to imply a tremendous suffering of feeling – a pathos – that belies their linguistically flat conception. This is the formal ingenuity of the play.

The play takes place on a small platform stage, with the setting for each scene indicated by a backdrop painted in the style of an old picture postcard. The action, which lasts just over an hour, starts innocuously, with chitchat about Budapest, who speaks which languages, and the weather, which "has been bad." Gradually, an unexplained menace makes its presence felt. When Paul and Eve go dancing, Paul has a seizure and collapses to the floor, his body twisted, his face contorted in a grimace. At the end of each scene, puffs of smoke rise up from holes in the stage floor. From Scene 10 on, the characters wear goggles over their eyes. Their skin is red with blotches; their clothes are soiled by ash and strange drippings. They grow more and more disoriented and desperate as the surface of reality itself seems to disintegrate, a process which Fornes extends by calling for the last two scenes to be presented twice, once by the actors themselves and once by the actors operating look-alike puppets of their characters on a tabletop puppet stage. In Scene 12 (repeated with puppets as Scene 13), Paul threatens to leave Eve, blaming her for his condition: "It is you who polluted me. I am clean of body and mind." She fights back, screaming "You are talking like a machine. You are saying what machines say." In the final scene (seen first with puppets, then actors), Paul and Eve pack for America and say good-bye to her father and the city. As they exit, "there is a brilliant white flash of light." And then a blackout.[1]

Figure 8 Two productions of *The Danube*, directed by Fornes: (top) at American Place Theatre in New York (1984), with Sam Gray as the Hungarian Mr. Sandor and Richard Sale as the American Paul Green; and (bottom) at Theater for the New City (1983), with Michael Sean Edwards as Paul Green, Margaret Harrington as Eve, and Arthur Williams as Mr. Sandor.

The Danube presents a gradual, ambiguous holocaust. Many have taken it to be a nuclear disaster, but the catastrophe is never actually identified. Its precise nature becomes the play's missing term. Critics who were not altogether baffled by the mystery could not resist the temptation to explain the play's sustained metaphor. "The message behind *The Danube*," wrote Michael Feingold (1984), "is that it is precisely our adaptive mechanism which may finally do us in, the human capacity for putting up with anything on the unspoken assumption that the human spirit will always survive." Critic Roger Downey (1988) cautioned against explicit interpretations: "Fornes is too canny a writer to link her drama to any single issue ... there's nothing in the play to suggest that the poison has its source in the outside world. A false relationship, a lived-out lie can sicken everything around." Una Chaudhuri discusses *The Danube* as a manifestation of what she calls "geopathology" in modern drama, the problematic relationship between character and place which "unfolds as an incessant dialogue between belonging and exile, home and homelessness" (Chaudhuri 1997: 15). For Chaudhuri, "the difference between being in a place and *belonging to a place* is suggested through the figure of tourism" in the play, evoked by Paul's status as a foreigner and sightseer in Eve's native Budapest and by the convention of the Hungarian language lessons. "What is at issue in the play is not cultural difference itself but a *view* of cultural difference that underestimates the poetic and personal demands of a truly nourishing relationship to place" (Chaudhuri 1997: 170).

Whatever the cause of the plague in the play, it generates a radical dissociation between a character's spirit, which in Fornes is always tied to the voice and vocality, and a character's physical body. This split is prefigured in the convention of the language tapes, which feature recorded voices with no bodies, and then capped by the convention of the puppet scenes. The characters in *The Danube* start the play as cardboard figures cut from the tropes of travel and translation, only to reveal a tremendous and alienated subjectivity as the disease spreads and worsens. "I don't have a mind. I don't have a soul," says Paul at the height of distress. "My Danube, you are my wisdom," says Eve as she bids her home farewell, "I don't know myself apart from you. I don't know you apart from myself." In this deceptively simple play, physical disease, spiritual despair, and geographical displacement compound each other to create a "drama of disembodied consciousness" (Chaudhuri 1997: 166) that is colored by a tremendous sense of loss.

"Irene time"

For Fornes, *The Danube* was "a tender farewell to western civilization as we witness its rapid destruction and the destruction of our planet."[2] The Hungarian language record inspired a sorrow in her for a "bygone era," which prompted her to set the play in 1938, ironically years before the first atomic bomb blast made such global destruction a real threat. Many other Fornes plays are also set before 1945, which is also the year that she emigrated from Cuba to the United States as a girl of 15. *Nadine*, the first play in *What of the Night?*, takes place in 1938. *Fefu and Her Friends* is set in 1935. The action of *Sarita* stretches from 1939 to 1947. Other Fornes plays hark back to an even earlier, bygone era. *Eyes on the Harem* begins in the last year of the Ottoman Empire, 1909, which is also the year in which Evelyn Brown wrote her diary. *A Visit* takes place in 1910. *Abingdon Square* goes from 1908 to 1917. *The Summer in Gossensass* takes place in London in 1891.

These settings in the past are more impressionistic than documentary, more an abstraction from the immediate present than a specifically historical setting, even in the plays – *Eyes on the Harem*, *The Summer in Gossensass* – based on historical subjects. A Fornes play tends to take place in an amorphous yesteryear that one artistic director once described simply as "Irene time."[3] There are very few references to actual historical events or famous people or specific geographical places. Her characters seem to exist in a world without proper names, one extracted from everyday reality and closed off by her imagination in a way that makes it self-contained and, in a sense, naïve. When asked why *Fefu and Her Friends* was set in 1935, Fornes explained her affection for:

> a kind of world which I feel is closer to the thirties than any other period. Simply because it is pre-Freud, in the way that people manifested themselves with each other there was something more wholesome and trusting, in a sense. They were not constantly interpreting each other or themselves ... Today, there is an automatic disbelieving of everything that is said, and

an interpreting of it. It's implied that there's always some kind of self-deception about an emotion.

(Marranca 1978: 109)

In the dramatic universe of "Irene time," characters exist outside the realm of a psychological realism that presents outward behavior as a social mask that conceals hidden motives. They operate without guile and speak without subtext. They respond to each other at face value, often with a simple, direct, even blunt honesty. Yet they have a tremendous depth of feeling, which may be vague or inchoate but often exerts a great pressure from within. They have souls, rather than egos. That is, they are spiritual beings before they are social creatures; that makes them vulnerable, but it also results in an intimacy and a tenderness that is their hallmark.

Mud (1983)

Mud takes place in a bone-white wooden room atop a promontory of soft red earth under a vast blue sky. Mae and Lloyd, unkempt, dirt poor, uneducated, and in their twenties, have lived together in this rural shack since the day Mae's father took Lloyd in as an orphan. Left to fend for themselves when the father died, Lloyd takes care of the pigs and farms the field and Mae irons clothes and makes the meals. As Mae explains, "I don't know what we are. We are related but I don't know what to call it. We are not brother and sister. We are like animals who grow up together and mate" (Fornes 1986: 28). The play depicts what happens when Mae attempts to rise up out of the mud and, in effect, become human, a condition she imagines in simple terms: "I'm going to die in a hospital. In white sheets. You hear? Clean feet. Injections. That's how I'm going to die. I'm going to die clean" (Fornes 1986: 19).

Both Mae and Lloyd are illiterate, but Mae is learning how to read from a primer about sea creatures, and she threatens to leave Lloyd when she finishes school. At the start of the play, he is weak, feverish, and impotent from an undiagnosed infection. Mae consults a doctor and returns with a prescription and a medical pamphlet that she cannot read, so she brings home a man in his fifties named Henry to read it for them. Henry struggles with the technical jargon, but he has "a natural sense of dignity" that fuels Mae's

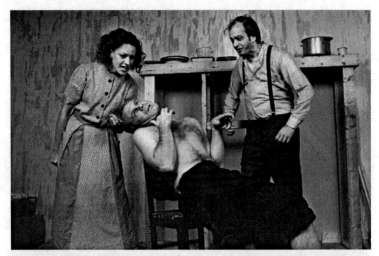

Figure 9 Two productions of *Mud*, directed by Fornes: (top) at Theater for the New City (1983) and (bottom) Milwaukee Repertory Theatre (1991). Scene 16: Mae (Patricia Mattick) confronts Henry (Alan Nebelthau) over her stolen money as Lloyd (Michael Sollenberger) urges her on. The final tableau: the dying Mae (Rose Pickering) reaches for the light as Lloyd (James Pickering) and Henry (Tom Blair) look on.

yearning to learn. "Sometimes I feel hollow and base. And I feel that I don't have a mind. But when I talk to you I do. I feel I have a mind," she explains as she confesses her love and invites him to move in and share her bed, displacing Lloyd. From here forward, the rivalry between these two needy men mounts until – as in many Fornes plays – it erupts in a violent act of passion. When Mae gets fed up and leaves – "I work too hard and the two of you keep sucking my blood. I'm going to look for a better place to be" (39) – Lloyd grabs a shotgun, follows after her, and shoots her. In the final moments, he returns with the blood-drenched Mae in his arms, and as life drains out of her, she echoes her textbook:

> Like the starfish, I live in the dark and my eyes see only a faint light. It is faint and yet it consumes me. I long for it. I thirst for it. I would die for it. Lloyd, I am dying.
>
> (Fornes 1986: 40)

When *Mud* premiered in 1983, Mae became the most pronounced manifestation of the Fornes Innocent to date, mainly because her effort to learn how to read is tantamount to bringing herself into being. She feels hollow, base, empty, but when she meets Henry she recognizes that "some people make you feel that you have something inside you. Inside your head." Like the starfish in her reader, she perceives only a faint light, which she pursues with heroic determination. For the Innocent, this pursuit often involves some aspect of mastering a language. Mae is learning how to read. Leticia in *The Conduct of Life* "would like to be a woman who speaks in a group and have others listen" (Fornes 1986: 70). Leopold in *Tango Palace* must learn the scripted wisdom on Isidore's index cards. The characters in *The Danube* are not students per se, but their existence is conditioned by the conceit of the language lesson. This acquisition of language – the spare, unsophisticated language of Evelyn Brown's diary, Mae's reader, or *The Danube*'s language tapes – is the outward sign of the interior process of coming to thought that defines the Innocent. For Fornes characters, especially explicit learners like Mae and Leticia, this process is a matter of gaining

access to a world beyond the corporeal self and a means of investing it with the subject's verbal presence. Mae and Leticia both pursue this sphere of linguistic access, out of the belief that knowledge and its articulation will not only refashion their world but also redress their invisibility in it.

(Garner 1994: 191)

In Fornes, to become a speaking subject is to make oneself visible, present, alive.

Sarita (1984)

Sarita is a romantic tragedy that verges on chamber opera. The action takes place in a Cuban-American household in the South Bronx where Sarita, age 13, lives with her mother Fela. They practice Santería, the syncretic Afro-Caribbean religion that fuses Spanish Catholicism with Yoruba polytheism; they maintain a home altar for Oshun, the patron saint of Cuba, also known as the Virgin of La Caridad del Cobre. Punctuated by a dozen songs, the play's twenty short, episodic scenes chart the unhappy course of young Sarita's love for Julio, a heartless man who abuses her affection again and again until she can stand it no more. By the second scene, Julio has left Sarita and she is pregnant from sleeping around with other boys. She refuses to marry her mother's older tenant Fernando to save her honor, and in the fifth scene, she leaves home to reunite with Julio, abandoning her infant son to her mother's care.

Julio – or Sarita's passion for him – exerts a kind of demonic possession over her that makes her so desperate that at the end of the first act she is ready to jump off the Empire State Building. A GI from Cleveland named Mark intervenes; they fall in love and marry. But in the second act, the pattern continues, only now each time she succumbs to Julio, she is betraying her husband's trust as well as her own self-respect. The ordeal becomes unbearable. She prays to God for deliverance. Eventually, when Julio tries to blackmail her by threatening to reveal her infidelity, she grabs a knife and stabs him. As he dies in her arms, she sings "Don't leave me, Papi," pleading, pressing money into his hands, prying open his eyes, and kissing him again and again. The final scene finds Sarita, age 21, in a mental hospital receiving visits from Fernando and then Mark. Numb, eerily calm now, she speaks of "this thing I have inside me. Something I cannot tear off. It is a bad growth that will not die."

Figure 10 *Sarita* at INTAR in New York (1984), directed by Fornes. Scene 3: young and pregnant, Sarita (Sheila Dabney, in school uniform) resists her mother Fela's (Carmen Rosario) effort to get her to marry the older Fernando (Rodolfo Diaz). Donald Eastman's set design for the INTAR production.

She takes Mark's hands and asks what will happen to her, as the lights fade to black.

Sarita – clearly another Fornes Innocent – suffers her desire for Julio the way the characters in *The Danube* suffer the poisoned atmosphere that stifles all of Budapest. Her passion is absolute and irremediable, in a manner that recalls the heroines of Lorca or Racine.

> Sarita is destroyed, the question is why, and the play not only refuses an answer but presents the question so it only surfaces after the show's over. Partly this is because of the poetic con- viction of each moment of action and image, flowing so neces- sarily from the one before. Partly it's because of the music, which deflects the analyzing mind with sensuousness. Partly it's because we allow the characters ... to take us over – even though they do it through our compassion, not our empathy.
>
> (Munk 1984: 95)

This compassion is linked to the ontological imperative that defines Sarita and other Fornes heroines. "Other people don't have to learn how to be," she says to her mother. "But I'm a savage. I have to learn how to lead my life." In Fornes, this compulsion to civilize the self and master the conduct of life often leads to violence and cata- strophe, as if the extremity of feeling must ultimately be matched by an equally extreme act of violence.

The "emotigraph" as unit of construction

When *Sarita* premiered in 1984, one critic compared it to Georg Büchner's proto-expressionist play *Woyzeck* because of its "use of short, episodic scenes and terse, often symbolic and enigmatic dia- logue" as well as its focus on a protagonist succumbing to madness (Syna 1984). "I love the way that Büchner doesn't tell you very much," Fornes said of *Woyzeck* in 1986:

> He is so economical. He leaves out the details that are garbage, that you don't need. You don't really know what is wrong, even when Woyzeck is talking to the ground. You can say he is crazy, but is he? He is not painting a picture of a crazy man,

necessarily. He just depicts a kind of agony, almost like a triptych. You have this picture and you have that picture and you have that picture and it shows the passion of Saint Sebastian.[4]

This comparison to the visual composition of the triptych sheds light on Fornes's dramaturgy. As early as *The Successful Life of 3*, she experimented with composing a play out of short, rapid-fire scenes juxtaposed one after the next. Her 1980s plays took this strategy further by making regular use of a new unit of dramatic construction: a brief, momentary, static scene that offers an emotional snapshot or cross-section of a changing dramatic situation.

Scenes 5 and 6 of *Sarita* are good examples. In Scene 5, lights come up dim on Sarita wearing a coat and beret, a bundle of clothes under her arm, leaning over her mother sleeping in an overstuffed chair. Without waking her, Sarita explains in a few words that she is leaving to be with Julio and asks her to take care of her son. A teddy bear sits on the couch. "Don't worry, Mami. I'll take care of myself," she says in a low voice and exits. Scene 6 is even more abbreviated. Lights come up on a small upper level of the set to reveal Sarita and Julio (seen for the first time in the play) sitting side by side on the floor with their arms around each other. The stage direction indicates that "they face front and smile tenderly as if they are looking at each other in a mirror." Drums play. Neither of them speaks. After half a minute or so, lights fade and the scene is over.

These miniature scenes – "merely flashes, bolts of illumination" (Munk 1984) – became so characteristic of Fornes's playwriting that they ask for their own nomenclature, and so, for reference purposes, I call them "emotigraphs" in order to emphasize their brevity, their pictorial quality, and their affective content. Each one "is like a gasp, so short it is over in the time it takes for a blush to go" (Kellaway 1989). They operate on the principle of a tableau, but they last longer and have a more contemplative dimension. Whether as brief as a few seconds or as long as a few minutes, these vignettes are always rigorously composed, iconographic, marked by stillness, and pulsing with emotion. If there is dialogue, often only one character speaks and then privately, intimately, or in a detached manner. Sometimes an emotigraph takes the form of a song presented as a self-contained scene, as in Scene 4 of *Sarita* when Fela leans back on the sofa, arms stretched out at her side, and sings a lament for her "first love," Sarita's father, a merchant marine who left her and never came back.

When placed one after another, Fornes's emotigraphs operate like the panels of a triptych. Each has its own integrity as an image, but when seen in a sequence, a more complex picture emerges. The spectator "connects the dots," projecting both a narrative and an emotional progression into the "space" between the scenes. In Scene 17, Mark sits at the table in Sarita's small apartment, studying from a large textbook. A key is heard in the door, and to Mark's surprise, Julio steps in, wearing a blue suit. He stands in profile, motionless, and explains that he has come to return his key because "he shouldn't have a key that's not the key to my place." Julio slowly squats to within six inches of the floor, drops the key, and backs out of the room, leaving the door open as lights fade on the scene. When they come up again, for Scene 18, Sarita is standing exactly where Julio was a moment before, staring at the key on the floor. Mark still sits there, but now with his head on the table, passed out, a shot glass and liquor bottle at his side. Reversing Julio's gesture, she slowly bends to the floor and picks up the key.[5] The stage direction reads: "She is dejected." At this late moment in the play, the sequence is harrowing, signaling in the most economical terms that it is impossible for Sarita to free herself from her love for Julio. A prisoner of desire, her suffering rises to the level of martyrdom.

Of *Sarita*'s twenty scenes, eight are emotigraphs. While this is Fornes's most insistent experiment with this form of theatrical shorthand, she includes them in many other plays. Scene 8 of *Mud* is an emotigraph that captures the romance in Mae's relationship with Henry. As she sits at the table snapping beans, he comes up behind her, covers her eyes, and places a small package in her hands. She opens it to find a lipstick, which Henry pushes up out of the tube and hands back to her. She puts on lipstick – presumably for the first time in her life – as he holds up a hand mirror for her to see. They kiss, and she sighs, "Oh, Henry." Other playwrights might more readily include such a sequence in a longer scene, but Fornes distills the dramatic situation down to "a single emotive moment" that frees "characters from explaining themselves in a way

Figure 11 Mud at Signature Theatre Company (1999), directed by David
Esbjornson. Scene 8 as emotigraph: Deirdre O'Connell as Mae
and John Seitz as Henry.

that attempts to suggest interpretations of their actions" (Marranca 1984: 30). The hallmark of Fornes's playwriting, the emotigraph exemplifies the use of silence and stillness throughout her work as a crucible of character and a formal device that invites the audience to contemplate rather than analyze the dramatic situation onstage.

The Conduct of Life (1985)

The Conduct of Life begins with an emotigraph that introduces Fornes's most troubling idealist. Lights come up on a bare-chested man wearing riding boots and military breeches doing jumping jacks "as long as it can be endured." When he is exhausted, he dries himself with a towel and explains in a soliloquy that he is a 33-year-old lieutenant with great ambition: "Man must have an ideal, mine is to achieve maximum power. That is my destiny" (Fornes 1986: 68). He resolves to overcome all obstacles in his quest, including one that will prove formidable: "My sexual drive is detrimental to my ideals. I must no longer be overwhelmed by sexual passion or I will be degraded beyond hope of recovery" (Fornes 1986: 68). In this regard, Orlando is similar to Sarita. Both are defined by an uncontrollable desire that dispirits them and hurts those around them. Sarita's agonizing passion imbues her with the virtue of the penitent, but Orlando's will-to-power and insatiable libido lead to the degradation that he fears, one that defies compassion as it finds expression in the form of violence against women, a sadistic sexual violence against an orphan named Nena and a cruel emotional violence against his wife Leticia.

Most of the play's nineteen scenes take place in Orlando's home in an unnamed Latin American country ruled by a military junta. The first half alternates between scenes at home in the living room and dining room – Leticia talking on the phone with her friend Mona; Olimpia, the feisty household servant, haggling over money to buy a pressure cooker; Orlando discussing politics with his friend and fellow officer Alejo – and scenes which depict Orlando's capture, incarceration, and repeated sexual assault of Nena, a destitute 12-year-old girl he kidnaps off the street. At first, he locks her in a warehouse and visits periodically to beat her, rape her, and leave enough food to keep her alive. Midway through the play, Orlando sneaks Nena into his own house and installs her in the basement, where he continues to rape her. All this while, his military career advances due to his work as a torturer of political prisoners.

Leticia's gradual recognition of Nena's presence in the house parallels her gradual recognition of Orlando as a professional torturer. Eventually, she confronts him about the screams coming from the basement; Orlando defiantly insists that Nena will become another servant in their home. In the play's final scene, as Olimpia and Nena look on, Orlando accuses Leticia of taking a lover; he interrogates her like one of his prisoners and manhandles her sexually until she breaks away, takes out a gun, and shoots Orlando dead. Then, Leticia faces Nena and places the murder weapon in her hands, steps back, and says, "Please ... " Nena looks at the gun "in a state of terror and numb acceptance" as the lights fade to black.[6]

The Conduct of Life is a play about the circulation of power – within the domestic sphere and social hierarchy of the home and within the political sphere and military hierarchy of the police state. These realms are homologous: each is a metaphor for the other; each is defined by Orlando's sadistic use of either rape or torture to dominate others and to gain control over his own sexual impulses. His effort to master the self – to tame the beast within and, as Sarita says, "learn how to be" – makes him akin to other Fornes agonists, but his ruthless brutality, graphically depicted onstage, forestalls the compassion they often inspire. Orlando's decision to bring Nena from the warehouse into his home can be seen as an effort to domesticate what he calls his "desire to destroy and to see things destroyed and to see inside of them." He puts a new cotton dress on Nena, claims to love her, and allows Olimpia to care for her, but his abuse is so palpably heinous that "it is hard not to see Orlando as monstrous and the three women as his victims" (Sofer 2006: 449).

Much of the scholarship on *The Conduct of Life* examines its "successful deconstruction of the inextricable intermixing of violence, gender, sexuality, and power that marks this historical moment" (Wolf 1992: 31).[7] Alluding to the image of the loathsome in *Fefu and Her Friends*, Catherine Schuler argues that Fornes "turns the stone over and reveals aspects of male psychology and heterosexual intimacy that are profoundly disturbing," chiefly that "our society condones, encourages, and even venerates male brutality, and violence against women has for centuries been a strategic device that preserves traditional gender hierarchies" (Schuler 1990: 226). Other critics have drawn on theorists such as Julia Kristeva, Teresa de Lauretis, and Elaine Scarry in order to argue that the female characters are not altogether without agency, that class differences foreclose an easy solidarity between them, and that the operation of power, desire, and violence in the play reveals gender identity as unstable, fluctuating, and performative. Stacy Wolf (1992: 29), for instance, argues that "Orlando, for example, rapes Nena in an attempt to assert masculine subjectivity from his feminized subject position as tool of the military state" and that "Leticia's class privilege constructs her as male in relation to the maid Olimpia and Nena, but, at the same time, the unfulfillment of her desire for Orlando maintains her position of feminine passivity."[8]

The rhetoric of space/the space of rhetoric

When Fornes directed the original production of *The Conduct of Life* at Theater for the New City in 1985, she took full advantage of the tremendous depth of one of the theaters there. As a result, the script stipulates an unusually specific groundplan that consists of a series of receding playing areas: 1) a living room downstage with archways that lead to the rest of the house; 2) a dining room centerstage, ten feet deep and eighteen inches above the living room; 3) a hallway upstage of that, with a door at either end and further elevated; 4) a basement room with an old mattress on the floor; and finally 5) a warehouse where Orlando first incarcerates Nena, set up on a narrow platform over the basement all the way upstage. The depth of the playing space requires the audience to look through the living room and dining room – "areas of public sociability" (Worthen 1989: 175) – to see the cellar and warehouse upstage, the clandestine sites of rape and torture. In this way, the stage space "provides a visual emblem of the hierarchy of power in the play" (Worthen 1989: 175) and "spatializes the vertical connections between the State's monopoly on violence and intimate violence within the domestic space" (Kintz 1991b: 97).

Nena's physical location onstage comes forward from warehouse to basement to dining room to living room in a gradual way that parallels Leticia's dawning recognition of Nena's presence,

Orlando's true profession, and the political crisis in her country. This progressive movement downstage constitutes a scenographic variation on the process of coming to thought in other Fornes plays. Initially, in the warehouse, Nena embodies that vague intimation of knowledge that rises to the surface of consciousness and seeks articulation through the use and command of language. She has been so thoroughly objectified by Orlando's violence that she lacks the agency of speech until Scene 15. Then, when she does speak for the first time, she has the longest speech in the play, a five-minute monologue that chronicles her life on the streets and abduction by Orlando. She blames herself for her condition because she is dirty, echoing Sarita when she says, "the dirt won't go away from inside me." She concludes on an astonishing note:

> I want to conduct each day of my life in the best possible way. I should value the things I have. And I should value all those who are near me. And I should value the kindness that others bestow upon me. And if someone should treat me unkindly, I should not blind myself with rage, but I should see them and receive them, since maybe they are in worse pain than me.
>
> (Fornes 1986: 85)

The humility and equanimity in this monologue are all the more remarkable for Nena's status as "the ultimate victim within the play's spectrum of representation" (Cubilié 2005: 55). She does not speak again in the play.

Leticia has a different, more explicit relationship to language. She wants to command political rhetoric as a public speaker. In Scene 2, she asks Orlando's colleague Alejo to teach her "elemental things" so that she might one day go to university and study political science because "I would like to be a woman who speaks in a group and have others listen" (Fornes 1986: 70). She practices for this by memorizing political speeches from a book and reciting them out loud. For Leticia, as for Mae in *Mud*,

> language transforms the world it takes as its subject, marking its environment with human reference and with the framing contours of human perception, elevating its speaker as well as

what it purports to describe from the grayness of unarticulated, merely bodily life.

(Garner 1994: 191)

But in the world of Fornes plays, the emergence of the speaking subject poses a threat to the status quo that is often met with violence. In the play's final moments, when Orlando attacks Leticia, pulling her hair and molesting her, she reaches for a gun and kills him. Only then does Leticia look Nena in the eye and speak to her for the first time in the play, placing the gun in her hands and saying only "Please ... " The ambiguity of this gesture and Nena's mute response as the lights fade resist narrative closure. What matters is that Nena has risen to the surface and come face to face with Leticia.

Notes

1 In fact, the play was commissioned by Theater for the New City for inclusion in a Nuclear Freeze Festival. The first two times that Fornes directed the play – at Padua Hills in 1982, under the title *You Can Swim in the Danube, but the Water Is Too Cold* and at TNC in 1983 – the play ended with a backdrop showing a giant mushroom cloud, prompting Erika Munk (1983) to observe "all the obviousness that Fornes has worked to avoid catches her by the back of the neck." By the time Fornes staged the play at American Place Theatre in 1984, she changed the script to call for a less explicit "brilliant white flash of light."

2 This statement was part of a program note by Fornes included in the playbill for the Theater for the New City production.

3 The informal term comes from a personal interview (July 14, 1986) with Phyllis Jane Rose, artistic director of At The Foot of the Mountain when Fornes directed *Fefu and Her Friends* there.

4 Interview with this author conducted 1986 October 11.

5 The published version of the play indicates that Sarita enters at the start of this scene, but in the original INTAR production, the lights came up on Sarita in place.

6 While many critics have understood Leticia's putting the gun in Nena's hands as an effort to dissociate herself from her violent act and even to exercise class privilege and shift responsibility to Nena, others have seen it as a plea for Nena to shoot Leticia in turn, "(possibly) asking help of her double in ending her own torment" (Austin 1989: 84). As if to clarify the matter, Fornes added a stage direction to the play when it was anthologized in 1987, indicating that Leticia is "hoping [Nena] will take

the blame" (Osborn 1987: 72). Nena's "numb acceptance" still preserves a measure of irresolution.

7 Almost twenty years after the play's premiere, at a different "historical moment," Stephen J. Bottoms (2004b) updated the play's dissection of gender, class, and power by arguing that "*The Conduct of Life* may be constructively re-read as offering valuable insights" (21) into the torture of Iraqi prisoners by low-ranking US soldiers, several of them female, at Abu Ghraib prison. With Orlando's "fear of emasculation and disempowerment" as a point of reference, he speculates that the Americans' humiliation of their Iraqi prisoners was "an expression of their own relative powerlessness" (25) as low-ranking "country boys" far from home, an enactment – by female and male soldiers alike – of the compulsive masculinity demanded by the military.

8 *The Conduct of Life* has attracted a quantity of scholarly thought that cannot be fully represented here. For a wide range of theoretical responses to the play, see Bottoms 2004b, Cubilié 2005, Garner 1994, Kintz 1991a, Lee 1996, Schuler 1990, and Wolf 1992.

8   Key play: *Abingdon Square* (conquering the vagueness)

Fornes began teaching at Padua Hills in 1978 and at INTAR in 1981. By the mid-1980s, she was being invited to teach workshops for playwrights groups, drama departments, and theater conferences all over the USA and eventually in India, Australia, Mexico, and elsewhere. David Henry Hwang attended the first Padua workshop in 1978, the summer before his senior year at Stanford. Sarah Ruhl participated in a two-week Fornes workshop in Taxco, Mexico in 1998. In the intervening twenty years, hundreds of playwrights studied with Fornes, for a day, a few weeks or months, some for years. It would be difficult to over-estimate her influence on American playwriting during this time. She left a strong impression on her students, in part because "she encouraged a very ruthless search for honesty: a profound unlocking of the verbal and visual imagination" (Svich 2009: 2). At the INTAR Lab, where she was affectionately known as La Maestra, she inspired a generation of Latina/o playwrights, many of whom carved out significant careers and extended her legacy by becoming teachers in their own right. Eduardo Machado, who worked on his "Floating Island" plays as a member of the Lab, went on to head major playwriting programs at Columbia and then NYU and to succeed Max Ferra as Artistic Director of INTAR for six years (2004–10). "To say that she changed me would be an understatement," he wrote in a 2007 memoir (Machado and Domitrovich 2007: 213): "She, more than anyone, altered the course of my career, my life, my very way of being."

Teaching playwriting

Fornes sought to nurture what she called the writer's "creative system" through an extensive series of exercises that helped "students to attain a writer's concentration and to permit themselves the freedom to enter an inspired state."[1] Musicians practice scales, dancers work at the barre, artists carry sketchbooks or attend life-drawing classes, she often pointed out, but playwrights are expected simply to sit down and write – often from a standpoint that is more analytical than creative. Fornes's exercises – rooted in memory, daydreaming, and free association – were designed to bypass a writer's rational mind in order to gain direct access to the imagination. Students were coached to trust and accept whatever came to mind, however arbitrary or mysterious or personal it might first seem, and to follow the impulse wherever it might lead.

The INTAR Lab met three times a week for thirteen weeks each year. The Padua Hills workshop usually ran for a month. As invitations to teach elsewhere grew, Fornes tailored her teaching to fit the constraints of different sponsors and her own busy schedule, but the structure of a single class session remained much the same. It lasted three or four hours and began with a half-hour of stretching, breathing, and relaxation exercises intended to quiet the mind. Students then gathered around a table or at individual desks, and Fornes instructed them to close their eyes and concentrate on their breathing as she led them in a guided visualization. For example, she might ask them to think back to a time in their lives before the age of 12 that had some connection with water or to imagine a face in close-up and examine its every detail.

Once an image had been given time to register, students were told to open their eyes, take up pen and paper, and record what they saw. This might take the form of a groundplan or map, a rough sketch of the people in a room or some outdoor place, a drawing of a character's face, a prose description of what is happening, or lines of dialogue. Soon, students were encouraged to begin writing a scene or a monologue, triggered by a line of neutral dialogue that Fornes often found in a newspaper or magazine at hand that day. The room then grew quiet as everyone – including Fornes – was left to write on their own for much of the remaining class time. Now and again, based on the level of concentration in the room, Fornes interrupted with a fresh line of random dialogue or the instruction to jump forward or back in time and start a new scene. In the last half hour, volunteers read from that day's output. Fornes refrained from direct critical comments on the writing, but she did respond with general observations.[2]

For newcomers to Fornes's teaching, the extended physical warm-up at the start of a class, the attention to breathing, and the instruction to close your eyes and let the mind wander were often discomfiting at first but then became central to the writing routine. As Alisa Solomon observed, Fornes:

> invited us to engage playwriting as a carnal enterprise – like sex or eating, an activity that involved discernment and skill but that sprang from deep, organic urges. We needed to learn to hear them rumble through us. The idea sounded a little nutty, but made perfect sense in the doing of it. Theatre is an embodied art form after all, and Irene didn't think a playwright's words could be made flesh on the stage if they hadn't somehow started out that way.
>
> (Svich 2009: 26)

Fornes's approach to teaching playwriting was influenced by for-mative theater experiences in the early 1960s. As a member of the playwrights unit of the Actors Studio and a student in an acting class taught by Gene Frankel, she was introduced to the acting technique known as the Method, the Americanization of the Stanislavsky System closely associated with Lee Strasberg, the actor, teacher, and influential head of the famous Actors Studio.

> My writing changed when I first found out what the principle of Method is. My writing became organic. I stopped being so manipulative. In *Tango Palace* I felt I knew what needed to happen in a scene and that the writing was serving me. You can see the moments when a character is speaking for my benefit rather than from their own need. The first play that I wrote that was influenced by my understanding of the Method was *The Successful Life of 3*. What one character says to another comes completely out of his own impulse and so does the other character's reply. The other character's reply never comes from

some sort of premeditation on my own part or even the part of the character. The characters have no mind. They are simply doing what Strasberg always called "moment to moment." There I was applying the Method technique for the actor to my writing and it was bringing something very interesting to my writing.

(Cummings 1985: 52)

A cornerstone of Strasberg's Method is the use of "affective memory" (also known as "emotional memory"). This practice, controversial to some and misunderstood by many, helps actors develop truthful emotional responses for a character by summoning correlative personal experiences from memory and applying them to the dramatic situation in a scene. David Lee Strasberg, the acting master's son, revisited the confusion around emotional memory in a 2009 blogpost:

What the heck was Lee Strasberg going on about? How do trained actors get in touch with real and powerful emotions despite the well-conditioned human tendency to repress them? Here's how: You start by releasing physical tension in the body (Relaxation will be a topic for another entry). You place your-self at the time you wish to experience and you ask questions: What do I see? What do I hear? What do I smell? What do I taste? What do I feel on my skin? Is it hot? Cold? Where do you feel that temperature? What part of the body? What am I wearing? Can I feel the fabric? Is there anyone else there? Can I see them? Hear them? What do they look like? What does their voice sound like? And so on. That is the exercise. Really. That's it. There is the scary secret uncloaked. Like most great things, its genius is in its simplicity.[3]

These questions are much like the ones that Fornes used to prompt her students in the middle of a guided visualization. Following Strasberg (and Stanislavsky before him), Fornes understood that powerful emotions often become associated with the sights, sounds, smells, and textures of the moment when they first occur. Before an experience fades from memory, these sensory details encode and register its affective content in the form of a complex image. Fornes adapted the idea of affective memory to the teaching of playwriting, creating exercises to gain access to the mysterious and elusive realm of the unconscious and discover raw material there that was more vivid, immediate, and truthful than the conscious mind can fabricate. As she explained, "You open your creative system to whatever enters into it, rather than imposing something on it. And you enter into another kind of world. It's a passive but very rich state" (Weiss 1986).

Lovers and Keepers (1986)

One of the plays that came out of the writing that Fornes did along with her INTAR Lab students was *Lovers and Keepers*, a suite of three short musical plays with Hispanic characters that recalls the traditional Spanish form of the zarzuela. The project teamed Fornes as lyricist with a trio of Latin American composers: Francisco Rodriguez, Fernando Rivas, and the famous percussionist and bandleader Tito Puente, the "King of Latin Jazz." Rivas also arranged the music, which mixed Afro-Cuban and Latin rhythms with tangos and ballads and even a catchy tune about chicken soup. After an early workshop in upstate New York, Fornes directed the premiere in April 1986 for INTAR's twentieth anniversary season and then a follow-up production that fall at City Theatre in Pittsburgh. She never returned to the work.

Each of the three plays offers a sympathetic portrait of love and marriage. In a program note for the Pittsburgh production, Fornes described the characters in *Lovers and Keepers* as "the non-heroes in our society: the ordinary (Fred and Fina), the unfortunate (Tato), the humble and giving (Elena, Clara), the aged with a gift for life (Nick and Toña)." They are the "salt of the earth," dull, even a bit dim-witted, but still subject to a depth of feeling that achieves special poignancy when expressed in song, lending them a dignity that they might otherwise seem to lack.

In each play, a marriage weathers a threat or crisis and emerges renewed by abiding love. *Fred and Fina* telescopes the ups and downs of twenty-three years of marriage into twenty-five minutes, twelve scenes, and five songs. The compression of the action is so severe that it recalls *The Successful Life of 3*, but comic nonchalance is replaced by genuine emotion. In the end, bitterness and recrimination give way to tenderness and generosity as Fred and Fina look back over their lives together and proclaim themselves content, admitting "I wouldn't mind if I would die here like this with you." *Tato, Elena, and Clara*, the least developed play, is a portrait of anguish. Tato is tortured by his lack of intelligence, which makes him slow at work and the object of ridicule. Despondent, he prepares to commit suicide, but the simple thought of his wife Elena stops him and he returns home to ask her forgiveness in song. "Life is so frail," he sings, and she stops folding laundry to offer love and consolation.

Toña and Nick, the most delightful of the three, turns the basic task of changing a tire into a Herculean feat. Toña and Nick are an old married couple. She has a stutter; he is confined to a wheelchair. In the first scene, Toña notices an ad in the newspaper for a sale on tires, so they decide to buy new tires to fix their car and go for a Sunday drive. Given their infirmities and limited finances, this turns out to be a logistical challenge, but they persevere in the face of each new obstacle and sing a bouncy tune "Yes We Can" to keep their spirits up. When Nick stays outside after nightfall so that the new tires are not stolen, he catches cold and takes to bed. Soon, he is unconscious and dying. Toña sings a painful lament as she spoons medicine into his mouth. A change in the music signals his recovery and a happy ending. In the last scene, we see Nick, all bundled up, and Toña in the front seat of their cardboard cut-out car, with their friends Fred and Fina (from the first play) in the back as they finally head out for their long-awaited drive.

Lovers and Keepers offers a "simple reaffirmation of humankind's need to find a mate with whom to ward off the plagues of time" (Marinelli 1987). The plays have the whimsy of Fornes's 1960s plays, but the specter of death in each play (abortion, suicide, sickness) grounds them in a world of serious consequences. They "take simplicity to the very edge of simplemindedness in their precise rendering of ordinary moments of love, anger, fear and nurture ... she evokes deeper truths than any summary of the modes surface could suggest" (Rawson 1986). For all of its charm, *Lovers and Keepers* did not gel as a unified whole for most reviewers. "Every moment in the piece is rewarding – Fornes is apparently incapable of making a dull moment onstage – but the rewards fall in different directions, rather than adding up" (Feingold 1986).

Abingdon Square: genesis and production history

For the beauty of its visual composition, the excruciating ordeal of its young heroine, and the masterful way in which it takes shape through the spectator's own imagination, *Abingdon Square* needs to be seen as central in Fornes's body of work. It, too, grew out of a playwriting exercise, one designed to demonstrate the staying power of images that come from other writers. Fornes asked her INTAR students "to close their eyes and let something come to them from the work that others in the class had written; something that had been vivid to them when they heard it." When Fornes did this, she saw a young girl from another writer's work who was auditioning for a silent movie at the turn of the century:

> When I visualized the girl in my mind there was something different about her. She was in a very dark room with her head down on the table, and there was a young man next to her in some kind of military uniform of the turn of the century. And he said to her that "he" would give her enough money to live for the rest of her life if she left the country but that if she stayed she would never see the child again. Then she told the young man that she had no intention of leaving the country and then she said "you tell him that, Son." She called him son but I had no idea why, because she was too young to be his mother.
>
> (Wasserman 1988: 23)

In subsequent classes, Fornes continued to write about this young girl, following her in her mind's eye and even imagining that she saw her on the streets of New York. One day, waiting for her bus uptown to teach at INTAR, Fornes spotted the girl at a fruit stand in the actual Abingdon Square and watched as she furtively ducked around the corner into a building there; only later, when she found herself writing a scene about a rent receipt, did she realize that the girl must have been on her way to a secret rendezvous (Tallmer 1965).

Eventually, Fornes had more than eighty separate bits of writing which she began to sift through, taking "the ones where the images had been the strongest and had made the most impact on me" and arranging and re-arranging them "like making a collage" (Wasserman 1988: 27). She wrote new fragments, rewrote and edited others, and shaped them into a rough draft of the play, which received a workshop at the Seattle Repertory Theatre in 1984. The play lay dormant until a staged reading in the spring of 1987 paved the way for the play's world premiere that October in New York by Women's Project and Productions. A year later, Fornes directed a revised version of the play at Studio Arena Theatre in Buffalo. In 1992, at the invitation of the San Diego Repertory Theatre, she translated a play of hers into Spanish for the first time and then directed *Abingdon Square/La Plaza Chica* with a bilingual cast that performed the play eight times in Spanish after several weeks of performances in English.[4] Fifteen years after that production, veteran local critic Anne Marie Welsh harkened back to it as "arguably the finest production of the last two decades in San Diego."[5]

Abingdon Square attracted more international attention than any other Fornes play. There were productions in Toronto and Sydney, and in 1989, Nancy Meckler directed a co-production in London by Shared Experience and the Soho Poly Theatre that transferred to the National Theatre's Cottesloe Theatre. The London production, which attracted widespread and mainly positive discussion in the press, served as a belated introduction of Fornes's work to British audiences. Conspicuous to many reviewers was Fornes's signature "technique of compressing meaning into images, rather than elaborating it into extended drama" (Taylor 1990). "The action is fragmented into countless tiny, inconsequential scenes which stop just as they are starting to hot up. The language is sparse, sometimes elaborately formal, and there are many moments which throb with a portentous but always elusive significance" (Spencer 1989). The play was characterized as "a deeply conventional tale, but the spare, bony writing has an almost surrealistic intensity" (Peter 1989) and "a delicate tone-poem of a play which blends shadow and light, texture and mood with the delicacy of an adagio" (Rose 1991: B2). "What is extraordinary is how much Ms. Fornes leaves out: circumstantial detail is cut to the bone ... Her prime concern, through studied language and distilled images, is to show destructive passion bursting through a formal, elegant surface" (Billington 1989).

Abingdon Square: Marion as Fornes Innocent

The action takes place between 1908 and 1917, mainly in the living room of a well-to-do house on 10th Street in Greenwich Village. The room is elegant and sparsely furnished with a sofa and two armchairs, a small writing desk, a chess table, and two tall pedestals holding large ceramic vases. In Fornes's productions, the set designed by Donald Eastman was shallow and wide and backed by a broad, undecorated wall, giving it the abstract, presentational quality of the skene of classical Greek tragedy. Long thin wooden floorboards accentuated the horizontal dimension. Two sets of French doors opened out onto a small terrace garden.

The story unfolds through a series of thirty-one brief, often enigmatic scenes. The first takes the abbreviated form of an emotigraph: a teenage girl in a simple dress stands inside the French doors, enraptured, as a well-dressed older gentleman on the terrace sings Handel's "Where'er You Walk;" when he finishes, she whispers "Psssst!" and stretches her hand out to him as the lights fade. A moment later, in the second scene, this same young girl runs into the living room squealing with laughter as she is chased around the room by a handsome adolescent boy her age. He grabs a piece of candy from her, pops it into his mouth before she can get it back, and they collapse on the floor together in playful frolic. A moment later what she says comes as a surprise: "I love you, Mike! I love you. I don't love you as a mother does, though. I love you as a sister loves a brother. I must be a mother to you. You should have a mother. You need a mother" (Fornes 1988: 2). In these first two scenes, Fornes withholds formal exposition about these characters and their relationships in favor of activating the audience's curiosity with evocative yet incongruous stage pictures.

The young girl is Marion, unschooled, orphaned at 15 by the death of her parents and soon to be married to Juster, a 50-year-old widower and father of her playmate Michael. At the start, Marion anticipates this marriage much like a novitiate preparing to take holy orders and enter a convent: "In this house," she says, "light comes through the windows as if it delights in entering here. I feel the same. I delight in entering here" (Fornes 1988: 2). Once married, she hopes to continue private study with her cousin Mary "because of all the years I was not able to go to school, I feel I don't yet comprehend a great many things." This familiar yearning for learning stems from a spiritual anxiety that afflicts many Fornes characters. "I feel sometimes that I am drowning in vagueness – that I have no character. I feel I don't know who I am," she tells her aunt Minnie, and this lack of identity motivates a routine of disciplined study. She goes to the attic, stands on her tiptoes grasping a rope overhead, and recites poetry until she collapses, exhausted and drenched in sweat.

> I come to this room to study. I stand on my toes with my arms extended and I memorize the words till I collapse. I do this to strengthen my mind and my body. I am trying to conquer this vagueness I have inside me. This lack of character. The numbness. This weakness – I have inside of me.
>
> (Fornes 1988: 4)

Just as Marion imagines herself as a beam of light that delights in entering Juster's house, her recitation is a passage from the second canto of Dante's *Purgatorio* that describes an oncoming beam of light – "A light so swiftly coming through the sea/No winged course might equal its career." – that as it approaches reveals itself as the light of a ministering angel with wings opened wide. While rendered all but incomprehensible by her anguished delivery, Marion's choice of catechism associates her ordeal with the epic journey of the spirit through hell and purgatory towards paradise and salvation. But Marion, unlike Dante, lacks a Virgil to guide and teach her, and so, she must, as Sarita says, "learn how to be" on her own. The effort of the Innocent to bring her self into being often entails a process of coming to thought, one that is liberating but often leads to madness and catastrophe. In *Abingdon Square*, that process involves Marion's imagination. Like one of Fornes's students, Marion gains access to her own "creative system" and what she finds there comes to life.

Abingdon Square: the process of imagination

In Scene 5, six months after getting married, Marion and her cousin Mary are huddled over her schoolbooks when something happens that sets the course for the rest of the play. Mary tells a story she has heard about two sisters in New Paltz who both live openly with one husband. Marion and Mary literally cannot imagine this. They puzzle over the notion of these three together in the same bed making love, titillated and troubled by it all at once. Just as Marion makes the judgment that the husband is a sinner who will go to hell, she drops to her knees to beg God's forgiveness, confessing to Mary in a panic, "I thought about it. I imagined it! I did" (Fornes 1988: 3). Excited, Mary quizzes her about what she saw, pressing for the lurid details until Mary, too, gasps suddenly and falls to her knees: "Oh Marion. Now I have sinned too. Will God forgive us?" In naïve desperation, the two girls clutch each other tight lest God strike them dead right then and there.

In its depiction of a schoolgirl's naïve sexual fantasy, this is as delightful a scene as any Fornes ever wrote. For Marion though, it represents a rupture of innocence by an act of mind that is just as real and irrevocable as the loss of virginity itself. The very next scene confirms this in a deft and subtle way. In a tableau of domestic tranquility, Marion sits at the desk writing in a diary, Michael sprawls on the floor reading, and Juster sits in a chair and reads out loud from a book about horticulture:

> If you wish to see it for yourself, take a pencil and push the pointed end into the open mouth of the flower and downward toward the ovary and the honey, just as a bee would thrust in its tongue. If it is a young flower you have chosen you will see the two anthers bend down as if they knew what they were doing, and touch the pencil about two inches from the point leaving a smudge of golden pollen on it. A day later, the stigma will have lengthened and, if you would, then push your pencil in again ...
>
> (Fornes 1988: 3)

Neither Michael nor Marion seem to pay attention to Juster, who reads with scientific dispassion, but this technical description of cross-pollination, coming moments after Marion and Mary have tried to imagine three lovers in bed, pulses with the splendid danger of erotic literature. The audience's imagination picks up where Marion's left off in Scene 5 and assigns the subtextual libidinal energy in the botany text to the adolescent girl writing in her diary (and, for that matter, to the adolescent boy reading nearby).

The rest of Act One traces the awakening of Marion's sexual identity through a process of imagination that draws on the audience's attribution of thoughts, feelings, and impulses to Marion before they are made explicit in word or deed. Scene 7 reveals Marion in the attic reciting her catechism from Dante – as if to mortify sexual urges that she has not even articulated yet. In Scene 9, Michael teaches Marion to dance to a music hall rag. Their enjoyment is so exuberant that it sparks the idea of a taboo romance between them, but when Juster comes home from work, he claps along with the music as he watches them dance. But then, in Scene 10, when Michael sneaks up behind Marion writing in her diary, she closes the book and clasps it to her chest as if caught in the midst of something private or forbidden. When Michael insists that diaries are for recording things that are true, Marion tells him, "This diary is to write things that are not true. Things that are imagined. Each day I write things that are imagined." She confides in Michael that she is writing "the story of a love affair" between a young man whose name begins with the letter F and a young girl. "Who is she?" he asks. "Me!" is her one-word answer. Michael quizzes her for details – where they first met, how often they meet, whether she will kiss him – and when he asks if her fantasy lover is real, she says, "He is real, as real as someone who exists." The play pivots on this tenet of Fornes's drama: what is imagined is real.

The next scene, another wordless emotigraph, is straight out of nineteenth-century romantic melodrama:

> Scene 11. Three months later. October, 1910. It is morning. Marion enters right, carrying a hooded cloak. She walks left furtively and looks around. She puts on the cloak, lifting the hood over her head, covering her face. She looks around again and exits right hurriedly.
>
> (Fornes 1988: 5)

Is Marion actually sneaking out for a clandestine rendezvous or is this a page from her diary sprung to life? What the play insists is that it makes no difference, a point brought home two scenes later when a distressed Marion confesses to Michael that she spotted her imaginary lover in a bookshop and that she went back again and again to spy on him until one day he waited around a corner and surprised her. Her sense of sin at this moment is just as absolute as when she first imagined the illicit lovers of New Paltz. "I'm ashamed of myself," she says, "I'm a worthless person ... I have to do penance." But as the rest of the play demonstrates, it is already too late for that. Marion has sexual urges to which she will eventually succumb. Like Sarita, like Orlando, she judges herself harshly for this weakness, but the play itself, through the clinical precision of its form, refuses to judge her.

Two scenes later, Frank (as she now calls him) appears outside the French doors and enters the house. Terrified and excited both at once, Marion touches his face, as though to see if he is real. She sends him away, insisting that she loves her husband and will always be faithful to him, but when Frank departs, she sits on the sofa and sobs. Juster enters and, seeing her distress, holds her and strokes her hair as she stares blankly into space. That is the elegiacal end of the first act. Its fifteen scenes offer Fornes's most painstaking, step-by-step representation of the process of coming to thought, configured here as an act of imagining rather than rote learning. A vague idea or sense of possibility, a voice or a glimmer of light just beyond the threshold of perception, gradually gains clarity and definition, rising to the surface of consciousness through some effort to learn or to command language. What starts as naïve fantasy becomes "as real as someone who exists."

In the second act, the nature of the action – and the audience's contribution to it – changes as Marion's passions are pursued and her idealism compromised. In Scene 18, Marion has an odd, one-time sexual encounter with a workman who has come to repair a window. She becomes pregnant as a result, and Juster thinks the child is his. Frank returns after a four-year absence, and Marion commences an extra-marital affair with him at a rented apartment on Abingdon Square. The rest of the act, unusually plot-driven for a Fornes play, traces a conventional line of events. Juster discovers her infidelity, throws her out of the house, and refuses to let her see her infant son. Michael, torn between father and friend, enlists in the army. The affair with Frank sours. Both Marion and Juster grow distraught to the point of madness, leading to a violent confrontation. Juster comes to the love nest on Abingdon Square to kill Marion but cannot bring himself to do it. He suffers a stroke on the spot, which leaves him in a coma. Marion cares for

Figure 12 Abingdon Square at Studio Arena Theatre in Buffalo (1988), directed by Fornes. The final tableau: Marion (Susan Gibney) cradles the dying Juster (Edwin Owens) as Michael (Andrew Colteaux) looks on. Donald Eastman's set design for Juster's house on 10th Street.

him day and night until one day Juster revives. He panics at the sight of her but then calls her back a moment later on the verge of death. They proclaim their love for each other as Michael enters in his army uniform and stands with them. Marion, cradling Juster in her arms, sobs "He mustn't die! He mustn't die!" And the play is over.

Abingdon Square is a romantic tragedy in which Marion is caught between two undeniable and irreconcilable absolutes: the noble and pure spirit represented by Juster's townhouse on 10th Street and the anarchic sexual freedom represented by the apartment on Abingdon Square. Here again, Fornes invites comparison to the passionate heroines of Lorca and Racine. Marion judges herself a sinner for her carnal instincts, even before they come to life as a lover named F, but she cannot deny them, and because they spring from her imagination – and, significantly, from what the audience imagined for her – they have a truthfulness that cannot be dismissed. Her efforts to reconcile opposite claims and achieve her own subjectivity lead to a suffering of feeling that is heroic even as it leads to a kind of madness.

"The Poetry of Space in a Box:" scenography and Fornes's orchestration of space

In *Abingdon Square*, and throughout Fornes's body of work, psyche is spatial. As the first director of her plays, Fornes composed meticulous stage images that configure theatrical space as both a visual frame and an outward extension of her protagonist's state of mind. In this effort, she was particularly well-served by her ongoing collaboration in the 1980s and early-1990s with a trio of designers: Donald Eastman (scenery), Anne Millitello (lighting), and Gabriel Berry (costumes). Together, they helped Fornes to articulate an onstage environment that operated like an emotional echo chamber, amplifying a character's subjectivity, making stillness dynamic rather than static, and activating space in expressionistic terms. All three worked on *Sarita* at INTAR in 1984, Fornes's production of *Hedda Gabler* at the Milwaukee Repertory Theatre in 1987, and *Abingdon Square* at Studio Arena Theatre in 1988, as well as numerous other Fornes productions involving one or two of them and other designers.

In Fornes's productions, domestic interiors were sparsely furnished with plain pieces of furniture surrounded by empty space. The accoutrements of realistic décor – side tables, bookshelves, stools, lamps and lighting fixtures, knickknacks – were rare. Walls were often tall and imposing, undecorated but heavily textured, featuring baseboards, molding, pilasters, lintels, an occasional shelf, and other architectural details. Many sets included alcoves, vestibules, or other recesses that could isolate a character within the main playing area. Inspired by the tiny interiors of Giotto paintings, Donald Eastman's set for *The Trial of Joan of Arc in a Matter of Faith* (1986) was a small, gray, abstract cubicle with even smaller niches and a window well wide and deep enough that Joan could climb up on the ledge and achieve a limited asylum within her cell. Sandra Woodall's set for *Oscar and Bertha* at the Magic Theatre included two tiny, self-contained bedrooms no bigger than a walk-in closet, which were shuttered off from view, when desired, by a short curtain.

While actual doors were rare on a Fornes set, doorways, archways, and passageways leading to other barely discernible spaces deeper within were common. *Evelyn Brown (A Diary)* (1980) and *The Conduct of Life* (1985), both staged at Theater for the New City, featured playing areas that were unusually deep, accentuating the sense of interiority and isolation further upstage. In a different way, *Fefu and Her Friends* takes the audience deeper inside Fefu's house when it divides the audience into four groups and guides them to the library, the kitchen, and the bedroom. Sometimes, a smaller, secondary setting – Sarita's kitchen, Marion's Abingdon Square apartment – was concealed on a raised platform behind the tall wall of the main set, giving it a diorama quality when lighted by itself and framed by darkness. Isidore's personal shrine in *Tango Palace*, ringed by a string of flower-shaped light bulbs and decorated with a miscellany of theatrical props, is a precursor for this space-within-a-space, which can even be seen in the puppet stage that figures in the last two scenes of *The Danube*. One radical manifestation of this scenographic trope was in Eastman's design for Fornes's *Hedda Gabler* in Milwaukee, which included an odd-looking, white, polygonal chamber prominently situated upstage center that turned out to be the stove called for by Ibsen. At the end of Act Three, Hedda entered this little chamber through a small door to burn Lovborg's manuscript and was herself engulfed in the orange light of the flames.

These formal characteristics of the typical Fornes set – long, straight lines and flat textured surfaces; isolated, iconic pieces of furniture; a lack of decorative detail; and architectural elements that lead deeper inside – gave the interior settings for her plays an austere, abstract quality, even as the characters who occupy these rooms engage in familiar, everyday activities and household chores. Characters come and go with the logic of realism, but the rooms themselves feel separate and disconnected from the outside world. If there were windows, they were often high on a wall or otherwise offered a limited view of the outside. This hermetic, self-contained quality helped Fornes to accentuate the spiritual turmoil of her characters. At one moment, she would set off a character from the physical environment with empty space, and at another, she positioned an actor outside a window, against a wall, behind a chair, under a bed, down a hallway or in some other way that obscured her from view and absorbed her into the architecture. Through lighting, blocking, acting, and the use of music, the space seemed to expand and contract with the presence of the characters onstage.

The rhythm of changing figure–ground relationships over the course of the play reinforced the psychic connection between character and domestic setting and helped make the stage space feel like an inner sanctum or cell, both site and symbol of a character's most interior struggle. Always a place of confinement, this crucible of the spirit can be a private sanctuary (the attic on 10th Street, Sarita's kitchen) or a prison cell (the warehouse where Orlando keeps Nena, Joan's cell). It is the domain of the inner self, where spirituality and sexuality converge. It is a profoundly female space, a womb of the self, and the scenographic emblem of Fornes's greatest theme: the struggle of a woman to overcome a sense of weakness, insufficiency, or original sin and bring herself into being.

Notes

1 From a copy of Fornes's application for a Guggenheim fellowship to support assembling her exercises and comments on playwriting into a book to be called *The Anatomy of Inspiration*. This project never came to fruition.

2 For appreciations of Fornes as a teacher and examples of some of her exercises, see Delgado and Svich (1999) and Svich (2009).

3 "The Low-Down on the Emotional Memory Exercise," dated February 19, 2009 [http://www.strasberg.com/lstfi/index.php?option=com_content& view=article&id=52:the-low-down-on-the-emotional-memory-exercise& catid=35:uncategorized&Itemid=74] accessed January 2, 2010. David Lee Strasberg is Creative Director and CEO of the Lee Strasberg Theatre and Film Institute.

4 Playwright Mac Wellman brought *Abingdon Square* to the attention of San Diego Rep artistic director Doug Jacobs, who initially proposed that Fornes direct *Romeo and Juliet* with a bilingual cast that would perform it in Shakespeare's verse and then in Neruda's translation. Fornes demurred. She was wary, too, of rendering the WASP-ish world of *Abingdon Square* into Spanish, but once she did, she discovered "that the play really is a Latin American play, with strong traces of Catholicism, the juicier, more romantic Latin Catholicism" (Jones 1992: D-5).

5 Welsh, Anne Marie, "Between the scene changes, Maria Irene Fornes's 'Mud' is solid," *San Diego Union-Tribune* March 13, 2007: E-9.

Part IV

The 1990s

"Where are we in relation to all this?"

9   The Night Plays

For Fornes, the 1990s was a period of questioning, one in which her status as the most important "unknown" playwright in the United States took lasting root. Her productions of *What of the Night?* at Milwaukee Rep in 1989 and Trinity Rep in 1990 suggested she was on the verge of reaching a wider audience of resident regional theaters. In 1992, Yale Repertory Theatre presented *Fefu and Her Friends* and San Diego Repertory Theatre did *Abingdon Square*, but her incursion into the mainstream went no further. Even in New York City, she went ten years without a production after the 1987 premiere of *Abingdon Square*. She became more than ever an outsider artist, matron saint of the Off-Off Broadway tradition, an inspiration and revered model for two generations of vanguard theatermakers. Undaunted, she continued to write – including libretti for two operas and an ambitious cycle of four short inter-related plays – and to direct, if not at the prodigious pace of the 1980s. In what proved to be the last decade of her career, she remained a popular and influential teacher and continued to receive commissions, grants, awards, teaching invitations, and other accolades, including a season devoted to her work at New York City's Signature Theatre Company.[1]

While not a radical break with her earlier work, Fornes's 1990s plays took on new inflections and emphases. The figure of the Fornes Innocent is absent. In the calculus of pain, wearying disease replaces passionate outbursts of violence. Bonds of friendship, as in *Enter the Night*, *Terra Incognita*, *The Summer in Gossensass*, and *Letters from Cuba*, become more common than the consuming sexual obsessions of Sarita, Orlando, or Marion. Even when there is a sexual rivalry between friends, philia prevails over eros. And there is also a nagging distress about the state of the world that harkens back to *The Danube* (1983), which Fornes described as "a tender farewell to western civilization as we witness its rapid destruction and the destruction of our planet." In *Terra Incognita* (1997) three young American tourists are sitting around in a cafe in Spain when one of them observes: "If you look into a crystal ball and you ask, 'Crystal ball, will there be such a thing as the end of the world?' the crystal ball doesn't answer." As if to make his point, he asks the question of an imaginary crystal ball, gets no answer, and then turns to his friends and asks, "Is this the end of the world?" (Fornes 2007: 80). This same millennial anxiety hangs over *What of the Night?* (1989) and *Enter the Night* (1993), plays whose titles suggest a descent into the darkness of an unknown territory.

The specter of a world coming to an end is echoed by the threat of a life coming to an end. Disease is conspicuous in the plays of the 1990s, especially in *Enter the Night*, which includes the character of an amateur playwright named Jack who has an odd, depressing prediction of the future:

> One day every single person will be ill ... Everything in our minds will be illness, the ill, the dying. All art will be about illness. All plays will be about illness. And the ill. The characters will be defined by their illness. It is the characters' illnesses that will determine the plot. Instead of the ingénue, the romantic lead, the friend, the villain, the characters will be defined by their illnesses; the cancer victim, the AIDS victim, the tubercular, the diabetic. The person poisoned by industrial chemicals, in the air, in food. The central issue of the plots will be the development of the illness ...
>
> (Fornes 2008: 201)

This macabre fantasy goes on at length, to the point where Jack opines that "the best actors will be the ones who can reproduce the particular breathing for each illness" before he finally concludes, "The leading characters will have the illness most common among theatergoers. Since theatergoers prefer to have plays written about them. Plays will be funded by pharmaceutical laboratories." The expression here is extreme, to the point of achieving a dark, ironic humor, but the concern is not unusual in these later plays. Disease, disintegration, and moral, economic, and physical decay are very real threats in Fornes's later plays. Survival becomes a primary concern.

What of the Night? (1989)

In the summer of 1986, Fornes arrived for her annual stint at Padua Hills with a scene in which a woman named Nadine gives her son Charlie step-by-step instructions in how to iron a suit, teaching him to spit on the iron to see if it is hot, to use a damp cloth in order not to burn the fabric, and so on. From this kernel, Fornes wrote *The Mothers* and staged it at Padua Hills under a tree with a few pieces of furniture to serve as the outdoor home of the play's impoverished family. Not long after, Fornes was invited to write and direct a play for En Garde Arts, an experimental company that pioneered the development of site-specific theater in New York City. Founded in 1985 by Anne Hamburger, En Garde Arts specialized in commissioning playwrights and directors to create pieces for vacant Manhattan buildings that were in architectural turnaround. Charles Mee and Anne Bogart created *Another Person Is a Foreign Country* for an abandoned nursing home being redeveloped as luxury condominiums; Mac Wellman wrote *Crowbar* for a former porno house on 42nd Street on its way to becoming the New Victory Theatre; and Fornes wrote and directed *Hunger* as one of "Three Pieces for a Warehouse" that was being converted to an office building at 500 Greenwich Street in West SoHo. In March 1988, *Hunger* was performed on the seventh floor in a series of empty brick-walled rooms that Fornes chose to represent a dimly lit, cavernous shelter for the homeless.

Fornes came to imagine the characters in *Hunger* as the same as some in *The Mothers* only much later in life, so when the Milwaukee Repertory Theatre commissioned her to write a play to inaugurate their new black box theater, she decided to write a middle play for the same characters. She arranged for a workshop in August 1988 to develop the play with members of the Milwaukee Rep's resident and apprentice acting companies. By the time she arrived, three short plays had expanded into four, which she rehearsed for ten days and presented to an invited audience under the title *Give Us*

This Day. Fornes returned to Milwaukee to direct the world premiere in March 1989 under the new title *And What of the Night?* A year later, she directed a second production at Trinity Repertory Company in Providence, Rhode Island, during Anne Bogart's truncated one-year tenure as artistic director there. The play was a finalist for the Pulitzer Prize in 1990 and first published in 1993 (at which point Fornes dropped the word "And" from the title). In 1997, she directed *Springtime*, the second of the four plays, at Theater for the New City on a bill of one-acts with Edward Albee's *Counting the Ways* directed by Joseph Chaikin. Since then, the tetralogy has received scant attention.

By a strict historical timeline, *What of the Night?* was conceived and developed in the latter half of the 1980s, but thematically it ushers in the work of the 1990s. Collectively, the four short plays are about "the human instinct for survival in an increasingly dim and horrifying context" (Clay 1990). As Fornes described it in the program for the Trinity Rep production:

> What inspired me to write this play is the overwhelming number of homeless, destitute, and ill who inhabit the streets and undergrounds of our cities and my state of confusion as to why this is happening. I fear for our future. I feel that we are becoming greedy and heartless. I don't understand what is leading us to these feelings and I can't imagine anything but disaster being the outcome of our mindlessness and heartlessness.

What of the Night? traces a path to that disaster.

The first play, initially titled *The Mothers*, then *Charlie*, and finally *Nadine*, takes place somewhere in the Southwest where a mother named Nadine and her children live in poverty outdoors in an empty lot with a few pieces of furniture. Her babe-in-arms Lucille is sick and needs medicine or she will die. Her hapless teenage son Charlie tries to help by mugging bums, stealing their clothes, and giving them to a menacing, small-time hoodlum named Pete to sell. But the few pennies he earns are insufficient so Nadine turns to having sex with Pete for money. Her 9-year-old daughter Rainbow brings home another mouth to feed, a feisty street kid named Birdie, who marries Charlie (despite their young ages). But

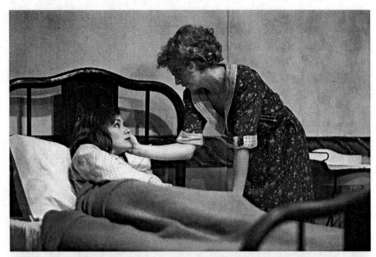

Figure 13 What of the Night? at Milwaukee Repertory Theatre (1989),
directed by Fornes. A scene from *Springtime*: Rainbow (Kelly
Maurer) takes care of the ailing Greta (Catherine Lynn Davis).
The final tableau from *Hunger*: the Angel (Thomas Van Voorhees)
brings rations for (from left to right) Ray (Daniel Mooney),
Charlie (Kenneth Albers), Birdie (Catherine Lynn Davis), and
Reba (Marilyn Frank).

Birdie wants "something from life," and in the end, she leaves, as Charlie begs her to stay and sobs and rubs his face in the dirt.[2]

The second play, *Springtime*, takes place twenty years later and chronicles in fourteen typical Fornes emotigraphs the sad romance between Rainbow, now 29, and her German lover Greta, who is desperately ill. Once again, the need for medical care prompts one of Nadine's children to turn to crime. Rainbow steals a watch from a wealthy man, who catches her and forces her into his service as part of a blackmail scheme. Unbeknownst to Rainbow, this man is her half-brother Ray, who was given up for adoption by Nadine at an early age. The love of Rainbow and Greta is sweet and tender, but Ray's presence in their lives comes between them. One day, Rainbow catches Greta with Ray. After a long silent good-bye, Rainbow leaves, ending a second play on a sad note of failed romance.

The third and strangest play of the four is *Lust*, which moves from "the fringes of society to the centers of power" (Clay 1990). It focuses on Ray, now an ambitious businessman moving up the corporate ladder. He is the embodiment of the heartless greed in the world that Fornes found so troubling. He marries the boss's daughter Helena, a high-strung woman so starved for affection that she seems barely to exist. They share a loveless marriage, as Ray becomes his father-in-law's partner and eventually takes over his business. In the middle of the play, there is a wildly theatrical sequence that presents a bizarre, erotic dream of Ray's. The action careens from a car-repair shop to a fire escape to a Chinese restaurant to the streets of Bolivia, as Ray has a rapid-fire series of sexual encounters. He masturbates against a bathroom mirror. He tells a woman to "measure my cock." He forces himself to watch as a boy burns hundred-dollar bills. A crow pecks at his face. Cold, heartless sex becomes the emblem of all rapaciousness, even when the dream sequence is over and Birdie enters the play as a companion Ray has hired to care for Helena. In the end, Ray, firmly in command, stops his father-in-law from shooting himself as Helena, fragile and forlorn, talks about how her father, now a broken man, always wished he had a son just like her.

The fourth play, *Hunger*, takes place in the future "after an economic disaster" so severe that all but a privileged minority live in prison-like warehouses for the dispossessed. Charlie, now a portly, slow-witted man of 76, is a low-level clerk in one such shelter. Ray, now one of the fallen, lives there with his mate Reba (a name that echoes Rainbow) and goes out at night scavenging for food or things he can sell. Birdie, now a woman of means, comes from "the Compound," the bunkered refuge of the ruling elite, to retrieve something taken by Ray. Charlie does not remember Birdie as his former wife or Ray as his brother. "It's different now," says Charlie. "The way a person thinks. The way a person is" (Fornes 2008: 158). An atmosphere of torpor and gloom prevails. Bodies shrouded in blankets line the walls. The characters are all damaged or wounded. Reba has a broken arm and needs medical treatment, but she will not sign a requisition form because, she says, it is better not to put your name down on paper. When Birdie returns with a loaf of bread for the others, she is handed a blanket and assimilated into the shelter. "A moment ago you felt you were different," says Reba. "But it won't take too long before you feel just like us" (Fornes 2008: 168). A bell sounds signaling mealtime in the shelter, and a stone Angel with a broken wing approaches and drops bloody animal entrails on the floor. Birdie gags and faints, Reba asks the Angel to bring Birdie "something she can eat," Charlie kneels and bows his head, and Ray sobs as the lights fade to black, prompting one reviewer to write: "As in Beckett, the juxtaposition of the cosmic and the prosaic, given equal weight, is devastating" (Clay 1990).

The four plays of *What of the Night?* present a process of enervation that leads to a world of perpetual hunger. Poverty leads to illness which leads to crime and degradation as well as to cruelty and betrayal. With its intergenerational characters, its apocalyptic focus on the human condition, and its effort to combine four separate plays into one, *What of the Night?* can be seen as Fornes's most ambitious playwriting experiment. The epic sweep of the action raises expectations for a strong central narrative on the order, say, of Tony Kushner's *Angels in America* (which premiered a couple years later). But as with so many other Fornes works, what holds the play together is a pervasive mood or feeling. Fornes does not offer an explicit political critique of late-stage capitalism so much as she mourns a world being drained of its humanity. The vision is bleak and dystopian. Sympathetic critics suggested there was no need for the whole to be greater than the sum of the parts. "You can't help but admire the writer's refusal to impose clarity on her confusion – as well as the imaginative strength to harness its swirl," wrote Carolyn Clay (1990). "If cohesion must sometimes be sacrificed to compassion, better that than the other way around." Kevin Kelly echoed this assessment in the *Boston Globe* (1990b):

> She keeps us riveted even when her scattering of images, emotions, language, and thoughts fails to coalesce ... But clarity here is not the measure, cohesion not the focus. *And What of the Night?* is deliberately scattered, half-irreal, half-pragmatic, its literary approach itself a metaphor for the blurred identities and blasted epoch the play creates.

Oscar and Bertha (1992)

In 1992, at San Francisco's Magic Theatre, Fornes directed the first and only full production of *Oscar and Bertha*, after workshops at the Guthrie Theatre in 1987 and at Padua Hills in 1989. The play is an anomaly. It is not what this chapter would categorize as a "night play," nor is it like anything Fornes ever wrote. It belongs to a persistent vein of comic ribaldry that runs through *The Red Burning Light*, *A Visit*, and *Lust*, but it surpasses them in the extreme way that it couples emotional need with sexual appetite. Oscar and Bertha are a brother and sister whose sibling rivalry is so primal and so unchecked by the restraints of mature behavior that every interaction between them quickly devolves into physical combat or sexual assault. They are middle-aged adults, but they behave like absolute children.

Oscar is a mess of a human being. His speech is labored, his mind is slow, and he is confined most of the time to a wheelchair. Bertha is as sharp as Oscar is dull. She stands ramrod straight, her hair in a tight bun, a bundle of nervous energy beneath her stiff shell. They live together in a modest home, and the action begins when a frail, mousy woman named Eve answers their want ad looking for a live-in housekeeper. For brother and sister alike, it is lust at first sight. No sooner has Oscar begun to interview Eve than he starts making peeping sounds as he reaches over and pinches her breast like it was a bathtub squeeze toy, asking "Do the girls in Franklyn have a pretty little tit. Like a bird. That goes pip pip"

Figure 14 Oscar and Bertha at the Magic Theatre in San Francisco (1992), directed by Fornes. Regina Saisi as Eve and, behind her, Patricia Mattick as the ecstatic Bertha.

(Fornes 1991: 62). The rest of the play presents their crude and competitive efforts to seduce Eve or, failing that, simply to use her to relieve themselves sexually.

Their behavior is so narcissistic and infantile that it is neither erotic nor pornographic. Sex becomes the currency of attention and approval and Eve, as caregiver, serves as surrogate parent. In a typical sequence of juvenile one-upmanship, brother and sister brag about their sexual conquests until Oscar claims to have had sex with their mother even as a little baby:

> She was my woman. I owned her. I was her baby love – she never nursed you … I drank the milk that was intended for

you. I have your milk inside me. You never went near her. I lay in bed with her as she fed me. And we climaxed. Both of us. My baby penis was erect like a torpedo and I climaxed and so did she ... You think she enjoyed herself with Daddy? Ha! His cock was big but dull. My little penis was cheerful. She came so deeply and beautifully. And me. I turned to her and when my little penis touched her belly I came. She put her hand on my fat little butt and felt it pulsate with the throes of orgasm. She held me and she climaxed. We never kissed. Our love was pure.

(Fornes 1991: 81)

This is so devastating for Bertha that she drops to the floor in perverse denial and scurries about on all fours calling "Here! Doggy, doggy, doggy. Here! Doggy, doggy, doggy." This is comic pathos so ridiculous that it borders on the sublime.

Oscar and Bertha is a Punch-and-Judy show for actors instead of puppets, complete with pratfalls, verbal abuse, and slapstick violence using rolled-up newspapers. Fornes's grotesque becomes so extreme that it suggests "a fragility about her characters, a sense that they are perilously close to breaking. Once this is established, she seems to push them over the edge and then embrace them, as if she were saying that our vulnerability is what is most valuable about us" (Coates 1992). The action moves through a period of crisis towards a happy ending. Eve gets so sick that she is hospitalized. Oscar makes a clownishly heroic effort just to get out the door to look for work. Eve recuperates and returns home to Oscar and Bertha and a man from the bank named Pike, who rounds out the new family unit. "It's hell out there," says Eve, "Worse than here," and a moment later, some new transgression prompts another fight, and the four characters pull out their rolled-up newspapers and pummel each other with joyful abandon, a signal that life has returned to normal.

Enter the Night (1993)

Like *What of the Night?*, *Enter the Night* is a play about survival. It presents three characters: one cares for the sick, one is sick, one thinks he is sick. Tressa is a hospice nurse. Paula is a country farmer with a heart condition that threatens to kill her at any moment. Jack is a gay playwright so convinced he has AIDS that he gets tested again and again despite negative results. Here again Fornes uses illness as a metaphor for a deeper affliction, a profound existential despair in the face of loss and loneliness, a spiritual malaise from which there seems to be only two forms of relief: love and theater.

Enter the Night was commissioned by New City Theatre in Seattle, where it received its world premiere in April 1993. In typical fashion, the playwright used this first production as the occasion to complete a draft of the script, which she continued to develop in her June 1994 workshop production at the Dallas Theater Center. The New York premiere was directed by Sonja Moser in December 1999 as part of the Signature Theatre Company's Fornes season. Again, critical response was more respectful than laudatory. "Though the languorous flatness of 'Enter the Night' can be bothersome, there's something intriguing, even admirable about Fornes' refusal to juice things up," wrote veteran Seattle critic Misha Berson (1993b), "Her images and words leave a subliminal imprint on your mind; the symbolism bobs to the surface later." Michael Feingold (1999), after 25 years of reviewing Fornes in New York, commented: "Rock-solid and evanescent as quicksilver, the play's as maddening as it is hypnotic; I think it's either my favorite Fornes play or the only one I can't stand."

Enter the Night began as a work-in-progress titled *Dreams*, a series of monologues that Fornes jotted down when the voices of friends came to her in her sleep "telling me things about themselves, things I wouldn't have otherwise known" (Berson 1993a). The finished play retains a similar liminal sense of being situated between dream and awake, between fantasy and reality, and also between theater and life. The play takes place in Tressa's roomy but hermetic loft apartment. In a rare nod to the Aristotelian unity of time, Fornes confines the action to a 24-hour span; a nocturnal mood prevails throughout, even in a scene that takes place in the afternoon. In the first scene, Tressa comes home at 6:30 a.m. from an all-night nursing shift, turns on the radio, gets a cup of coffee, and proceeds to change from her street clothes into the pants, jacket, and slippers of a male Chinese peasant. "I think I'm a cross-dresser," she later explains with utter nonchalance. "People dress in a certain way. Feel in a certain way. It's natural to me to dress this way. I feel whole. It soothes me" (Fornes 2008: 181). There's nothing outwardly flamboyant about Tressa's male guise; as she says, it is a matter of comfort, just as her job as nurse is about "making people comfortable ... so they can bear their pain ... their agony." This need for soothing comfort and the action of providing it is the driving force in the play.

Soon after Tressa arrives home from work, her friend and houseguest Paula awakens from a restless sleep. Paula has come down to the city to visit friends, attend a party, interview for a job, apply for a loan to save her failing farm, and see a cardiologist about her failing health. When Jack arrives with croissants for breakfast, the play's triangle of friends – "a trio of left-hand gloves trying vainly to make a pair" (Feingold 1999) – is complete. For the remainder of the first act and the four scenes of the second act, small talk and routine chores alternate with ritual enactments and cathartic outbursts of emotion. An undercurrent of sexual tension runs between the three friends, but it never erupts into outright conflict, as it does in *Sarita*, *Mud*, *Abingdon Square*, and *Oscar and Bertha*. Here, compassion trumps desire. Tressa, Paula, and Jack

> love each other selflessly and deeply. They suffer from self-inflicted wounds, suffer even more perhaps from witnessing each other's suffering, discovering that love's at best an ano-dyne, not a cure. But love they do, and their mutual affection pervades *Enter the Night* with a warmth, a palpable radiant energy, that somehow contradicts the demonstrable, depressing facts of their existence, an existence haunted by disease, real and imagined, by labors unrewarded, constant fear, hope denied.
>
> (Downey 1993)

The play is a testament not only to the soothing balm of friendship but also to the restorative power of theater. On two occasions, the action gives over to an extended play-within-the-play. In the first act, Jack convinces Paula and Tressa to read aloud the rough draft of a clumsy, amateur play he has written about two happily married Vermont farmers who are thinking of moving to the city and wonder where they will keep their cows. Paula and Tressa clap with delight when they reach the end, and Jack takes a ceremonial bow. He has been overwhelmed by the recent death of his lover Joey from AIDS. Writing the play, he insists, "has saved my life. It has made me calm, be still. I don't spend nights roaming around the city anymore" (Fornes 2008: 186).

The second theatrical enactment comes at the beginning of the second act. Without introduction or explanation, Tressa, in her Chinese male garb, and Jack, dressed as an urchin girl, act out a montage of scenes from D.W. Griffith's 1919 silent-film classic *Broken Blossoms*. Tressa plays Huang, the immigrant Chinese shopkeeper in an East London slum who rescues the helpless Lucy (originally played by Lillian Gish and here by Jack) from the abuse of her drunken father, the boxer Battling Burrows. Huang cares for Lucy – dressing her in a clean white blouse, adorning her with a crown of flowers, giving her a doll – only to have her die in his arms in the end, the victim of her father's violence. Tressa and Jack's gestures and movements are exaggerated in the histrionic manner of silent-film acting, and organ music from the film swells and pulses throughout. Paula enters in the middle of their private dumbshow and watches them unnoticed, a bit like a voyeur. "Is this something you do?" she asks when they are done, and Tressa explains that her dressing as a man is calming for Jack and, in a manner that is paradoxically chaste and erotic, "very satisfying" for both of them.

As nurse, as silent-film "Oriental," as cross-dresser, and most of all as loving friend, Tressa's role is to take away pain, to bring serenity, to soothe a restless soul that cannot sleep. But this, the play suggests, is also the function of art. Allusions to theater, film, and literature continue through the play's disjointed second act, culminating in a final extended quotation from the 1937 Hollywood movie *Lost Horizon*. Directed by Frank Capra and based on the novel by James Hilton, it tells the story of Shangri La, a mythical paradise hidden away in the Himalayas until accidentally discovered by Westerners. As the movie soundtrack plays, first Paula and then Tressa and Jack join in and speak the lines of the wise and aged High Lama as he predicts an apocalyptic storm that "will rage until every flower of culture is trampled" and then be followed by a "long age of desolation." Only the tiny, secluded utopia of Shangri La will survive this apocalypse so that it might become the future seed of "a

new world stirring in the ruins, stirring clumsily but in hope-
fulness, seeking its lost and legendary treasures and they will all be
here preserved as if by a miracle for a new renaissance" (Fornes
2008: 217).

At the heart of *Enter the Night* there is a profound melancholia
and an insistent belief that the love of true friends and the act of
performance will provide some palliative care until such time as a
genuine civil society can be reborn. The need for such relief is great.
The play ends with a brief segment that Fornes added before the
1999 New York premiere.[3] Paula waits to say good-bye to Jack,
who enters wrapped in a blanket, saying, " ... I'm tired ... I can't
go back to sleep" as his head reaches for the pillow and he lets out a
soft cry. *Enter the Night* aches with this same wish for peace of
mind in a dark time.

Manual for a Desperate Crossing (*Balseros/Rafters*) (1997)

Music was always an important part of Fornes's work. *Promenade*
was an early exemplar of the Off Broadway musical. Numerous
other plays, notably the INTAR plays *Cap-a-Pie*, *Sarita*, and *Lovers
and Keepers*, featured numerous songs. But not until the 1990s did
Fornes collaborate with a composer on a contemporary opera. She
did it twice. In 1995, Fornes began work on a libretto commissioned
by Miami-Dade Community College, South Florida Composers
Alliance, and Florida Grand Opera. Inspired by recent events, it
harkened back to *Cap-a-Pie*, both in its Hispanic subject matter and
its use of interviews as source material for the text. For this new
work, Fornes and others interviewed more than two dozen balseros
(rafters), political and economic refugees who left Cuba under
duress on makeshift rafts and survived crossing the Florida straits to
find a new life in the USA. Hundreds who attempted this same
ninety-mile journey were lost at sea, and the piece paid tribute to
the heroism and the hardships of planning and carrying out such a
dangerous escape. With this in mind, Fornes titled her libretto
Manual for a Desperate Crossing, but when the opera premiered in
Miami in 1997, it was presented simply as *Balseros/Rafters*.

The opera was composed by Robert Ashley, a pioneer of experimental music since the 1960s, celebrated for his work in creating

new operas for video and television. Generally, "Ashley's music consists of dramatic songs delivered by characters, singly and together, who spin long narrations sustained by live and electronic music and subtle or soaring choral passages" (Sabbatini 2005: 45). Known for his interest in vernacular speech, Ashley analyzed the interviews conducted for the Balseros Project with an ear towards the cadence and tonalities of Cuban Spanish. For her part, Fornes was drawn more to the resourcefulness of the rafters than the lingering geopolitical tensions between Cuba and South Florida. "I was mostly interested in how they did it," she said at the time of the premiere (Fleming 1997). Her libretto included extended passages detailing how the rafts were constructed and how the balseros distilled drinking water from seawater using a can as a stove, wood ripped from the raft as fuel, and a coil from a broken motor to capture condensing vapor. Even in this death-defying situation, Fornes's enduring interest in the mundane details of a mechanical task made itself known.

In her libretto, Fornes did not create individual characters with specific narratives that motivated their desire to leave Cuba. Instead, she focused on the common experience of the balseros and the four basic stages of the journey: 1) preparation for the crossing, including building the raft and gathering provisions; 2) departure, including the sadness of leaving one's homeland; 3) the difficult time at sea, including a terrible storm and an encounter with a huge ship that sailed close enough to gawk at the rafters and then moved away without offer of aid or rescue; and finally, 4) arrival in Florida and a search for a telephone to contact local relatives and a Coca-Cola to quench parched throats. Director Michael Montel staged the action on and around a large rectangular platform with a hydraulic lift that made it pitch and yaw like a raft adrift at sea. Large panels surrounding the playing area reflected colored light, abstract projected images in black-and-white, and portions of the libretto in Spanish. Ashley took a complex, multi-layered approach to the score. Five singers from Florida Grand Opera's Young Artist Program sang in English, as did four members of his own opera ensemble, except that Ashley's veteran collaborators sang at a much slower tempo, one that became as amorphous and hypnotic as ocean waves. At the same time, in vocal counterpoint, two actors spoke the libretto in spirited Spanish, while two onstage percussionists provided continuous Afro-Cuban rhythms that supplemented Ashley's recorded score for a synthesized orchestra.

As with *Promenade* three decades earlier, *Balseros/Rafters* bore the predominant stamp of the composer, all the more because this was the only new work since *Promenade* (except for the ten-minute play *Drowning*) that Fornes did not first direct herself. Nevertheless, as another portrait of survival, it resonates with her work in the 1990s, and its focus on Cuba, cultural identity, and leaving home give it a meaningful connection to *Cap-a-Pie*, *Sarita*, *Letters from Cuba*, and even obliquely to the "New World" aspects of *Terra Incognita*.

Terra Incognita (1997)

In 1990, with grants from the NEA Opera-Musical Theater program and Meet the Composer, INTAR commissioned Fornes and composer Roberto Sierra to write a music theater piece for the occasion of the Columbus Quincentenary in 1992. Preliminary versions of both the libretto and the score were given a workshop in the summer of 1991 at Storm King Art Center in the Hudson River Valley. While awaiting completion of the score, Fornes continued work on the script in workshop productions without music at the first-ever Dionysia Playwrights World Festival in Siena, Italy in the summer of 1992 and at Padua Hills in the summer of 1994. The finished "play-opera" – sung-through with piano accompaniment – finally received its world premiere in April 1997 in a joint production by two long-time Fornes supporters, Max Ferra and INTAR, and Julia Miles and the Women's Project. Critical response was negative. "The work gets so convoluted that it simply crumbles away in your hands," said *The Village Voice* (Feingold 1997). "Despite moments of bizarre vitality, this overladen work buckles under the weight of its ambitions," wrote the *New York Times* (Tommasini 1997). Nevertheless, *Terra Incognita* needs to be seen as another noble experiment in form that sheds light on Fornes's artistic concerns in the last decade of her career.

Terra Incognita takes place outdoors in the middle of the day, but the cloud of metaphoric night still hovers over it. Three young American travelers have arrived in Palos, Spain, the port from which Columbus sailed into the "unknown territory" of the New World in search of a shorter trade route to the East Indies. Amalia, her brother Rob, and their friend Georgia spend the morning in an outdoor cafe in typical tourist fashion: sipping coffee in the sun, jotting notes in a journal, consulting maps and guidebooks, sharing anecdotes about lost passports or language difficulties, and meeting the locals. In this instance, the two strangers they meet bring a historical dimension to the play that connects America in 1992 with the one Columbus "discovered" five centuries earlier. The first is a crazy, dirty vagrant named Burt, who punctuates his rambling thoughts about ancient cosmology with karate chops, manic laughter, and exclamations like "I'm a modern man." It gradually becomes evident that the delusional Burt thinks he is a manifestation of Christopher Columbus, just as the other stranger in the cafe, Steve, is an incarnation of Bartolomé de las Casas, the Dominican friar and Spanish colonist who chronicled the early European atrocities against the indigenous peoples of the Caribbean. Steve interacts with the others hardly at all; mainly he faces front and recites long passages from de las Casas's *History of the Indies* that document the greed and barbarism of the Spanish. The excerpt that ends the play is the most gruesome. It begins: "They entered the town and without sparing either children or elders or pregnant women or new mothers, they tore them to pieces as if they were sheep in their flock." And it ends: "I saw all the things that I have said and even more. I know the name of the guard and even his relatives in Seville" (Fornes 2007: 81).

The testimonial rhetoric here points to the play's questions about morality and personal responsibility in the face of violence, injustice, and oppression. "Where are we in relation to all this?" asks Amalia after Rob reads aloud several newspaper accounts of recent horrible events. The 1992 version of the script made explicit reference here to the Gulf War and the riots in Los Angeles after the Rodney King verdict.[4] Amalia wonders if the people they meet on their travels hold them personally responsible for the actions of their country: "Do they blame us for those things? Does the world hate us? Are we guilty of those terrible things? I don't want to think we're a part of it" (Fornes 2007: 52). The sentiment here harkens all the way back to the more carefree refrain in the Song of Ignorance from *The Successful Life of 3*: "Let me be wrong./But also not know it./Be wrong,/Be wrong,/And, oh, not to know it." But *Terra Incognita* lingers on the subject of ethics. When Rob complains about the terrible coffee in the cafe, Amalia accuses him of a kind of moral hypocrisy, that is, of feeling "superior and oppressed" or "righteous and ineffectual" at the same time. "You always have to blame someone else when things go wrong," she says. "It's a defect of my generation" is his coy reply. But Amalia is not so easily placated. She insists that the "malady" of making "someone else responsible for your own life" is "how the world ends. It just dies" (Fornes 2007: 68).

In a different way than *Manual for a Desperate Crossing*, *Terra Incognita* is a play about dislocation, being away from home, and relationship to place. Amalia, Rob, and Georgia get their bearings as tourists by looking for Palos on a map or recognizing the picture of a cafe in a guidebook as the one where they are sitting right then and there. Steve demonstrates how the ancient Greek geographer Eratosthenes first calculated the circumference of the earth by taking measurements at twelve noon on the summer solstice when the sun was directly overhead. Burt begins a long monologue full of nautical terms about how to sail a sailboat by pretending he is the mast and saying, "If I am the boat, then things are in relation to me." But *Terra Incognita*'s questions of ethical orientation – Amalia's "Where are we in relation to all this?" and Rob's "Will there be such a thing as the end of the world?" – are not so easily answered. They reflect Fornes's interest in the moral quandary of the individual in the face of an imperfect (disintegrating) world, a concern that first animated the plays of the 1960s. "Madness is lack of compassion," sang the prisoners 105 and 106 in *Promenade*. In *The Summer in Gossensass*, as Elizabeth Robins and Marion Lea speculate about Hedda's character, they hypothesize that "she lacks compassion ... she is not moved to experience the experience of others. Not moved to experience what another person is experiencing" (Fornes 2008: 53). And in *Terra Incognita*, Amalia attributes the world's ills to much the same culture of narcissism. Crying, almost hyperventilating with distress, she sings:

> I'm not talking about being nice.
> Just to know that others exist.
> To be curious about others.

To want to know about someone other than yourself ...
If you are not curious, you are alone.
What do you think bliss is?
To go outside yourself. That's all.
If you experience nothing but yourself
you'll feel no relief.
To get lost outside yourself is bliss.

(Fornes 2007: 53)

At the end of her long, emotional tirade, she leans forward and dips her finger in a glass of water, lets a drop fall on the table, points to it, and says, "If God could, he would come back and say, 'Look at this drop of water. Therein lies everything.'"

A Fornes play – more and more explicitly towards the end of her career – seeks to do what God would do. It dips the finger of the imagination into the well of the world, extracts a drop of experience, and finds the mysterious beauty of life therein.

Notes

1 A 2000 *New York Times* roundtable interview with Fornes and four other playwrights honored with seasons by Signature – Arthur Miller, Edward Albee, Horton Foote, and John Guare – highlighted her marginal status. When the discussion turned to the pressures and compromises faced by playwrights in the cultural mainstream, Fornes said,

> I am, in some ways, lucky that I'm not as successful or well known as the gentlemen who are with me here. What I mean by that is simply my work is not done on Broadway. My work is more Off Off Broadway, and not even Off Broadway ... it's almost like a different type of work.
>
> ("Reunion": AR5)

With unmentioned irony, Guare later referred to Fornes's "very, very bad experience in the commercial world" – 34 years earlier! – when Jerome Robbins "pulled the plug" on *The Office* days before it was to open on Broadway.

2 The play as performed in Milwaukee and Providence differs in significant ways from the published version described here. In production, the romance between Charlie and Rainbow was sketched more fully. Birdie still wanted to leave – but to go to a fashion show. And the play ended with a violent confrontation between Nadine and Pete, which

sent him into convulsions. Nadine took his gold jewelry and money as she berated him, "You bum! You have to die here, like a mountain of meat. You wanted to kill my Lucille."

3 Fornes made a number of changes for the productions of *Enter the Night* in Dallas in 1994 and New York in 1999. The play was initially set explicitly in Chinatown and ended with the extended quotation from *Lost Horizon*. Also, Tressa suspected that her patient was slowly being poisoned by his wife rather than dying of cancer, and Paula specialized in breeding and boarding Arabian horses. In addition to *Broken Blossom*, in the second act the characters also acted out the balcony scene from *Romeo and Juliet*.

4 The 1997 production eliminated these specific events in favor of more generic references to war, crime, and abuse. There are many other minor but suggestive differences in the initial acted script published in *Theater* in 1993 and the later libretto sung in 1997 and published by PAJ in 2007. For example, the earlier draft included a long harangue from Georgia about Edward Albee's *The Zoo Story* and how stupid it was for Peter to defend his park bench when Jerry was so obviously crazy and dangerous.

10 Coming to an end

The Fornes plays of the 1990s are not all gloom and doom. There is also a joyous metatheatrical focus on the process of playmaking and broader questions about writing, art, and creativity. *Enter the Night* has already been discussed in this context. After Tressa and Paula read Jack's play, they open a bottle of wine to celebrate. "May Art live!" toasts Tressa. "May Theatre live!" echoes Paula. "May Poetry live," says Jack. Here, and in *The Summer in Gossensass* and *Letters from Cuba*, Fornes celebrates the will to create and contemplates its meanings and mysteries. There is a retrospective dimension here, as if Fornes was reaching back to her roots for inspiration, guidance, or clarity. In 1968, the flamboyant, tyrannical Dr. Kheal outlined the terms of her vision – poetry, balance, ambition, energy, speech, truth, beauty and love, hope, cooking – and she returned to them again and again with a consciousness of purpose that meant that each play was composed for the aesthetic pleasure of an audience willing to engage the work on its own terms. Many of the plays – *Promenade*, *The Red Burning Light*, *Cap-a-Pie*, *Eyes on the Harem* – are overtly theatrical, adopting vaudeville or musical revue structures to link a series of songs, vignettes, monologues, and dances around a central theme. Others – *Tango Palace*, *Abingdon Square*, *Enter the Night*, *Letters from Cuba* – incorporate bits of pageantry and performance into the present-tense actions of the characters. Either way, a Fornes play is always putting on a show. As Emma says to Fefu and her friends as they prepare for their meeting, "Life is theatre. Theatre is life. If we're showing what life is, can be, we must do theatre." Sue nervously asks if she will have to act, and Emma replies with histrionic flair, "It's not acting. It's being. It's springing forth with the powers of the spirit. It's breathing" (Fornes 1992: 22).

The Summer in Gossensass (1998)

The first line of *The Summer in Gossensass* – "Ibsen said that anyone who wished to understand him must understand Norway" – signals what an unusual work it was for Fornes. Not only is the mention of Ibsen, the great nineteenth-century playwright and "father of modern drama," a rare citation of a historical figure, the play is one of very few she wrote about an actual historical event. *The Trial of Joan of Arc in a Matter of Faith* takes its text directly from historical records of Joan's trial. *Eyes on the Harem* examined Ottoman history broadly. The figures of Columbus and Bartolomé de las Casas haunt *Terra Incognita*, but *The Summer in Gossensass* is the only play in which Fornes imagined what historical characters might have said and done in the process of making history. Those characters are Elizabeth Robins and Marion Lea, two American-born actresses in London who went to great effort to mount the first English-language production of Ibsen's *Hedda Gabler*. Robins had already appeared in London productions of *The Pillars of Society* and *A Doll's House* when she and Lea managed to acquire the performance rights to Ibsen's newest work. At that point, Ibsen was an international celebrity in the prime of his career, and each new, potentially controversial play was hastily published and translated for production all over Europe. With the aid of William Archer and Edmund Gosse, Ibsen champions and rival translators, Robins and Lea produced and performed the play to great acclaim at the Vaudeville Theatre in April and May 1891. Bernard Shaw, Oscar Wilde, Thomas Hardy, and Henry James all attended the production, which came to be seen as "the one that influenced more remarkably than any other Ibsen's reception in England" (Gates 1994: 27). Robins went on to continued success in a number of Ibsen roles and a notable career as a feminist author and suffragist.[1]

Fornes's script incorporates a number of historical details, including technicalities of copyright law and the short-lived plan for Lily Langtry, mistress of the Prince of Wales and celebrity actress, to play Hedda Gabler in a rival production. But the overwhelming burden of the play centers on the enthusiasm of the two actresses to learn about and perform what would prove to be Ibsen's most admired play. The action begins in February 1891, just days after the world premiere of *Hedda Gabler* in Munich. Marion Lea, Elizabeth Robins, and her close friend Lady Florence Bell sit in the parlor of Robins's London home reading and speculating at length about the nature of Ibsen's latest heroine: "Do you think she fell from grace?" "Does she feel compassion?" "Does she have any redeeming qualities?" They have no reliable information to go on, just theater gossip and a newspaper review that describes Hedda as "a monster in female form" and "a horrid miscarriage of the imagination." That does not stop them from concluding that Hedda would be a highly desirable character to play onstage.

The remainder of the play sketches how Elizabeth and Marion come to present the London premiere. In Scene 3, they learn that a friend of a friend has a copy of the play in Norwegian, and, to their great distress, that the rights have been assigned to a different producer. In Scene 4, Elizabeth has acquired a copy of the untranslated play and struggles to use a Norwegian dictionary to make sense of the dialogue. Then, Marion arrives with a few random pages of the new English translation, which she has purloined from a wastebasket where the play is being rehearsed. With intense curiosity, Elizabeth and Marion read aloud the Act One scene between Hedda and Thea Elvsted, tentatively acting it out and then repeating it two more times, trying different acting styles (psychological realism, expressionism) in an effort to unlock the secrets of the play as a whole.

> Individual words, the placement of pauses, the phrasing of one character's question, the timing of another's entrance: Ibsen's smallest decision, mere craft in the context of a complete, action-filled play, have an overwhelming, almost magical significance for the women.
>
> (Robinson 1999: 115)

In Scene 5, another actor and Ibsen enthusiast named David arrives with a briefcase full of research and reads aloud from letters that reveal how the play was inspired by Ibsen's infatuation with Emilie Bardach, the 18-year-old Viennese girl he met in the Tyrolean village of Gossensass in the summer of 1889 (when he was 61).[2]

Each new fragment of documentary evidence, however imperfect or incomplete, feeds the imagination of Fornes's characters, prompting more and more penetrating questions and even a few false conclusions. At one point, they seem convinced that Ibsen himself will appear as a character in the play.

Their gradual discovery of the play *Hedda Gabler* advances through a series of approximations that parallel in an odd way Fornes's own creative process. In the beginning, Hedda is an unknown to them, a fascinating figment of Ibsen's imagination that prompts them to speculate about possibilities and gather what information they can in order to solve the mystery of her character. Fornes's method of writing a play often traces a similar path, except that her "research" was more internal than external, more a matter of observing images that bubble up from her unconscious than pouring over documents looking for information. In her playwriting workshops, Fornes always wrote along with her students, generating fragments of scenes stemming from vivid images in her mind. Subsequent writing followed characters of interest in an effort to find out who they were and what they were doing, as if to reveal more of what presumably was already there but not yet known by the playwright herself. A storehouse of raw material developed. Fragments coalesced into scenes and scenes began to fall into a sequence. Just as Elizabeth and Marion rehearse the Hedda–Thea scene without the full play in hand, Fornes always began to rehearse a play – including *The Summer in Gossensass* – before her script was complete. Rehearsal became another way to stimulate her imagination and discover more of the "terra incognita" of the world of the play.

In *The Summer in Gossensass*, the character of Vernon, Elizabeth's brother and a medical student, articulates this process when he describes a recent conversation with a woman dramatist:

> She said that a play is a riddle. A riddle that's in the head of the author. Something that intrigues the author but doesn't have a shape yet. It doesn't even have a question. And a riddle, of course, must have a question ... she says that, in the beginning, all the author has is that there is something to be discovered. That is all she has. And the writing of the play is its discovery. She says that by the time the author gets halfway through, she

knows what the question is. Then, answering the question begins to shape the play. She says every answer creates another question. And each answer makes the play grow. When the questions begin to dwindle, that means the play is coming to an end. The last question is the one whose answer doesn't invite another question. At the start, the subject haunts the writer. And at the end, the writer is in a state of bliss.

(Fornes 2008: 82)

On this model, Elizabeth and Marion can be seen as surrogate authors of Ibsen's play. In the beginning, what intrigues them is the riddle of the unknown Hedda. They ask question after question about her. Each new piece of evidence – a review, the text in Norwegian, an excerpt stolen from a wastebasket, quotations from Ibsen letters – leads to more questions and a closer approximation of the play until finally, at the end of Scene 5, Vernon arrives with a complete copy "fresh off the press – In English!" Elizabeth and Marion step forward to receive the holy grail and, the stage direction reads, they "emit a profound sigh," in the same "state of bliss" as the writer whose last question has been answered. The play has taken shape. By their inquiry, they have, in effect, brought it into being.

All that remains is for them to perform it. The last scene of Fornes's play shows Elizabeth, Marion, and their associates performing the last scene of Ibsen's play on April 20, 1891, right down to Judge Brack's famous final line, "People don't do such things." Then, anachronistically, Elizabeth steps forward from the curtain call to read from a tribute to Ibsen that she, in fact, gave 37 years later on March 12, 1928 to the Royal Society of Arts. A play full of documents and extended quotations ends with one last historical artifact.

Fornes and *Hedda Gabler*

Ibsen's masterpiece was a lifelong interest for Fornes. "It was the first play I read from start to finish without stopping," she said (Delgado and Svich 1999: 248), and as such, it became for her a touchstone of both dramatic tradition and artistic genius. In 1987, she directed Ibsen's play at the Milwaukee Repertory Theatre in a production that sought to liberate the text from its hermeneutic legacy and restore the ineffable to a character who, she felt, had been suffocated by a century of explication by critics, scholars, and translators. Referring to the Robins/Lea production, Fornes said, "The first really successful production of *Hedda* was done in England. My whole interpretation of the play questions that production and the influence it had on every other production and translation" (Paran 1987: 19). She fashioned a version of the play that resisted the received notion that Hedda was mainly the victim of a repressive late-nineteenth-century bourgeois society or that her psychopathology can be explained by her attachment to her father, her unwanted pregnancy, and other biographical factors.

Fornes aspired to revive the play's capacity to bewilder and amaze by somehow making Ibsen's heroine new and unknown. In *The Summer in Gossensass*, that is exactly what she did by positing two actress characters who have only a vague presentiment of who Hedda is and a zealous desire to find out. In their effort to bring

Figure 15 Ibsen's *Hedda Gabler* at Milwaukee Repertory Theatre (1987), directed by Fornes. Marie Mathay as Hedda Gabler. Set design by Donald Eastman. Lighting design by Anne Militello. The cubicle (center), with raised door and inset window, represented the stove, which Hedda entered to burn Lovborg's manuscript.

Hedda into being, there is an echo of the process of coming to thought that defines the Fornes Innocent.

> As the characters in *The Summer in Gossensass* develop the skills needed to recognize their instincts, then scan their vocabulary for sufficiently vivid ways of expressing them, they are, in fact, learning to read all over again. Fornes traces every stage of that education, so that, as we listen to her characters, we enter their minds, seeming to witness the birth of ideas and, even more important, the struggle to sustain them, make them intelligible to others, and translate them into action.
>
> (Robinson 1999: 118)

The Summer in Gossensass had a typically long gestation for a Fornes play. She began writing during a 1995 residency at the University of Iowa, where an early version was presented with the title *Ibsen and the Actress*. Work continued that summer at Padua Hills and in the fall at the Audrey Skirball Foundation in Los Angeles. At Women's Project and Productions in New York, Fornes directed a staged reading in February 1997 and then the world premiere in April 1998. A few weeks before opening, Fornes told scholar Susan Letzler Cole (2001: 179) that she had done more revision on the play than any other, in part "because there are no emotional relationships ... it's almost as if I'm learning how to write a play in which personal relationships are secondary to the longing and desire for this play." Cole's account of the rehearsals for *The Summer in Gossensass* suggests that finishing the script was a difficult process. On an almost daily basis, Fornes responded to the work of the actors by cutting, adding, or changing lines, often on the spot in rehearsal. The pattern of perpetual revision became frustrating enough to prompt one actor to confess "I wish I was the script" at a company meeting ten days before opening. "'You wish you were the script?' Fornes asks. 'Yes,' the actor replies. 'I wish I was the script because it's gotten more attention than we have'" (Cole 2001: 180).

This anecdote reinforces the extent to which *The Summer in Gossensass* needs to be seen as a metadrama, a play about writing a play. Fornes claimed that she set out to make a point about "the question of interpretation and misinterpretation" (Delgado and Svich 1999: 251), but the emphasis shifted:

Through revisions in rehearsal, the play has changed. The logic used to rely more on storyline. Now the logic, the movement of the play, is different. The plot *is* the characters' understanding of the play and what playwriting is and what drama is. That is the evolution of the play, of how an author can create, based on a real person or an invented character. It's like a theory of how one creates a play. That is what is forming the movement of the play.

(Cole 2001: 182)

Reviewers of the 1998 Women's Project production took the play to task for this very reason, describing it as "a disconcerting hybrid of naturalistic settings, formal language, dreamlike eruptions of bizarre behavior, and nonlinear narrative ... less like a play than a graduate seminar in dramaturgy" (Shewey 1998), "a discussion group at a dramaturgical society and about as exciting to watch" (Winer 1995), and "Fornes's ars poetica, tossing off enough apothegms about playwriting, acting, and the sources of artistic inspiration to rank as an act of literary criticism more than a play" (Feingold 1998).

In writing *The Summer in Gossensass*, Fornes was looking back at the first play she ever read in order to think out loud about what a play is and how it is created. There is a retrospective impulse there – a return to a point of origin – that is also evident in *Letters from Cuba*.

Letters from Cuba (2000)

Letters from Cuba is Fornes's last play. When the play premiered in 2000, she was beginning to show signs of a mental confusion that worsened over the next few years to the point where she could no longer take care of herself. After living alone in her Greenwich Village apartment for four decades, in 2005 she moved in briefly with one sister and then the other and then, her dementia worsening, into an adult care home in Oneonta, New York.[3] She left several projects unfinished, including an adaptation of Gertrude Stein's *The Autobiography of Alice B. Toklas* commissioned by the Acting Company with the working title *27 Rue de Fleurus*.

Fornes's most intimate, personal play, *Letters from Cuba* could hardly have been a more fitting way to end her writing career. With sweet nostalgia, it harkens back to her familial roots in Cuba and her theatrical roots in Greenwich Village. Just as her very first playwriting effort, *La viuda (The Widow)*, drew on family letters that Fornes brought with her to the USA in 1945, *Letters from Cuba* takes much of its text from 30 years of correspondence with her brother Rafael back in Havana. The play was commissioned for the ninth season of the Signature Theatre Company, a New York theater founded by James Houghton in 1991 with a unique mission: to celebrate a veteran American playwright by dedicating a full season to his or her work. Romulus Linney was the first-ever Signature honoree, and he was followed in the 1990s by Lee Blessing, Edward Albee, Horton Foote, Adrienne Kennedy, Sam Shepard, Arthur Miller, John Guare, and then Fornes in 1999–2000. Her Signature Season – which included a double-bill of *Mud* and *Drowning*, directed by David Esbjornson; the New York premiere of *Enter the Night*, directed by Sonja Moser; and the world premiere of *Letters from Cuba* – was an effort to recognize Fornes's legacy as a great American playwright, despite her lack of main-stream success. As it turned out, it became the capstone on her forty-year career.

Figure 16 Maria Irene Fornes with four other American playwrights featured by Signature Theatre Company: (from left to right) Arthur Miller, John Guare, Edward Albee, Horton Foote.

Letters from Cuba is more a theater poem than a play. Typically, it is composed of brief, fragmentary scenes, twenty-one in all, many of them typical Fornes emotigraphs that invoke a meticulously composed stage image, imbue it with feeling, sustain for a minute or two, and then dissolve into the next crystalline moment of being. In performance, the piece lasts barely an hour. Her strategy is lyrical and not narrative. She indicates as much in the first scene when the character Marc wonders out loud, "How does one write a poem?" He gets this reply from his friend Joseph:

> I've been writing poetry. And I've been saying words in my head to see if word spirits would come, like move in, like to join other words that were there. If they would do that then, to see if they would come in to form a poem. I think that's how poems get written. I think that's how difficult things get done. We can't really do them. We can't do difficult things. We can do easy things. But the difficult ones come to us by themselves. It's just that to learn to listen to them is difficult. We just have to learn to listen and to let them come in easy as if the words would come out by themselves because they want to make a poem. Because they desire to make a poem. As if words had desires, and they want to join other words to express something ... of beauty or longing or despair.
>
> (Fornes 2007: 10)

Here again, Fornes articulates a principle of her own work. The task of the artist is to leave the door open for "word spirits" to enter and then, with as little willful intervention as possible, to allow them to join together to form a poem – or a play – that expresses deep emotion. This is unquestionably her method in *Letters from Cuba*, a gossamer of everyday dialogue, Latin music, free-form dance, and shifting light that reaches a simple, subtle epiphany. The play demonstrates a lightness of touch that makes it feel tender and inchoate. Nothing holds it together except for the feeling it expresses: a powerful yearning for love, for home and family, and for aesthetic beauty.

The play takes place both in Cuba and New York City. The main part of the set is a sparsely furnished Manhattan apartment shared by three young artist friends: Marc, an aspiring poet; Joseph, a designer; and a beautiful dancer named Fran. As designed by Donald Eastman for the original Signature production, this plain white room was symmetrical and spacious, with doors, walls, windows, corners, and floorboards that created enough unadorned rectangles to give it an abstract dimension. There was even an upstage alcove that recalled the cell-like inner sanctum in so many Fornes sets created by Eastman and others. On an upper stage high above the main playing area, a wide ledge with a short wall represented the rooftop of the building in Havana where Fran's brother Luis lives. This is where he comes, sometimes under a blanket of stars, to relax with his son Enrique or his friend Gerardo and also to recite the letters he sends to Fran, his beloved sister in New York, letters that Fornes culled from hundreds she herself received from her brother in Cuba.

The play makes no direct reference to Castro or the Cold War politics separating Cuba and the United States in Fornes's adult life, but as the action pivots back and forth between apartment below and rooftop above, it becomes clear they are worlds apart. Bridging that gap is the poetic action of the play. In one scene, Luis drops a letter from the roof so that it lands in the apartment below; Fran retrieves it and they read it together in unison. In another, Luis enters the New York apartment, takes Fran in his arms and dances an elegant ballroom turn with her, and then walks out, all without her ever knowing he was there. Time in the play is just as elastic as space. The letters from Cuba span enough time for one to announce the birth of Luis's son Enrique ("the laziest baby in the world") and another to be written years later by Enrique himself as a young man. But time in New York City does not seem to advance more than a matter of days or weeks for the trio of friends there. Little is known about them except that both Marc and especially Joseph are in love with Fran. Their rivalry is tame by comparison to other romantic triangles in Fornes, erupting into nothing worse than a pillow fight. Joseph pines for Fran and stares at her adoringly as she dances in their wide-open apartment, but as in *Enter the Night* the friendship of the three is what really matters. "Romantic love can be lasting," says Joseph. "But the love of a friend is the most lasting" (Fornes 2007: 20).

The love of place is just as powerful in the play. From the beginning, Luis's letters speak of his intention to leave Cuba for

Figure 17 Letters from Cuba at Signature Theatre Company in New York (2000), directed by Fornes. In Cuba (above), Luis (Chris de Oni) reads a letter to his sister Fran (Tai Jimenez) in New York (below), as Joseph (Peter Starrett) looks on.

New York, but as his friend Gerardo says, "I still feel if I left here, I would die. Because I belong here, and if I went elsewhere, I wouldn't recognize anything around me and I would die" (Fornes 2007: 29). The gravitational pull of the familiar is formidable, but eventually, with the encouragement of young Enrique, Luis breaks free and makes it to New York. In the play's final moments, Joseph and Fran come together in a brief, gentle embrace, and then Enrique calls from offstage for his father to come and join him. Stifling a sob, Luis leaves the rooftop, and a moment later a hidden panel in the apartment wall swings open like a magic door; father and son step through a flood of light to greet Fran and her friends as a stirring version of "Guantanamera," the epitome of Cuban song, pulses louder and louder. In the Signature production, this final sequence – as it turned out, Fornes's last-ever stage picture – was stunning in its beauty and cathartic in its fusion of joy and sorrow. Whether this family reunion is fantasy or reality matters little. Desire, emblematized by music, poetry, dance, and a lifetime of letters, has proven its ability to transcend time and space. Fornes's two homes, Cuba and New York, are pushed together like the yes-and-no of Dr. Kheal, "opposites, contradictions compressed so that you don't know where one stops and the other begins" (Fornes 1971: 72).

Legacy

Letters from Cuba, Fornes's last project as a director as well as playwright, serves as a final reminder of just how inseparable those practices were for her. Her lack of formal education and her dyslexia, her early inclination to become a painter, and her immersion in the interdisciplinary art forms and styles Off-Off Broadway in the 1960s, all contributed to an aesthetic that was as visual and aural as it was literary. Her work demonstrates an undeniable fascination with language and the power of speech as well as a corresponding lyricism achieved with a deceptively simple vocabulary and an often elliptical style of dialogue. The central action of her work is the effort to bring self into being by gaining command of language, be it a stack of pre-programmed index cards, a Vietnamese wedding ceremony, a Hungarian language lesson, a reading book about starfish and hermit crabs, memorable speeches by politicians, a diary full of "things that are imagined," or the script of *Hedda Gabler*. Still, Fornes composed her plays in time and space as much as in words, working with designers and actors to create stage pictures resonant with emotion. Hers was always a total theater, albeit on a small scale and often a modest budget. Her plays only ever took their true shape through the process of her staging them.

This raises questions about Fornes's legacy. "The fact remains that her playtexts will generally be more accessible, self-contained, and thus available in ways that her role as a director and teacher of playwriting is not ... Fornes's genealogy and impact remain at risk, as if there were a cultural amnesia surrounding the force of her impact" (Alker 2009: 209). In recent years, efforts have been made to preserve and perpetuate Fornes's theater beyond her own career. The Theatre on Film and Tape archive at the New York Public Library for the Performing Arts at Lincoln Center, the 1999 volume of anecdotes and appreciations called *Conducting a Life*, a Fornes website (http://www.mariairenefornes.com), a documentary-in-the-making

by Michelle Memran titled *The Rest I Make Up*, and related projects are all valuable resources, as is the growing body of scholar-
ship on her work. In 2007 and 2008, Bonnie Marranca and PAJ
Publications issued two new volumes of Fornes plays. In 2010, New
York University and INTAR celebrated Fornes's 80th birthday with
a series of staged readings and panel discussions, and that same
year, the Halcyon Theatre in Chicago devoted a full season to
Fornes, including the first productions of *What of the Night?*, *The
Summer in Gossensass*, and *Letters from Cuba* not directed by
Fornes herself. Still, more than a decade after her Signature season,
her plays remain largely untouched by directors and theaters with a
national profile, even as they continue to appeal to university theater groups and alternative, local, Off-Off-type companies in cities
around the United States.

Fornes's enduring legacy, difficult to measure, may well be in her
influence on playwrights and playwriting. This is most obvious in
her role as playwriting teacher at INTAR, at Padua Hills, and in
workshops all over the USA and abroad. Her exercises designed to
create an "anatomy of inspiration" emboldened her students to trust
their imaginations and to withhold willful manipulation of their
material for as long as possible so that a new play might reveal
itself on its own terms. As those she has taught became teachers
themselves, her methods and values have spread far and wide. Just
as inspiring is the influence of the work itself, as evidenced in trib-
utes by writers who achieved much greater success. Paula Vogel, a
major playwriting teacher in her own right, claimed: "In the work
of every American playwright at the end of the 20th century, there
are only two stages: before she or he has read Maria Irene Fornes –
and after" (Shewey 1999). Tony Kushner put it in categorical terms
when he said: "America has produced no dramatist of greater
importance than Maria Irene Fornes ... Her plays and productions
profoundly altered my understanding of what theater is; what it
aims at accomplishing; what it may demand of its audience; how it
speaks to the political through the personal and vice versa; and the
role that beauty plays in the political, redemptive, transformational
power of art" (Delgado and Svich 1999: xxxiii).

This is not hyperbole. For many playwrights, directors, other
theater artists, and spectators, Fornes opened up a realm of creative
possibilities that they either failed to imagine or were hesitant to

trust. Her lifetime of theater practice and lasting body of work tes-
tify to an artist's uncompromising commitment to her own way of
seeing. To summon Dr. Kheal one final time:

> Well, we each have our way. I know we can only do what is
> possible. I know that. We can only do what is possible for us to
> do. But still it is good to know what the impossible is.
>
> (Fornes 1971: 70)

Drowning as paradigm

Over the course of her career, Fornes accepted a number of invitations to contribute short pieces to anthology projects. *Green Pants*
is a bit of comic pornography that she wrote for *Oh! Calcutta!*, the
1969 Off Broadway erotic musical revue that gained notoriety for its
liberal use of nudity. The sketch, which was not included in the
actual production, presents a mother warning her daughter about
going out with her boyfriend – "If you itch, you'll have to
scratch." – and ends up with two couples copulating with stylized
abandon. In 1986 at INTAR, Fornes produced "Box Plays," a
showcase for playwrights in her Hispanic Playwrights-in-Residence
Laboratory, each of whom wrote for a tiny forced-perspective box
set. She included on the bill her own play *Art*, "a staged political
cartoon" (Solomon 1986) about two men in suits who watch dispassionately as a woman is torn to pieces nearby. *The Audition* was
commissioned for "The Square," a project presented in 2000 by the
Mark Taper Forum's Asian Theatre Program that gathered sixteen
pieces about Asian-American characters in relation to non-Asian-
American characters, all of them set in a public square in an urban
Chinatown. In Fornes's offering, a young Chicano actor coaches
two struggling Asian actors – "You want the Spanish, Ranchero,
Chicano or Cholo accent?" – who are auditioning for Hispanic roles
in a movie ("Mifune played Mexican. So can we. You teach us how.
We do it. We give you two per cent.") These all proved to be
occasional works of nominal importance, but another short play,
Drowning, is a miniature masterwork, on par with the "dramati-
cules" Beckett wrote towards the end of his career. It encapsulates
enough of Fornes's work as a whole to be seen as a paradigm of her
theater, and thus will serve as a summary conclusion to this study.

Fornes wrote *Drowning* at the height of her career in the mid-1980s as her contribution to an interesting experiment in commissioning new plays. Anne Cattaneo, dramaturg for the Acting Company, wanted to incorporate contemporary playwriting into the company's largely classical repertoire, so she invited a dozen leading American playwrights to adapt short stories by Anton Chekhov into ten-minute plays. Under the collective title *Orchards*, this anthology – including pieces by Spalding Gray, John Guare, David Mamet, Wendy Wasserstein, Michael Weller, Samm-Art Williams, and Fornes – was staged by Robert Falls and performed by the Acting Company in repertoire with *As You Like It* on a grueling 60-city tour that ended with a three-week run at the American Place Theatre in New York.

Fornes was assigned a short story called "Drowning" and given carte blanche to adapt it as she wished. Subtitled "A Little Scene," Chekhov's sketch presents the tale of a derelict who approaches a pedestrian waiting by the side of a river and offers to "impersonate" a drowning man for a small fee ("Two rubles for drowning myself with my boots on, one ruble – without them."). He badgers and bargains until a third man appears and takes the odd fellow up on his offer. He then proceeds to pull off his boots, jump in the cold river, flail about spastically for a minute, sink, resurface, climb out of the water, collect his fee, and walk off without further comment, wet and shivering. That is the whole story, which Fornes found bewildering at first:

> I didn't know if such a thing was actually practiced or if it was just an allegory for how far a human being will go to survive … I almost asked for another story, but I began to feel more and more moved by that man and his drowning act. I would think of how he walked away afterward – this large man, dripping with water, unwanted, who performed for an audience who didn't even care to see him. The rejection, the loneliness. I didn't read the story again, but that sense of feeling like a monster stayed with me.
>
> (Weiss 1986)

Around this time, Fornes gave her students a playwriting exercise that asked them to close their eyes and allow the image of a face to come into their minds. As usual, Fornes participated along with her students and found that a blubbery, barely human face came to her, one which she associated with the drowning man in the story (who Chekhov describes as "a stocky individual with a terribly ravaged, bloated face"). The image brought with it the feeling of rejection and loneliness she found in the story. Never one to question her creative impulses, Fornes forged her adaptation.

"This must be made by a person."

Drowning takes place at a cafe – "probably in Europe," the text says[4] – where two large, dowdy figures sit at a small wooden table waiting for a friend to arrive. One of them stares, as if transfixed, at a folded newspaper on the table between them. Eventually, he asks what it is. His companion tells him it is a newspaper, and the first responds, "It is beautiful. May I touch it?" And when he does, a tear comes to his eye and he says in utter wonder, "This must be made by a person." This exchange would seem ridiculous if not for the physical appearance of the two characters: they are well dressed, one in a beige jacket and olive hat, the other in a brown suit and hat, but their roly-poly bodies are stuffed into their clothes, "large and shapeless, like potatoes." Their heads are gnarly, rubbery, hairless bulbs. At another moment, Fornes says they resemble seals or sea lions. They have warts on their faces and reddish, watery eyes. "Their flesh is shiny and oily ... When they breathe their bodies sweat."

Fornes begins the play with this ontological conundrum. Who or what are these characters? Their dress and behavior is civilized. But their physiology is almost amphibian. They seem human and not-human at the same time. Their speech and gestures are slow and deliberate, mechanical without quite being robot-like, but their senses are finely tuned to the world around them. One of them is an odd variation on the archetypal figure of the Fornes Innocent, a character who lacks formal education but seeks knowledge and a command of language as a way of achieving presence in the larger world. There is something immature or embryonic about the Fornes Innocent, and the names of the characters in *Drowning* suggest as much. The one fascinated by the newspaper is called Pea. His friend is Roe.

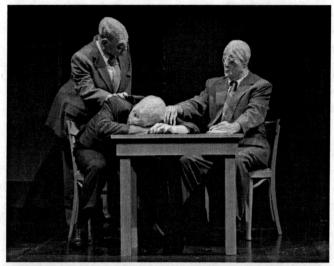

Figure 18 Two productions of *Drowning*: (top) at Magic Theatre in San Francisco (1992), directed by Fornes; and at Signature Theatre Company in New York (1999), directed by David Esbjornson. Patrick Morris (top, head on table) and Marc Damon Johnson as Pea; Dennis Ludlow (top, seated) and Philip Goodwin as Roe; and Regina Saisi (top) and Jed Diamond as Stephen.

Pea's sub-human intelligence becomes clear when he points to a picture in the newspaper and asks, "What is snow?" Roe explains what snow is, but then he confuses Pea anew when he points to a picture of a snowman. Pea describes the snowman as "awkward," but it turns out he does not really know what the word "awkward" means and he meant to say "strikingly wonderful." He thinks that the snowman "must be a very nice man," prompting Roe to explain that the snowman is not a real man: "He is an imitation of a man. It is snow that has been packed to look like a man." Pea's difficulty in comprehending what he sees in the newspaper – an imitation (in the form of a photograph) of an imitation of a man (made out of snow) – is a sign of Fornes's interest in both the politics and the logistics of representation.

When Pea spots a picture of a woman named Jane Spivak in the paper, he is mesmerized by her beauty and all the more confused about the nature of his existence. He says he looks more like the snowman than the woman, but Roe explains that the snowman, "when it gets warmer, will melt. She will not. And you will not" – because each of them is made of "human flesh." Pea says he "would like to look at her. In the flesh" and touches her newsprint image with an odd, erotic tenderness that signals the play's main event: Pea is falling in love with Jane Spivak. Fornes is a sensualist and a romantic. In her plays, love, like language, is transformative. It alters reality and puts a character's very being in jeopardy. In Scene 3 of *Mud*, when Mae professes her love for Henry and asks him to move in and share her bed, she wonders, "Why is it that some people make you feel stupid and some people make you feel smart. Not smart, because I am not smart. But some people make you feel that you have something inside you. Inside your head." Here, the intimation of a knowledge that is not yet known, a key trait of the Fornes Innocent, is explicitly linked with the feeling of love.

Scene 2 of *Drowning* takes place a few minutes after Scene 1 and is only two lines long. Pea sleeps on the table. Roe sits to his left and their friend Stephen stands over Pea:

STEPHEN (*REFERRING TO* PEA): He is very kind and he could not do harm to anyone.

ROE: Yes. And I don't want any harm to come to him either because he's good.

And the lights fade. This is a typical Fornes emotigraph, a fundamental unit of construction that zeroes in "on a few choice lines surrounding a point of crisis or discovery – lines most other playwrights would dismiss as too banal" (Kalb 2000). It is rigorously composed, framed by silence, iconographic, and reverberant with emotion, like a pebble tossed into a still pond sending out ripples. And in this instance, it reflects not only the feeling that has overtaken Pea but also the compassion of his companions, who do not wish to see him suffer. These blob-like characters are animated by a deep well of humanity.

The third and final scene makes *Drowning* a theatrical triptych that might be subtitled "the Passion of Pea." Disheveled and distraught, at moments "short of air," Pea sits and talks to Roe about his feelings for the woman he first glimpsed in the newspaper a month earlier. "She is a mystery to me," he says, " I love her. She is close to my heart the way only an animal can be. And as unfathomable." Somehow – Fornes does not want or need to provide the narrative details – he has met Jane Spivak and his affections have been rebuffed. His anguish is so severe that it prompts the play's most extraordinary moment, one that keeps the ontological question regarding who or what these characters are very much alive. "I am not a person," says Pea. "I am a bat. Look at my skin, see? It is too smooth and too dark. Touch it. This is not like human skin." And then he gets up, turns, exposes his buttocks to Roe, and says, "Look at that. My anus is violet. Put your finger on it. It is rough."

The gesture would be laughable if it was not so pathetic. Pea's abjection is absolute: "What is it that makes someone a link between you and your own life? I hold her close to me and she pushes me away. She finds me repulsive." And the irony is, of course, that in his bloated, oily-skinned, reptilian way, he is repulsive, but the combination of his innocence, his wonder and sense of beauty, and his absolute love for another have imbued him with a humanity that defies his outward appearance. "Is this why we have come to life? To love like this? And hurt like this?" He puts his head on the table, the image of woe. Stephen waddles on, and he and Roe stare at Pea with compassion, as they did in Scene 2. Finally, Roe makes the connection to Chekhov and the extended metaphor of the poor man who flails about in the river: "He's drowning. He hurts too much." And the lights fade to black.

All of this takes place in the span of three short scenes and less than twenty minutes onstage. In that time, Fornes creates a dramatic universe as large as life itself, puts at the heart of that universe a sentient creature in the throes of an unbearable feeling, and captures that condition of being in images and actions, both verbal and visual, which resonate with disturbing beauty and comforting truthfulness.

This is exactly what her theater does.

Notes

1 For a detailed account of the Robins/Lea production of *Hedda Gabler*, see Gates 1985. For book-length studies of Robins, see Gates 1994 and John 1995.

2 David reads brief excerpts from Ibsen's letters and from Emilie Bardach's diary, most of which are found in Michael Meyer's definitive biography of Ibsen (1967) in a chapter whose title – "The Summer in Gossensass" – seems to have provided the title for Fornes's play.

3 A diagnosis of Alzheimer's is presumptive. At least one member of Fornes's extended family thinks she has multi-infarct dementia brought on by a series of small strokes. As this book went to press, she continued to live in otherwise good health in upstate New York.

4 All quotations from *Drowning* can be found in the published version (pp. 55–62) found in *Orchards: Seven Stories by Anton Chekhov and Seven Plays They Have Inspired*, New York: Alfred A. Knopf, 1986.

Appendix A
Selected production history

Chronologies make an artist's career appear more orderly than it ever is. Plays take shape over time. Many Fornes works were conceived and drafted years before they were produced. And she often developed scripts over a series of workshops and even revised them after their initial productions. To assign them to a moment in time can be misleading.

The original production of each Fornes play is included here, as are workshops and readings (when known) and all productions directed by Fornes, including (in a separate section) plays by other playwrights that she directed. For Fornes's most frequently produced plays – *Mud*, *Fefu and Her Friends*, *The Conduct of Life*, *The Danube*, in that order – a limited number of other productions are listed. College and university productions are listed only if directed by Fornes.

Plays are listed in order of first full production, even when preceded by workshops or readings. All productions directed by Fornes are indicated with a **. Productions marked with a ++ indicate that there was another Fornes work on the same bill.

La viuda (*The Widow*) (1961)

1961   New York NY (details unknown)
1963   (radio broadcast) Universidad de Mexico, Mexico D.F.

Tango Palace (1963) – originally titled *There! You Died*

1963   San Francisco Actors Workshop, Encore Theatre, San Francisco CA (dir. Herbert Blau)
1964   Actors Studio, East End Theatre, New York NY and Festival of Two Worlds, Spoleto, ITALY (dir. John Cappelletti)
1965   Firehouse Theatre, Minneapolis MN**++

1973   Theatre Genesis, New York NY**++ (co-directed with Michael
        Smith)
1997   7 Stages Theatre, Atlanta GA (dir. Anders Cato)
2010   (staged reading) The 2010 New York Fornés Festival, Cherry Lane
        Theatre, New York NY++ (dir. Gisela Cardenas)

The Successful Life of 3 (1965)

1965   Firehouse Theatre, Minneapolis MN++ (dir. Charles Morrison III)
1965   Open Theatre, Sheridan Square Playhouse, New York NY (dir.
        Joe Chaikin, Richard Gilman)
1967   Judson Poets' Theater, Judson Memorial Church, New York NY++
        (dir. Lawrence Kornfeld)
1968   Studio Theatre, Amsterdam, HOLLAND (dir. Huib Broos)
1969   Traverse Theatre Club, Glasgow, SCOTLAND
1970   The Little Arhus Theatre, Svalegange, DENMARK
1971   The Odyssey Theatre, Los Angeles CA
1972   The Proposition, Cambridge MA
2010   (reading) The 2010 New York Fornés Festival, Goldberg Theatre,
        New York NY (dir. Zishan Uruglu)

Promenade (1965) – music by Al Carmines

1965   Judson Poets' Theater, Judson Memorial Church, New York NY
        (dir. Lawrence Kornfeld)
1969   Promenade Theatre, New York NY (dir. Lawrence Kornfeld)
1970   Cricket Theatre, Minneapolis MN (dir. Paul Boesing)
1983   Theatre Off Park, New York NY (dir. Albert Harris)
2010   (concert presentation) Legacy: The Musicals of Off-Broadway at
        New World Stages, New York NY (dir. Pamela Hall)

The Office (1966)

1966   (closed in previews) Henry Miller Theatre, New York NY
        (dir. Jerome Robbins)

A Vietnamese Wedding (1967)

1967   Washington Square Methodist Church, New York NY**
1968   The Changing Scene, Denver CO
1969   Cafe La MaMa, New York NY**++

The Annunciation (1967)

1967   Judson Poets' Theater, Judson Memorial Church, New York NY**++

Dr. Kheal (1968)

1968	New Dramatists Committee, New York NY (dir. Remy Charlip)
1968	Village Gate and Judson Memorial Church, New York NY (dir. Remy Charlip)
1968	Berkshire Theatre Festival, Stockbridge MA (dir. Gordon Rogoff)
1968	Act IV, Provincetown MA
1968	The Changing Scene, Denver CO (dir. Michael Smith)
1973	Theatre Genesis, New York NY** (co-directed with Michael Smith)
2010	(staged reading) The 2010 New York Fornés Festival, Cherry Lane Theatre, New York NY++ (dir. Gisela Cardenas)

The Red Burning Light Or: Mission XQ3 (1968)

1968	Open Theatre, European tour, Zurich-Milan-Copenhagen (dir. Fredric de Boer)
1969	Cafe La MaMa, New York NY**++ (co-directed with Remy Charlip, Ken Glickfield, Fredric de Boer, and James Barbosa)

Molly's Dream (1968) – music by Cosmos Savage

1968	(workshop) Boston University-Tanglewood Workshop, Lenox MA (dir. Edward Setrakian)
1968	(workshop) New Dramatists Committee, New York NY**
1973	New York Theater Strategy, Manhattan Theatre Club, New York NY**
2003	SoHo Rep, New York NY (dir. Daniel Aukin)
2003	Boston Theatre Works, Tremont Theatre, Boston MA (dir. Dani Snyder)

The Curse of the Langston House (1972)

1972	Cincinnati Playhouse in the Park, Cincinnati OH**

Aurora (1974)

1974	New York Theatre Strategy, Theatre of the Riverside Church, New York NY**

Cap-a-Pie (1975) – music by José Raul Bernardo

1975	INTAR, New York NY**

Fefu and Her Friends (1977)

1977	New York Theatre Strategy, Relativity Media Lab, New York NY**
1978	American Place Theatre, New York NY**

1979	Padua Hills Playwrights Festival, Claremont CA**
1979	Pasadena Community Arts Center, Brookside Theatre, Pasadena CA**
1979	University of Wisconsin, Parkside, Parkside WI**
1981	Eureka Theatre, San Francisco CA (dir. Alma Becker)
1981	The Empty Space, Seattle WA (dir. M. Burke Walker)
1982	Victoria College for the Arts, Melbourne, AUSTRALIA (dir. Ros Horin)
1983	Paradise Island Express, Washington Project for the Arts, Washington DC (dir. Deirdre Lavrakis)
1983	Theatre Off Park, New York NY
1984	Blind Parrot Productions, Blackbird Theater, Chicago IL (dir. Janice St. John)
1985	Théâtre des Cinquantes, Paris, FRANCE (dir. Lucienne Hamon)
1986	At The Foot Of The Mountain, Minneapolis MN**
1987	At The Foot Of The Mountain, Minneapolis MN**
1989	New City Theatre, Seattle WA**
1992	Yale Repertory Theatre (Winterfest), New Haven CT (dir. Lisa Peterson)
1992	Amersfoort, THE NETHERLANDS (dir. Moniek Merkx)
1996	(single-set version) Muhlenberg College, Allentown PA**
1999	Santa Fe Stages, Santa Fe NM**
2001	Chickspeare Theatre Company, Charlotte NC (dir. Anne Lambert)
2001	Actor's Express, Atlanta GA (dir. Wier Harman)
2010	(reading) The 2010 New York Fornés Festival, Theater for the New City, New York NY (dir. Billy Hopkins)

Lolita in the Garden (1977)

| 1977 | INTAR, New York NY** |

In Service (1978)

1978 Padua Hills Playwrights Festival, Claremont CA**

Eyes on the Harem (1979)

| 1979 | INTAR, New York NY** |

Evelyn Brown (A Diary) (1980)

| 1980 | Theater for the New City, New York NY** |

A Visit (1981)

1981	Padua Hills Playwrights Festival, Claremont CA**
1981	Theater for the New City, New York NY**

The Danube (1983)

1982	Padua Hills Playwrights Festival, Claremont CA**
1983	Theater for the New City, New York NY**
1984	American Place Theatre, New York NY**
1984	City Theatre, Pittsburgh PA (dir. Jed Allen Harris)
1985	Eureka Theatre, San Francisco CA (dir. Susan Marsden)
1988	Organic Theater Company, Chicago IL (dir. Blair Thomas)
1988	New City Theatre, Seattle WA (dir. John Kazanjian)
1991	Schauspielhaus, Vienna, AUSTRIA (dir. Marlene Streruwitz)
1993	Links Hall Studio, Chicago IL (dir. Shira Piven)
1994	Shared Experience at Wolsey Studio Theatre, Ipswich and the Gate Theatre, London, ENGLAND (dir. Nancy Meckler)
2001	Genesis West, Center Stage Theater, Santa Barbara CA (dir. Michael Smith) ++
2000	Infernal Bridegroom Productions, Atomic Café, Houston TX (dir. Jason Nodler)
2003	Kitchen Dog Theater, Black Box Theatre, Dallas TX (dir. Dan Day)

Mud (1983)

1983	Padua Hills Playwrights Festival, Claremont CA**
1983	Theater for the New City, New York NY**
1983	Omaha Magic Theatre, Omaha NE**
1985	Empty Space, 2nd Space, Seattle WA (dir. Craig Latrell)
1986	Court Theatre, Chicago IL
1989	InterAct Theatre Company at the Annenberg Centre for the Performing Arts, Philadelphia PA (dir. Seth Rozin)
1989	At The Foot of the Mountain, Cedar-Riverside People's Center, Minneapolis MN (dir. Wendy Knox)
1990	Magic Theatre, San Francisco CA (dir. Mary Forcade)
1990	New City Theatre, Seattle WA**
1991	Milwaukee Repertory Theatre, Milwaukee WI**
1991	Source Theatre, Washington DC (dir. Pat Murphy Sheehy)
1991	Kitchen Dog Theatre, Dallas TX (dir. Dan Day)
1992	Grazer Orpheum, Graz, AUSTRIA (dir. Bernd Hagg)
1992	Piven Theatre at Victory Gardens Theater, Chicago IL (dir. Joyce Piven)

1993	Horizon Theater, Cologne, GERMANY (dir. Jonathan Fox)
1995	Other Theater, Judith Anderson Theater, Chelsea, New York NY (dir. Mary Forcade)
1997	Fritz Theatre, San Diego CA (dir. Tim West)
1999	Signature Theatre, New York NY++ (dir. David Esbjornson)
2001	Genesis West, Center Stage Theater, Santa Barbara CA++ (dir. Maurice Lord)
2001	Infernal Bridegroom Productions, Axiom Theater, Houston TX (dir. Jason Nodler)
2001	Source Theatre, Washington DC (dir. Pat Murphy Sheehy)
2003	Arcola Theatre, London, ENGLAND (dir. Tiffany Watt-Smith)
2003	The Corn Exchange, Project Arts Centre, Dublin, IRELAND (dir. Annie Ryan)
2007	The Hypokrites, The Building Stage, Chicago IL (dir. Sean Graney)
2009	Cutting Ball Theater, San Francisco CA (dir. Paige Rogers)
2009	Tron Theatre, Glasgow, SCOTLAND (dir. Andy Arnold)

Sarita (1984) – music by Leon Odenz

1984	INTAR, New York NY**
1987	Loraine Hansbury Theater, San Francisco CA (dir. Stanley E. Williams)
1988	(reading) Soho Poly, London, ENGLAND (dir. Ros Shelley)
1988	Wisdom Bridge Theatre, Chicago IL
1991	Unicorn Theatre Company, Berkshire Theatre Festival, Stockbridge MA (dir. Kim Rubinstein)
2010	The Catastrophic Theatre, Houston TX (dir. Jason Nodler)
2010	Halcyon Theatre, Lincoln Square Theatre, Chicago IL (dir. Gina LoPiccolo)

No Time (1984) – early version of *The Conduct of Life*

1984	Padua Hills Playwrights Festival, California Institute for the Arts, Valencia CA**

The Conduct of Life (1985)

1985	Theater for the New City, New York NY**
1987	Moving Target Theatre, Washington DC (dir. Michael David Fox)
1988	Organic Theater Company, Chicago IL (dir. Thomas Riccio)
1994	Fritz Theatre, San Diego CA (dir. Karin Williams)

1994	Theater LaB Houston, Houston TX (dir. Edith Pross)
1996	Centro Cultural de la Raza, San Diego CA (dir. Sam Valdez)
1996	Gardner Stages, Los Angeles CA (dir. Dona Guevara Hill)
1999	Cara Mia at Deep Ellum Center for the Arts, Dallas TX (dir. Marisela Barrerra)
2000	Rooster Theater, New Orleans LA (dir. Harry Hoffman)

Drowning (1985)

1985	(part of "Orchards") Acting Company, national tour and New York NY (dir. Robert Falls)
1988	Padua Hills Playwrights Festival, Pacific Design Center, Los Angeles CA (dir. Roxanne Rogers)
1992	Magic Theatre, San Francisco CA**++
1999	Signature Theater, New York NY++ (dir. David Esbjornson)

The Trial of Joan of Arc in a Matter of Faith (1986)

| 1986 | Theater for the New City, New York NY** |

Lovers and Keepers (1986) – music by Tito Puente and Fernando Rivas

1985	(workshop) Woodstock NY**
1986	INTAR, New York NY**
1986	City Theatre Company, New City Theatre, Pittsburgh PA**
1989	Blind Parrot Productions, Chicago IL and El IV Festival de Teatro Hispano, Minorca Playhouse, Coral Gables FL (dir. David Perkins)

Art (1986)

| 1986 | (part of "Box Plays) Hispanic Playwrights-in-Residence Laboratory, INTAR, New York NY** |

The Mothers (1986) – early version of *Nadine*

| 1986 | Padua Hills Playwrights Festival, Santa Monica CA** |

Abingdon Square (1987)

1985	(workshop) Seattle Repertory Theatre, Seattle WA**
1987	Women's Project and Productions, Inc., American Place Theatre, New York NY**
1988	Studio Arena Theatre, Buffalo NY**

1989   Theatre Passe Muraille, Toronto, Ontario, CANADA. (dir. Peter Hinton)

1989   Shared Experience and Soho Poly Theatre, London, ENGLAND (dir. Nancy Meckler)

1990   Next Theatre, Evanston IL (dir. Eric Simonson)

1990   National Theatre, Cottesloe Theatre, London, ENGLAND (dir. Nancy Meckler)

1990   Belvoir Street Theatre, Sydney, and Melbourne International Festival, Melbourne, AUSTRALIA (dir. Ros Horin)

1991   Source Theatre, Washington DC (dir. Elizabeth Robelen)

1992   (bilingual production) San Diego Repertory Theatre, San Diego CA**

2003   Piven Theatre Workshop, Evanston IL (dir. Jessica Thebus)

2004   Open Fist Theatre Company, Los Angeles CA (dir. Martha Demson)

Hunger (1988)

1988   En Garde Arts, "Three Pieces for a Warehouse," 500 Greenwich Street, New York NY**

What of the Night? (1989) – *Nadine, Springtime, Lust, Hunger*

1988   (workshop, under the title *Give Us This Day*), Milwaukee Repertory Theatre, Milwaukee WI**

1989   Milwaukee Repertory Theatre, Milwaukee WI**

1990   Trinity Repertory Company, Providence RI**

2010   (staged reading) The 2010 New York Fornés Festival, Cherry Lane Theatre, New York NY (dir. Marya Ferrer, Jacquelyn Landgraf, and Kay Matschullat)

2010   Halcyon Theatre, Lincoln Square Theatre, Chicago IL (dir. Margo Gray)

Lust (1989)

1995   Colour Clinic, Traverse Theatre, Edinburgh, SCOTLAND (dir. Morvin McLean)

Springtime (1989)

1997   Theater for the New City, New York NY**

Oscar and Bertha (1992)

1987   (workshop) Guthrie Theatre, Minneapolis MN**

1989   Padua Hills Playwrights Festival, California State University-
        Northridge, Northridge CA**
1992   Magic Theatre, San Francisco CA**++

Enter the Night (1993)

1993   New City Theatre, Seattle WA**
1993   Dallas Theater Center, Dallas TX**
1999   Signature Theatre, New York NY (dir. Sonja Moser)

Terra Incognita (1997) – music by Roberto Sierra

1991   (workshop) Storm King Art Center, Storm King NY**
1992   (workshop) Dionysia Festival at the Public Palace, Siena, ITALY**
1993   Yale Cabaret Theatre, New Haven CT (dir. Jonathan Moscone,
        music by Kim Sherman)
1994   Padua Hills Playwrights Festival, Woodbury University,
        Burbank CA**
1997   INTAR and Women's Project and Productions, New York
        NY**Women

Manual for a Desperate Crossing (Balseros/Rafters)
        (1997) – music by Robert Ashley

1997   Florida Grand Opera, Miami FL (dir. Michael Montel)
2010   Halcyon Theatre, Lincoln Square Theatre, Chicago IL (dir. Coya Paz)

The Summer in Gossensass (1998)

1994   (workshop, under the title *Ibsen and the Actress*) Iowa
        Playwright's Workshop, University of Iowa, Iowa City IA**
1995   Padua Hills Playwrights Festival, University of Southern
        California, Los Angeles CA**
1997   (workshop) Women's Project and Productions, New York NY**
1998   Women's Project and Productions, New York NY**
2010   (staged reading) The 2010 New York Fornés Festival, Theater for
        the New City, New York NY (dir. Alice Reagan)
2010   Halcyon Theatre, Lincoln Square Theatre, Chicago IL (dir. Lavina
        Jadhwani)

The Audition (1998)

1998   Theater for the New City, New York NY**
2000   (part of "The Square") Mark Taper Forum Asian Theater Workshop
        at Actors' Gang Theater, Los Angeles CA (dir. Lisa Peterson)

Letters from Cuba (2000)

2000   Signature Theatre, New York NY**
2010   Halcyon Theatre, Lincoln Square Theatre, Chicago IL (dir. Juan Castañeda)

*

Maria Irene Fornes – as director of plays by others

In addition to directing the original productions of her plays from 1968 on (as listed above), Fornes also directed the following plays by other playwrights:

1981   *Life Is Dream* by Pedro Calderón de la Barca (trans./adapt. by Fornes). INTAR, New York NY
1982   *Exile* by Ana María Simo. INTAR, New York NY
1986   *Cold Air* by Virgilio Piñera (trans./adapt. by Fornes). INTAR, New York NY
1987   *Hedda Gabler* by Henrik Ibsen (adapt. by Fornes). Milwaukee Repertory Theatre, Milwaukee WI
1987   *Uncle Vanya* by Anton Chekhov (adapt. by Fornes from trans. by Marian Fell). Classic Stage Company, New York NY
1990   *Going to New England* by Ana Maria Simo. INTAR, New York NY
1990   *Dogs* by Leo Garcia. West Coast Ensemble, Los Angeles CA
1990   *Shadow of a Man* by Cherrie Moraga. Eureka Theatre, San Francisco CA
1992   *It Is/It Is Not* by Manuel Pereiras Garcia. Theater for the New City, New York NY
1995   *Any Place But Here* by Caridad Svich. Theater for the New City, New York NY

Appendix B
Plays in publication

Most Fornes plays reached publication in fits and starts. From one publication to the next, she sometimes made changes in the texts. While these were usually minor, comparison of different editions can be suggestive.

La viuda (The Widow) (1961)

In *Teatro cubano: Cuatro obras recomendadas en el II Concurso Literario Hispanoamericano de la Casa de Las Américas*. Havana: Casa de las Américas, 1961.

Tango Palace (1963)

In *Playwrights for Tomorrow: A Collection of Plays*, Volume II. Ed. Arthur H. Ballet. Minneapolis: University of Minnesota Press, 1966.
In *Concepts of Literature*. Ed. James William Johnson. Englewood Cliffs: Prentice Hall, 1971.
In *Promenade and Other Plays*. Ed. Michael Feingold. New York: Winter House, 1971. Revised edition New York: Performing Arts Journal Publications, 1987.

The Successful Life of 3: A Skit for Vaudeville (1965)

In *Playwrights for Tomorrow: A Collection of Plays*, Volume II. Ed. Arthur H. Ballet. Minneapolis: University of Minnesota Press, 1966.
In *Eight Plays from Off Off Broadway*. Eds. Nick Orzel and Michael Smith. New York: Bobbs Merrill, 1966.
In *Promenade and Other Plays*. Ed. Michael Feingold. New York: Winter House, 1971. Revised edition New York: Performing Arts Journal Publications, 1987.

Promenade (1965)

In *The Bold New Women*. Ed. Barbara Alson. Greenwich: Fawcett, 1966.
In *The New Underground Theatre*. Ed. Robert J. Schroeder. New York: Bantam, 1968.
Promenade. New York: Metromedia On Stage, 1969 (acting edition with Al Carmines score).
In *Promenade and Other Plays*. Ed. Michael Feingold. New York: Winter House, 1971. Revised edition New York: Performing Arts Journal Publications, 1987.
In *Great Rock Musicals*. Ed. Stanley Richards. New York: Stein and Day, 1979.

The Office (1966)

Unpublished.

A Vietnamese Wedding (1967)

In *Promenade and Other Plays*. Ed. Michael Feingold. New York: Winter House, 1971. Revised edition New York: Performing Arts Journal Publications, 1987.
In *Literature: An Introduction to Fiction, Poetry and Drama*. Ed. X.J. Kennedy. New York: HarperCollins, 1991.

The Annunciation (1967)

Unpublished.

Dr. Kheal (1968)

In *Yale/Theatre* 1 (Winter 1968): 32–40.
in *The Best of Off Off-Broadway*. Ed. Michael Smith. New York: Dutton, 1969.
In *Promenade and Other Plays*. Ed. Michael Feingold. New York: Winter House, 1971. Revised edition New York: Performing Arts Journal Publications, 1987.
In *A Century of Plays by American Women*. Ed. Rachel France. New York: Richard Rosen Press, 1979.

The Red Burning Light Or: Mission XQ3 (1968)

In *Promenade and Other Plays*. Ed. Michael Feingold. New York: Winter House, 1971.

Molly's Dream (1968)

In *Promenade and Other Plays*. Ed. Michael Feingold. New York: Winter House, 1971. Revised edition New York: Performing Arts Journal Publications, 1987.

In *The Off Off Broadway Book: The Plays, People, Theatre*. Eds. Albert Poland and Bruce Mailman. New York: Bobbs-Merrill, 1972.

The Curse of Langston House (1972)

Unpublished.

Aurora (1974)

Unpublished.

Cap-a-Pie (1975)

Unpublished.

Fefu and Her Friends (1977)

In *Performing Arts Journal* Vol 2 No 3 (Winter 1978): 112–40.

In *Word Plays*. Ed. Bonnie Marranca and Gautam Dasgupta. New York: PAJ Publications, 1980.

Fefu and Her Friends. New York: PAJ Publications, 1990.

In *Stages of Drama: Classical to Contemporary Theater*. Ed. Carl H. Klaus, Miriam Gilbert, and Bradford S. Field, Jr. New York: St. Martin's Press, 1995.

In *Teatro: 5 autores cubanos*. Ed. Rine Leal. Jackson Heights: Ollantay Press, 1995. [in Spanish as *Fefu y sus amigas*.]

In *The Harcourt Brace Anthology of Drama* (2nd ed.). Ed. W.B. Worthen. Fort Worth TX: Harcourt Brace College Publishers, 1996.

Lolita in the Garden (1977)

Unpublished.

In Service (1978)

Unpublished.

Eyes on the Harem (1979)

Unpublished.

Blood Wedding (1980) – trans./adapt. of Garcia Lorca

Unpublished.

Evelyn Brown (A Diary) (1980)

Unpublished.

A Visit (1981)

Unpublished.

Life Is Dream (1981) – trans./adapt. of Calderón

Unpublished.

The Danube (1983)

In *Plays from Padua Hills 1982*. Ed. Murray Mednick. Claremont, Calif: Pomona College, 1983.
In *Maria Irene Fornes: Plays*. New York: PAJ Publications, 1986.

Mud (1983)

In *Maria Irene Fornes: Plays*. New York: PAJ Publications, 1986.
In *The HBJ Anthology of Drama*. Ed. W.B. Worthen. Fort Worth: Harcourt Brace Jovanovich College Publishers, 1993.

Sarita (1984)

In *Maria Irene Fornes: Plays*. New York: PAJ Publications, 1986.

The Conduct of Life (1985)

In *Maria Irene Fornes: Plays*. New York: PAJ Publications, 1986.
In *On New Ground: Contemporary Hispanic-American Plays*. Ed. M. Elizabeth Osborn. New York: Theatre Communications Group, 1987.
In *Telling Tales: New One-Act Plays*. Ed. Eric Lane. New York: Penguin, 1993.
In *Literature: The Evolving Canon*. Ed. Sven P. Birkerts. Boston: Allyn and Bacon, 1993.
In *Modern Drama: Plays/Criticism/Theory*. Ed. W.B. Worthen. San Diego: Harcourt Brace College Publishers, 1995.
In *Drama and Performance: An Anthology*. Ed. Gary Vena, Andrea Nouryeh. New York: HarperCollins College Publisher, 1996.

In *Plays Onstage: An Anthology*. Eds. Ronald Wainscott, Kathy Fletcher. Boston: Pearson/Allyn & Bacon, 2006.
In *Teatro cubano actual: dramaturgia escrita en Estados Unidos*. Ed. Alberto Sarrán and Lillian Manzor. La Habana: Ediciones Alarcos, 2005. [Translated into Spanish as *Conducta de la vida*.]

Drowning (1985)

In *Orchards: Seven Stories by Anton Chekhov and Seven Plays They Have Inspired*. New York: Alfred A. Knopf, 1986.
In *Orchards*. New York: Broadway Play Publishing, 1987.

Cold Air (1986) – trans./adapt. of play by Virgilio Piñera

Cold Air. *Plays in Process* Vol 6 No 10. New York: Theater Communications Group, 1985.
In *New Plays USA 3*. Eds. James Leverett and M. Elizabeth Osborn. New York: Theatre Communications Group, 1986.

The Trial of Joan of Arc in a Matter of Faith (1986)

Unpublished.

Lovers and Keepers (1986)

Lovers and Keepers. Plays in Process Vol 7 No 10. New York: Theater Communications Group, 1987.

Art (1986)

Unpublished.

Abingdon Square (1987)

In *American Theatre* (February 1988): 1–10 (inserted playscript).
In *Plays International* Vol 5 No 9 (April 1990): 42–49.
In *Womenswork*. Ed. Julia Miles. New York: Applause, 1989.
(in Spanish) *La Plaza Chica*. Los Angeles: Libertoas, 1994.
In *From the Other Side of the Century II: A New American Drama, 1960–1995*. Eds. Douglas Messerli and Mac Wellman. Los Angeles: Sun & Moon Press, 1998.
Abingdon Square. København: Green Integer, 2000.
In *A Theatre for Women's Voices: Plays & History From the Women's Project at 25*. Ed. Julia Miles. Portsmouth NH: Heinemann, 2003.
In *What of the Night?: Selected Plays*. New York: PAJ Publications, 2008.

What of the Night? (1989)

In *Women on the Verge: Seven Avant-Garde Plays*. Ed. Rosette C. Lamont. New York: Applause (1993).

In *What of the night?: Selected Plays*. New York: PAJ Publications, 2008.

Springtime (only) in *Antaeus* No 66 (Spring 1991): 81–90.

Springtime (only) in *Facing Forward*. Ed. Leah D. Frank. New York: Broadway Play Publishing, 1995.

Springtime (only) in *Amazon All Stars: Thirteen Lesbian Plays, With Essays and Interviews*. Ed. Rosemary Keefe Curb. New York: Applause, 1996.

Oscar and Bertha (1992)

In *Best of the West: An Anthology of Plays From the 1989 & 1990 Padua Hills Playwrights Festivals*. Eds. Murray Mednick, Bill Raden, and Cheryl Slean. Los Angeles: Padua Hills Press, 1991.

Enter the Night (1993)

In *Plays for the End of the Century*. Ed. Bonnie Marranca. Baltimore MD: The Johns Hopkins University Press, 1996.

In *What of the Night?: Selected Plays*. New York: PAJ Publications, 2008.

Terra Incognita (1997)

In *Theater* Vol 24 No 2 (1993): 99–111.

In *Padua: Plays From the Padua Hills Playwrights Festival*. Ed. Dan Tucker. Los Angeles: Padua Playwrights Press, 2003.

In *Letters from Cuba and Other Plays*. New York: PAJ Publications, 2007.

Manual for a Desperate Crossing (Balseros/Rafters) (1997)

In *Letters from Cuba and Other Plays*. New York: PAJ Publications, 2007.

The Summer in Gossensass (1998)

In *What of the Night?: Selected Plays*. New York: PAJ Publications, 2008.

The Audition (1998)

Unpublished.

Letters from Cuba (2000)

In *Letters from Cuba and Other Plays*. New York: PAJ Publications, 2007.

Bibliography

Aaron, Jules (1979) "Padua Hills Playwriting Workshop," *Performing Arts Journal*, 3.3: 121–27.

Alker, Gwendolyn (2009) "Teaching Fornes: Preserving Fornesian Techniques in Critical Context," *Theatre Topics* 19.2: 207–21.

Alson, Barbara, ed. (1966) *The Bold New Women*, Greenwich, CT: Fawcett Publications, Inc.

Antholis, Kary (1985) "'The Danube': Few Memorable Moments," *The Stanford Daily* 28 May.

Aronson, Arnold (2000) *American Avant-garde Theatre: A History*, London: Routledge.

Austin, Gayle (1989) "The Madwoman in the Spotlight: Plays of Maria Irene Fornes," in Lynda Hart (ed.) *Making A Spectacle: Feminist Essays on Contemporary Women's Theatre*, Ann Arbor: University of Michigan Press.

Banes, Sally (1982) "The Birth of the Judson Dance Theatre: 'A Concert of Dance' at Judson Church, July 6, 1962," *Dance Chronicle* 5.2: 167–212.

——(1983) *Democracy's Body: Judson Dance Theater, 1962–1964*, Ann Arbor, MI: UMI Research Press.

——(1987) *Terpsichore in Sneakers: Post-modern Dance*, Middletown, OH: Wesleyan University Press.

——(1993) *Greenwich Village 1963: Avant-garde Performance and the Effervescent Body*, Durham, NC: Duke University Press.

Barnes, Clive (1969) "Theater: 'Promenade,' Wickedly Amusing Musical," *New York Times* 5 June: 56.

——(1974) "Stage: Fornes 'Aurora'," *New York Times* 30 September: 53.

——(1982) "'A Visit' that Went Wrong," *New York Post* 2 January: 10.

Berson, Misha (1993a) "'Voices' Direct Her Writing," *Seattle Times* 16 April: 19.

——(1993b) "'Enter the Night': Nocturnal Ruminations on Fear and Loneliness," *Seattle Times* 22 April: D2.

Betsko, Kathleen and Rachel Koenig (eds.) (1987) *Interviews with Contemporary Women Playwrights*, New York: Beech Tree Books.

Bigsby, C.W.E. (1985) *A Critical Introduction to Twentieth-Century American Drama Volume 3: Beyond Broadway*, Cambridge: Cambridge University Press.

Billington, Michael (1989) "Tragedy in Sepia of a Child Bride," *Guardian*.

Blau, Herbert (1999) "Water under the Bridge: From *Tango Palace* to *Mud*," in Marc Robinson (ed.) *The Theater of Maria Irene Fornes*, Baltimore, MD: Johns Hopkins University Press.

Blumenthal, Eileen (1984) *Joseph Chaikin: Exploring at the Boundaries of Theater*, Cambridge: Cambridge University Press.

Bottoms, Stephen J. (1997) "'Language Is the Motor': Maria Irene Fornes's *Promenade* as Text and Performance," *New England Theatre Journal* 8: 45–71.

——(2004a) *Playing Underground: A Critical History of the 1960s Off-Off-Broadway Movement*, Ann Arbor: University of Michigan Press.

——(2004b) "Sympathy for the Devil?: Maria Irene Fornes and the Conduct of Life," *The Journal of American Drama and Theatre*, 16.3: 19–34.

Breslauer, Jan (1994) "A Mecca Is Reborn," *Los Angeles Times* 17 July: Calendar 8.

Case, Sue-Ellen (1988) *Feminism and Theatre*, New York: Methuen.

Chaudhuri, Una (1997) *Staging Place: The Geography of Modern Drama*, Ann Arbor: University of Michigan Press.

Clay, Carolyn (1990) "Hell on Earth," *Boston Phoenix* 18 January: Sec. 2, p. 3.

Coates, Mari (1992) "All Wound Up with Nowhere To Go," *San Francisco Sentinel* 19 March: 26.

Cohn, Ruby (1995) "Reading and Teaching: Maria Irene Fornes and Caryl Churchill," in *Anglo-American Interplay in Recent Drama*, Cambridge: Cambridge University Press, 1995.

Cole, Susan Letzler (1992) *Directors in Rehearsal: A Hidden World*, New York: Routledge.

——(2001) *Playwrights in Rehearsal: The Seduction of Company*, New York: Routledge.

Colpitt, Frances (2002) "Thick & Thin: Hans Hofmann," *Art in America* 90.12 (December 2002): 102–3.

Confessore, Lynda Leonard (1968) "The Judson Poets' Theater: A Descriptive Study," Master of Arts thesis available as PDF document at http://www.judson.org/Stephen_Bottoms_Interviews.html (accessed 25 January 2009).

Crespy, David A. (2003) *Off-Off-Broadway Explosion: How Provocative Playwrights of the 1960s Ignited a New American Theater*, New York: Backstage Books.

Cubilié, Anne (2005) *Women Witnessing Terror: Testimony and the Cultural Politics of Human Rights*, New York: Fordham University Press.

Cummings, Scott T. (1985) "Seeing With Clarity: The Visions of Maria Irene Fornes," *Theater* 17.1 (Winter 1985): 51–56.

——(1988) "Notes on Fefu, Fornes, and the Play of Thought," *Ideas and Production* Issue 8: 91–103.

——(1989) "Maria Irene Fornes," in *American Playwrights Since 1945: A Guide to Scholarship, Criticism, and Performance.* Ed. Philip C. Kolin. Westport, CT: Greenwood Press: 111–23.

——(1994) "Fornes's Odd Couple: *Oscar and Bertha* at Magic Theatre," *Journal of Dramatic Theory and Criticism* 8.2: 147–56.

——(2006) *Remaking American Theater: Charles Mee, Anne Bogart and the SITI Company*, Cambridge: Cambridge University Press.

Curb, Rosemary (1986) "Scenes of the Times," *Women's Review of Books* 3.9 (June 1986): 10.

Delgado, Maria M. and Caridad Svich (eds.) (1999) *Conducting a Life: Reflections on the Theatre of Maria Irene Fornes*, Lyme, NH: Smith and Kraus.

Dolan, Jill (1988) *The Feminist Spectator as Critic*, Ann Arbor, MI: UMI Research Press.

Downey, Roger (1988) "Berlitz meets Beckett," *Seattle Weekly* 22 June.

——(1993) "Theater of the Superb," *Seattle Weekly* 28 April.

Dramatists Guild Quarterly (1988) "The Playwright in the Regional Theater" [roundtable discussion in Spring 1988 issue], 9–16.

Drukman, Steven (2000) "Notes on Fornes (With Apologies to Susan Sontag)" *American Theatre* 17.7: 36–39, 85.

Eder, Richard (1979) "Stage: Intar Presents 'Eyes on the Harem,'" *New York Times* 25 April: C17.

Falk, Florence (1980) "Turning (House)Work into Art," *Soho Weekly News* 2 April: 57+.

Farfan, Penny (1997) "Feminism, Metatheatricality, and Mise-en-scène in Maria Irene Fornes's *Fefu and Her Friends*," *Modern Drama* 40.4: 442–53.

Feingold, Michael (1974) "The Tragic Mustache," *Village Voice* 19 September: 76.

——(1979) "The Magic Seraglio," *Village Voice* 7 May: 104.

——(1981) "Fornescations," *Village Voice* 30 December: 69–70.

——(1984) "Found in Translation," *Village Voice* 20 March: 83.

——(1986) "Fornes's Incompatibles," *Village Voice* 29 Apr: 92.

——(1997) "Missing Connections," *Village Voice* 8 April: 97.

——(1998) "Show Businesses," *Village Voice* 14 April: 129.

——(1999) "Women's Stresses," *Village Voice* 14 Dec: 83.

Fleming, John (1997) "Adrift on a Sea of Drama," *St. Petersburg Times* 19 May: 1D.

Fornés, María Irene (1971) *Promenade and Other Plays*, New York: Winter House.

——(1977) "'I Write These Messages That Come,'" *The Drama Review* 21 (December 1977): 25–40.

——(1986) *Plays*, New York: PAJ Publications.

——(1988) *Abingdon Square*, inserted playscript in *American Theatre* 4.11 (February 1988).

——(1991) *Oscar and Bertha* in *Best of the West*, Murray Mednick, Bill Raden, and Cheryl Slean, eds., Los Angeles: Padua Hills Press.

——(1992) *Fefu and Her Friends*, New York: PAJ Publications.

——(2007) *Letters from Cuba and Other Plays*, New York: PAJ Publications.

——(2008) *What of the Night?: Selected Plays*, New York: PAJ Publications.

Frame, Allen (1984) "María Irene Fornés," *Bomb* 10 (Fall 1984): 28–30.

Garfield, David (1980) *A Player's Place: The Story of the Actors Studio*, New York: Macmillan.

Gargano, Cara (1997) "The Starfish and the Strange Attractor: Myth, Science, and Theatre as Laboratory in Maria Irene Fornes's *Mud*," *New Theatre Quarterly* 13.51: 214–20.

Garner, Jr., Stanton B. (1994) *Bodied Spaces: Phenomenology and Performance in Contemporary Drama*, Ithaca, NY: Cornell University Press.

Gates, Joanne E. (1985) "Elizabeth Robins and the 1891 Production of *Hedda Gabler*," *Modern Drama* 28:4 (December 1985): 611–19.

——(1994) *Elizabeth Robins, 1862–1952: Actress, Novelist, Feminist*, Tuscaloosa: University of Alabama Press.

Geis, Deborah R. (1990) "Wordscapes of the Body: Performative Language as Gestus in Maria Irene Fornes's Plays", *Theatre Journal*, 42.3: 291–307.

Gener, Randy (2003) "Dreamer from Cuba," *American Theatre* 20.7 (September 2003): 22+.

Gilman, Richard (1971) "Introduction" to *Promenade and Other Plays*, New York: Winter House, 1–3.

——(1985) "30 Years of Off-Off Broadway," a supplement to the *Village Voice* 21 May: n.p.

Gussow, Mel (1972) "New Group to Offer Plays by Women," *New York Times* 22 February: 44.

——(1981) "The Stage: 'A Visit,' a Musical Trip Back to 1910," *New York Times* 30 December: B6.

Harrington, Stephanie (1966) "Irene Fornes, Playwright: Alice and the Red Queen," *Village Voice* 21 April: 1, 33–34.

Hill, Holly (1980) "Three Portraits of Women," *Other Stages* 17 April: 7.

Huerta, Jorge (2000) *Chicano Drama: Performance, Society, Myth*, Cambridge: Cambridge University Press.

Jenner, C. Lee (1979) "Bosporous Belles," *Other Stages* 3 May: 9.

John, Angela V. (1995) *Elizabeth Robins: Staging a Life*, New York: Routledge.

Jones, Welton (1992) "'Square' Writer Is Acclaimed Yet Little Known," *San Diego Union* 15 January 1992: D-1+.

Kalb, Jonathan (2000) "Letters from Cuba," *New York Press* 14 March.

Kellaway, Kate (1989) "Theatre: *Abingdon Square*," *Observer* 11 June.

Kelly, Kevin (1990a) "Seeking to Sail the Mainstream," *Boston Globe* 7 January: A1+.

——(1990b) "At Trinity, a Dramatic and Visual Knockout," *Boston Globe* 13 January: 9+.

Kent, Assunta (1993) "*And What of the Night?*: Maria Irene Fornes's Apocalyptic Vision of America at the Millennium," *Journal of Dramatic Theory and Criticism* 7.2 (Spring 1993): 132–47.

——(1996) *Maria Irene Fornes and Her Critics*, Westport, CT: Greenwood Press.

Kerr, Walter (1969) "Hooray! He Gives Us Back Our Past," *New York Times* 15 June: 10.

Keyssar, Helene (1985) *Feminist Theatre*, New York: Grove Press.

——(1991) "Drama and the Dialogic Imagination: *The Heidi Chronicles* and *Fefu and Her Friends*," *Modern Drama* 34.1 (March 1991): 90–106.

Kiebuzinska, Christine (1993) "Traces of Brecht in Maria Irene Fornes' *Mud*," *The Brecht Yearbook* 18: 153–65.

Kintz, Linda (1991a) "Permeable Boundaries, Femininity, Fascism, and Violence: Fornes's *The Conduct of Life*," *Gestos* 6.11 (April 1991): 79–89.

——(1991b) "Gendering the Critique of Representation: Fascism, the Purified Body, and Theatre in Adorno, Artaud, and Maria Irene Fornes," *Rethinking Marxism* 4.3: 83–100.

Koppen, Randi (1997) "Formalism and the Return to the Body: Stein's and Fornes's Aesthetic of Significant Form," *New Literary History* 28.4: 791–809.

Kornfeld, Lawrence (1995) *Interview with Stephen Bottoms*, available as a PDF document at http://www.judson.org/Stephen_Bottoms_Interviews.html (accessed 25 January 2009).

Kroll, Jack (1969) "Apotheosis," *Newsweek* 16 June: 107.

——(1982) "The Best of Off Broadway," *Newsweek* 25 January: 71–73.

La Tempa, Susan (1983) "Fornes," *Dramatics* (October): 18–20+.

Lee, Josephine (1996) "Pity and Terror as Public Acts: Reading Feminist Politics in the Plays of Maria Irene Fornes," in Jeanne Colleran and Jenny Spencer (eds.) *Staging Resistance: Essays on Theatre and Politics*, Ann Arbor: University of Michigan Press.

Lester, Elenore (1965) "The Pass-the-Hat Theater Circuit," *New York Times* 5 December 1965: SM90.

Lopez, Tiffany Ana (2006) "Writing Beyond Borders: A Survey of US Latina/o Drama," in David Krasner (ed.) *A Companion to Twentieth-Century American Drama*, Malden, MA: Blackwell.

Machado, Eduardo and Michael Domitrovich (2007) *Tastes Like Cuba: An Exile's Hunger for Home*, New York: Gotham.

Mackenzie, Bob (1963) "Workshop Offers a Puzzling Pair," *Oakland Tribune* 2 December: D27.

Marinelli, Donald (1987) *High Performance* 36: 82–83.

Marranca, Bonnie (1978) "Interview: Maria Irene Fornes," *Performing Arts Journal* 2.3: 106–11.

——(1984) "The Real Life of Maria Irene Fornes," *Performing Arts Journal* 8.1: 29–34.

——(1992a) "The Aging Playwright and the American Theater," *Village Voice* 16 June: 94.

——(1992b) "The State of Grace: Maria Irene Fornes at Sixty-Two," *Performing Arts Journal* 14.2: 24–31.

Marranca, Bonnie and Gautam Dasgupta (1981) *American Playwrights: A Critical Survey*, New York: Drama Book Specialists.

Massa, Robert (1983) "Pomp and Circumstance," *Village Voice* 25 October: 98.

May, Hal and James G. Lesniak (1990) "Maria Irene Fornes," *Contemporary Authors* (New Revision Series) Detroit: Gale Research: 178.

Meyer, Michael (1967) *Ibsen: A Biography*, Garden City, NY: Doubleday & Company.

Mitchell, Lionel (1982) "'A Visit': An Erotic Play for Progressive Families," *New York Amsterdam News* 2 Jan: 24.

Moroff, Diane Lynn (1996) *Fornes: Theater in the Present Tense*, Ann Arbor: University of Michigan Press.

Morris, Steven Leigh (2002) "Surviving Brooklyn, and Finding a Voice Far Away," *New York Times* 22 December: AR7.

Munk, Erika (1980) "Let Us Now Praise Famous Women," *Village Voice* 21 April: 83.

——(1983) "Lost in Translation," *Village Voice* 8 March: 76.

——(1984) "Any Woman Can't," *Village Voice* 14 February: 95.

Murray, Piper (2001) "'They Are Well Together. Women Are Not.': Productive Ambivalence and Female Hom(m)osociality in *Fefu and Her Friends*," *Modern Drama* 44.4: 398–415.

O'Malley, Lurana Donnels (1989) "Pressing Clothes/Snapping Beans/Reading Books: Maria Irene Fornes's Women's Work," *Studies in American Drama, 1945–Present* 4: 103–11.

Onstad, Andréa J. (2009) "Conducting a Pedagogy: The Influence of Maria Irene Fornes's Teaching and The Padua Hills Playwrights Workshop and Festival on Three Contemporary Women Playwrights," unpublished dissertation, University of Missouri-Columbia.

Osborn, M. Elizabeth, ed. (1987) *On New Ground: Contemporary Hispanic-American Plays*, New York: Theatre Communications Group, 1987.

Paran, Janice (1987) "Redressing Ibsen," *American Theatre* 4.8 (November 1987): 14–20.

Pasolli, Robert (1967) "Theatre: The Successful Life of Three," *Village Voice* 1 June.

——(1968) "The New Playwrights' Scene of the Sixties: Jerome Max Is Alive and Well and Living in Rome ... ," *The Drama Review* 13.1 (Autumn 1968): 150–62.

——(1970) *A Book on the Open Theatre*, New York: Avon.

Peter, John (1989), "Theatre," *The Sunday Times* 11 June.

Poland, Albert and Bruce Mailman, eds. (1972) *The Off Off Broadway Book*, Indianapolis, IN: The Bobbs-Merrill Company.

Porterfield, Sally (2000) "Black Cats and Green Trees: The Art of Maria Irene Fornes." *Modern Drama* 43.2 (Summer 2000): 204–15.

Pottlitzer, Joanne (1988) *Hispanic Theater in the United States and Puerto Rico*, New York: Ford Foundation.

Rabillard, Sheila (1997) "Crossing Cultures and Kinds: Maria Irene Fornes and the Performance of a Post-Modern Sublime," *Journal of American Drama and Theatre* 9.2: 33–43.

Ramirez, Elizabeth C. (2000) *Chicanas/Latinas in American Theatre: A History of Performance*, Bloomington: Indiana University Press.

Rawson, Christopher (1986) "*Lovers and Keepers* is Innovative," *Pittsburgh Post-Gazette* 18 October 1986.

Renganathan, Mala (2010) *Understanding Maria Irene Fornes' Theatre*, Champaign, IL: Common Ground.

"Reunion of Playwrights Shaped in One Crucible" (2000) *New York Times* 24 September: AR5.

Richards, Stanley, ed. (1979) *Great Rock Musicals*, New York: Stein and Day.

Robinson, Marc (1997) *The Other American Drama*, Baltimore, MD: Johns Hopkins University Press.

——, ed. (1999) *The Theater of Maria Irene Fornes*, Baltimore, MD: Johns Hopkins University Press.

Rogoff, Gordon (1986) "Breaking the Faith," *Village Voice* 25 March 1986: 54.

Rollyson, Carl and Lisa Paddock (2000) *Susan Sontag: The Making of an Icon*, New York: W.W. Norton & Company.

Rose, Helen (1990) "Abingdon Square," *Time Out* 4–11 April.

Rose, Lloyd (1991) "Simmering Beneath the Surface," *Washington Post* 20 March: B2.

Ruhl, Sarah (2001) "Six Small Thoughts on Fornes, the Problem of Intention, and Willfulness," *Theatre Topics* 11.2 (September 2001): 187–204.

Sabbatini, Arthur J. (2005) "Robert Ashley: Defining American Opera," *PAJ* 80: 45–60.

Sainer, Arthur (1973) "Theatre: Molly's Dream," *Village Voice* 28 June.

Savran, David (1988) *In Their Own Words: Contemporary American Playwrights*, New York: Theatre Communications Group.

Schroeder, Robert J., ed. (1968) *The New Underground Theatre*, New York: Bantam Books.

Schuler, Catherine A. (1990) "Gender Perspective and Violence in the Plays of Maria Irene Fornes and Sam Shepard," in June Schlueter (ed.) *Modern American Drama: The Female Canon*, Rutherford, NJ: Fairleigh Dickinson University Press.

Sears, David (1974) "A Silly Intellectual Exercise," *The Villager* 2 October.

Shank, Theodore (1982) *American Alternative Theater*, New York: Grove Press.

Shewey, Don (1998) "The Women's Room," *The Advocate* 26 May: 93.

——(1999) "Her Championship Season," *The Advocate* 9 November: 74.

Smith, Michael (1965) "Theatre: The Promenade," *Village Voice* 15 April.

——(1966) "The Good Scene: Off Off-Broadway," *Tulane Drama Review* 32: 159–76.

——(1969) "Theatre: Promenade," *Village Voice* 12 June: 47.

Smith, Sid (1988) "Chicago Rediscovers a Theater Secret," *Chicago Tribune* 8 February: 2:3.

Sofer, Andrew (2006) "Maria Irene Fornes: Acts of Translation," in David Krasner (ed.) *A Companion to Twentieth-Century American Drama*, Malden, MA: Blackwell.

Solomon, Alisa (1986) "Box Variations," *Village Voice* 29 July: 81.

——(2003) "Long Night's Journey into Daze," *Village Voice* 4–10 June: 55.

Sontag, Susan (1963) *The Benefactor*, New York: Dell.

——(1986) "Preface," in *Maria Irene Fornes: Plays*, New York: PAJ Publications.

——(2008) *Reborn: Journals and Notebooks 1947–1963* (ed. David Rieff), New York: Farrar Straus Giroux.

Spencer, Charles (1989) "Marriage Lines," *Daily Telegraph* 9 June.

Stasio, Marilyn (1969) "Review of *Promenade*," *Cue* 14 June.

Svich, Caridad (2009) "The Legacy of Maria Irene Fornes: A Collection of Impressions and Exercises," *PAJ* 93: 1–32.

Syna, Sy (1979) "Eyes on the Harem," *Wisdom's Child* 30 April–6 May: 15.

——(1984) "Maria Fornes' Vision and Dabney's Talent Work Well in 'Sarita'," *New York Tribune* 1 February: 7B.

Tallmer, Jerry (1965) "Here Comes Irene Fornes," *New York Post* April.

Taylor, Paul (1990) "Square Roots," *Independent* 3 April 1990.

Teatro cubano: Cuarto obras recomendadas en el II concruso Literario Hispanoamericano de la Casa de las Américas (1961) La Habana, Cuba: Casa de las Américas.

Tommasini, Anthony (1997) "Taking On a Few Legends," *New York Times* 12 April: 20.

Wasserman, Ross S. (1988) interview in playbill for Studio Arena Theatre production of *Abingdon Square*.

Weber, Bruce (2003) "Somnolent Encounters of the Seductive Kind," *New York Times* 29 May: E5.

Weeks, Edith (2003) "The Long Run: A Performer's Life," NYFA Quarterly Summer 2003: http://camt.nyfa.org/level4.asp?id=230&fid=1&sid=51&tid=196 (accessed 3 June 2009).

Weiss, Hedy (1986) "What Fornes Sees Is What You Get," *Chicago Sun-Times* 22 June: 21.

Wetzsteon, Ross (1986) "Irene Fornes: The Elements of Style," *Village Voice* 29 April: 42–45.

——(2002) *Republic of Dreams: Greenwich Village: The American Bohemia, 1910–1960*, New York: Simon and Schuster.

Winer, Laurie (1995) "Padua Hills Festival: The Thrill is in the Discovery" *Los Angeles Times* 24 July: F1.

Winks, Michael (1986). "Encore," *The Pittsburgh Press* 28 September: 26–31.

Wolf, Stacy (1992) "Re/Presenting Gender, Re/Presenting Violence: Feminism, Form and the Plays of Maria Irene Fornes," *Theatre Studies* 37: 17–31.

Worthen, W.B. (1989) "Still Playing Games: Ideology and Performance in the Theater of Maria Irene Fornes," in Enoch Brater (ed.) *Feminine Focus: The New Women Playwrights*, Oxford: Oxford University Press.

Zinman, Toby Silverman (1990) "Hen in a Foxhouse: The Absurdist Plays of Maria Irene Fornes," in Enoch Brater and Ruby Cohn (eds.) *Around the Absurd: Essays on Modern and Postmodern Drama*, Ann Arbor: University of Michigan Press.

Index

Illustrations or captions are indicated in **bold**.